Margaret Cavendish

Oxford New Histories of Philosophy

Series Editors
Christia Mercer, Melvin Rogers, and Eileen O'Neill (1953–2017)

Advisory Board
Lawrie Balfour, Jacqueline Broad, Marguerite Deslauriers, Karen Detlefsen, Don Garrett, Robert Gooding-Williams, Andrew Janiak, Marcy Lascano, Lisa Shapiro, Tommie Shelby

*

Oxford New Histories of Philosophy provides essential resources for those aiming to diversify the content of their philosophy courses, revisit traditional narratives about the history of philosophy, or better understand the richness of philosophy's past. Examining previously neglected or understudied philosophical figures, movements, and traditions, the series includes both innovative new scholarship and new primary sources.

*

Published in the series
Mexican Philosophy in the 20th Century: Essential Readings
Edited by Carlos Alberto Sánchez and Robert Eli Sanchez, Jr.

Sophie de Grouchy's Letters on Sympathy: *A Critical Engagement with Adam Smith's* The Theory of Moral Sentiments
Translated by Sandrine Bergès. Edited and with an introduction by Sandrine Bergès and Eric Schliesser

Margaret Cavendish: Essential Writings
Edited by David Cunning

Margaret Cavendish

Essential Writings

EDITED BY DAVID CUNNING

OXFORD
UNIVERSITY PRESS

OXFORD
UNIVERSITY PRESS

Oxford University Press is a department of the University of Oxford. It furthers
the University's objective of excellence in research, scholarship, and education
by publishing worldwide. Oxford is a registered trade mark of Oxford University
Press in the UK and certain other countries.

Published in the United States of America by Oxford University Press
198 Madison Avenue, New York, NY 10016, United States of America.

© Oxford University Press 2019

CIP data is on file at the Library of Congress
ISBN 978-0-19-066406-0 (pbk.)
ISBN 978-0-19-066405-3 (hbk.)

To Professor Eileen O'Neill

CONTENTS

SERIES EDITORS' FOREWORD

Oxford New Histories of Philosophy speaks to a new climate in philosophy.

There is a growing awareness that philosophy's past is richer and more diverse than previously understood. It has become clear that canonical figures are best studied in a broad context. More exciting still is the recognition that our philosophical heritage contains long-forgotten innovative ideas, movements, and thinkers. Sometimes these thinkers warrant serious study in their own right; sometimes their importance resides in the conversations they helped reframe or problems they devised; often their philosophical proposals force us to rethink long-held assumptions about a period or genre; and frequently they cast well-known philosophical discussions in a fresh light.

There is also a mounting sense among philosophers that our discipline benefits from a diversity of perspectives and a commitment to inclusiveness. In a time when questions about justice, inequality, dignity, education, discrimination, and climate (to name a few) are especially vivid, it is appropriate to mine historical texts for insights that can shift conversations and reframe solutions. Given that philosophy's very long history contains astute discussions of a vast array of topics, the time is right to cast a broad historical net.

Lastly, there is increasing interest among philosophy instructors in speaking to the diversity and concerns of their students. Although historical discussions and texts can serve as a powerful means of doing so, finding the necessary time and tools to excavate long-buried historical materials is challenging.

Oxford New Histories of Philosophy (ONHP) is designed to address all these needs. It will contain new editions and translations of significant historical texts. These primary materials will make available, often for the first time, ideas and works by women, people of color, and movements in philosophy's past that were groundbreaking in their day, but left out of traditional accounts. Informative introductions will help instructors and students navigate the new material. Alongside its primary texts, ONHP will also publish monographs and collections of essays that offer philosophically subtle analyses of understudied topics, movements, and figures. In combining primary materials and astute philosophical analyses, ONHP will make it easier for philosophers, historians, and instructors to include in their courses and research exciting new materials drawn from philosophy's past.

ONHP's range will be wide, both historically and culturally. The series plans to include, for example, the writings of African American philosophers, twentieth-century Mexican philosophers, early modern and late medieval women, Islamic and Jewish authors, and non-Western thinkers. It will excavate and analyze problems and ideas that were prominent in their day but forgotten by later historians. And it will serve as a significant aid to philosophers in teaching and researching this material.

As we expand the range of philosophical voices, it is important to acknowledge one voice responsible for this series. Eileen O'Neill was a series editor until her death, December 1, 2017. She was instrumental in motivating and conceptualizing ONHP. Her brilliant scholarship, advocacy, and generosity made all the difference to the efforts that this series is meant to represent. She will be deeply missed, as a scholar and a friend.

We are proud to contribute to philosophy's present and to a richer understanding of its past.

Christia Mercer and Melvin Rogers
Series Editors

PREFATORY NOTES

I have used the following editions of Cavendish's work.

The worlds olio written by the Thrice Noble, Illustrious, and most Excellent Princess, The Duchess of Newcastle, second edition, printed by A. Maxwell in the year 1671. Note that the first edition was printed in 1655. The second edition contains some minor spelling and word changes, and I have used that edition here.

The philosophical and physical opinions written by Her Excellency the Lady Marchionesse of Newcastle, printed for J. Martin and J. Allestrye at the Bell in St. Pauls Church-Yard 1655.

Philosophical Letters, or, Modest Reflections Upon Some Opinions in Natural Philosophy Maintained By Several Famous and Learned Authors of This Age, Expressed by Way of Letters: By the Thrice Noble, Illustrious, and Excellent Princess, The Marchionesse of Newcastle. London, Printed in the Year, 1664.

Observations Upon Experimental Philosophy: To which is added The Description of a New Blazing World, Written By the Thrice Noble, Illustrious, and Excellent Princesse, The Duchess of Newcastle. The Second Edition. London, Printed by A. Maxwell, in the Year, 1668. Note that *Further Observations Upon Experimental Philosophy* and *Observations Upon the Opinions of Some Ancient Philosophers* are part of this 1668 volume.

Grounds of Natural Philosophy Divided into Thirteen Parts: with an Appendix containing Five Parts, Written By the . . . Duchess of Newcastle. London: Printed by A. Maxwell (1668). This also contains *Appendix to Grounds of Natural Philosophy.*

The description of a new world, called the blazing-world written by the thrice noble, illustrious, and excellent princesse, the Duchess of Newcastle. London: Printed by A. Maxwell (1668).

Bell in Campo, in *Playes written by the thrice noble, illustrious and excellent princess, the Lady Marchioness of Newcastle.* London: Printed by A. Warren, for John Martyn, James Allestry, and Tho. Dicas, 1662.

The She-Anchoret, in *Natures picture drawn by fancies pencil to the life being several feigned stories, comical, tragical, tragi-comical, poetical, romanicical, philosophical, historical, and moral: some in verse, some in prose, some mixt, and some by dialogues* / written by . . . the Duchess of Newcastle. London: Printed by A. Maxwell (1671).

Poems, and fancies written by the Right Honourable, the Lady Margaret Newcastle. London, Printed by T. R. for J. Martin, and J. Allestrye at the Bell in Saint Pauls Church Yard, 1653.

A True Relation of my Birth, Breeding and Life, in Margaret Cavendish, *The Life of William Cavendish, Duke of Newcastle, to which is added the True Relation of my Birth, Breeding and Life*, ed. C. H. Firth, London: George Routledge and Sons Limited (1880).

Note that I have kept all original punctuation, spellings, and mis-spellings, except in cases where a correction was needed for the sake of clarity.

Note also that in the footnotes to the various passages that appear in this edition, I have tried to err on the side of cross-referencing as many as possible of the related passages that appear in the Cavendish corpus.

Reference is made to selections from the following texts as well:

Mary Astell, *A Serious Proposal to the Ladies. Parts I and II*, ed. P. Springborg, Ontario: Broadview Literary Texts (2002). This was originally published in 1694.

Anne Conway, *Principles of the Most Ancient and Modern Philosophy*, ed. Allison P. Coudert and Taylor Corse, Cambridge: Cambridge UP (1996). This was originally published in 1692.

Ralph Cudworth, *True Intellectual System of the Universe*, Stuttgart-Bad Cannstatt: F. Fromann Verlag (1964). This was originally published in 1678.

The Philosophical Writings of Descartes, Volume I, ed. and trans. John Cottingham, Robert Stoothoff, and Dugald Murdoch, London: Cambridge UP (1985). This is abbreviated as "CSM 1."

The Philosophical Writings of Descartes, Volume II, ed. and trans. John Cottingham, Robert Stoothoff, and Dugald Murdoch, London: Cambridge UP (1984). This is abbreviated as "CSM 2."

The Philosophical Writings of Descartes, Volume III: The Correspondence, ed. and trans. John Cottingham, Robert Stoothoff, Dugald Murdoch, and Anthony Kenny, London: Cambridge UP (1993). This is abbreviated as "CSMK."

The Princess and the Philosopher: Letters of Elisabeth of the Palatine to René Descartes, ed. and trans. Andrea Nye, Lanham, MD: Rowman and Littlefield Publishers (1999).

Pierre Gassendi, *Fifth Objections*, in *The Philosophical Writings of Descartes, Volume II*, ed. and trans. John Cottingham, Robert Stoothoff, and Dugald Murdoch, London: Cambridge UP (1984).

Thomas Hobbes, *Leviathan*, ed. and trans. Edwin Curley, Indianapolis: Hackett Publishing (1994). This was originally published in 1651.

Thomas Hobbes, *Elements of Philosophy, the first section concerning body*, London: Printed by R. and W. Leybourn for Andrew Crooke, 1656.

David Hume, *An Enquiry Concerning Human Understanding*, ed. Tom L. Beauchamp, New York: Oxford UP (1999). This was originally published in 1748.

David Hume, *A Treatise of Human Nature*, ed. P. H. Nidditch, New York: Oxford UP (1978). This was originally published in 1739–1740.

David Hume, *Dialogues Concerning Natural Religion*, in J. C. A. Gaskin (ed.), *David Hume: Dialogues and Natural History of Religion*, Oxford: Oxford UP (1993). This was originally published in 1779.

Leibniz: Philosophical Essays, ed. and trans. Daniel Garber and Roger Ariew, Indianapolis: Hackett Publishing (1989).

John Locke, *An Essay concerning Human Understanding*, ed. P. H. Nidditch, New York: Oxford UP (1975). This was originally published in 1689.

Nicolas Malebranche, *The Search After Truth and Elucidations of The Search After Truth*, ed. and trans. Thomas M. Lennon and Paul J. Olscamp, Cambridge: Cambridge UP (1997). *The Search After Truth* was originally published in 1674–75.

Nicolas Malebranche, *Dialogues on Metaphysics and on Religion*, ed. Nicholas Jolley and trans. David Scott, Cambridge: Cambridge UP (1997). This was originally published in 1688.

Henry More, *An antidote against atheisme, or, An appeal to the natural faculties of the minde of man, whether there be not a God*, London: Printed by Roger Daniel, 1653.

Henry More, *The immortality of the soul, so farre forth as it is demonstrable from the knowledge of nature and the light of reason*, London: Printed by J. Flesher, for William Morden, 1659.

Spinoza: Complete Works, ed. Samuel Shirley, trans. Michael L. Morgan, Indianapolis and London: Hackett Publishing (2002).

Jean Baptiste van Helmont, *Oriatrike, or Physics Refined*, London: Printed for Lodowick Lloyd (1662).

Below is also included a section, "Early Modern Themes and Topics—for Instructors and Students," in which I attempt to abstract some of the central debate topics of the seventeenth and eighteenth centuries and point to passages in her corpus in which Cavendish weighs in on these.

CHRONOLOGY

1623   Margaret Lucas is born to Thomas Lucas and Elizabeth Leighton Lucas in the family home at St. John's Abbey in Colchester, Essex.

1625   Thomas Lucas dies. Charles I becomes King of England and marries the Catholic Henrietta Maria, the sister of Louis XIII of France, and the daughter of Marie de Medici.

1630   Hobbes begins his service as teacher of natural philosophy to William Cavendish.

1638   Anna Maria van Schurman publishes *The Learned Maid, or Whether a Maid May Be a Scholar* (in Latin). The English translation appears in 1659.

1639   Van Schurman engages a written correspondence with Princess Elisabeth of Bohemia and with Marie le Jars de Gournay, author of *The Equality of Men and Women* (in French, 1622).

1641   Descartes publishes *Meditations on First Philosophy*.

1642   The conflict between the Royalists and the Parliamentarians (or "Roundheads") turns into the English Civil War.
Lucas family home is sacked by Parliamentary sympathizers.

1643   Margaret joins the court of Henrietta Maria in Oxford.
Princess Elizabeth of Bohemia begins a philosophical correspondence with Descartes.

1644   Margaret escapes for Paris with Queen Henrietta Maria, not returning to live in England until 1660.

1645   Margaret marries William Cavendish, Marquis of Newcastle, in Paris.

1646   Margaret attends occasional meetings of the "Cavendish Circle," organized by William, and with participants including René Descartes, Thomas Hobbes, Marin Mersenne, and Walter

Charleton. The meetings of the Cavendish Circle take place through the 1660s.

1647   Cavendish's mother, Elizabeth Leighton Lucas, dies.

1648   Margaret and William move to Antwerp to live at the Peter Paul Rubens house. They remain in Antwerp through the 1650s.

1649   King Charles I is executed.

1650   Descartes dies on February 11 in Stockholm, Sweden.

1651   Hobbes's *Leviathan* is published.
       Margaret travels to London, where William is not welcome, to attempt to recover compensation for William's lost estate. The attempt is not successful.

1653   *Philosophicall Fancies. Written by the Right Honourable, the Lady Newcastle* is published.

1653   Henry More publishes *An Antidote Against Atheism*. More includes a glowing dedication "To the Honourable, the Lady Anne Conway." Her *Principles of the Most Ancient and Modern Philosophy* is published posthumously in 1690; it has a significant influence on the philosophy of Leibniz.

1654   Charles Cavendish dies, a mathematician and scholar, and the brother of William. Margaret and Charles had engaged in regular discussions of philosophy and other subjects.

1655   *The worlds olio written by the Right Honourable, the Lady Newcastle* is published. A revised edition appears in 1671.
       The philosophical and physical opinions written by Her Excellency the Lady Marchionesse of Newcastle is published.

1656   *Natures Picture drawn by fancies pencil to the life being several feigned stories, comical, tragical, tragi-comical, poetical, romancical, philosophical, historical, and moral: some in verse, some in prose, some mixt, and some by dialogues / written by . . . the Duchess of Newcastle* is published.
       This includes the biographical essay, "A True Relation of my Birth, Breeding and Life."

1659   Henry More publishes *The Immortality of the Soul*.

1660   The monarchy returns to England with Charles II as King.
       Margaret and William return to England and live at Welbeck Abbey. In the coming years they make regular visits to London.
       Margaret becomes an honorary member of the literary salon of Katherine Philips.

1662   *Playes written by the thrice noble, illustrious and excellent princess, the Lady Marchioness of Newcastle* is published.
       Orations of divers sorts accommodated to divers places written by the Lady Marchioness of Newcastle is published.
       Jean Baptiste van Helmont publishes *Oriatrike, or Physick Refined*.

1664   *Philosophical letters, or Modest Reflections upon some opinions in natural philosophy maintained by several famous and learned authors of this age, expressed by way of letters / by the thrice noble, illustrious, and excellent princess the Lady Marchioness of Newcastle* is published. *CCXI sociable letters written by the thrice noble, illustrious, and excellent princess, the Lady Marchioness of Newcastle* is published. This contains some of the earliest criticism of the plays of Shakespeare.

Margaret's views are discussed by More in his 1664/65 letter to Anne Conway.

Spinoza is writing *Ethics* through 1665; it is eventually published in 1677.

1665   William is made Duke of Newcastle. Margaret is named Duchess of Newcastle.

1666   *Observations upon experimental philosophy to which is added The description of a new blazing world / written by the thrice noble, illustrious, and excellent princess the Lady Marchioness of Newcastle* is published. An updated edition of *Blazing World* appears in 1668. *Womens Speaking Justified* is published by Margaret Fell Fox.

Mary Astell is born on November 16 in Newcastle, England. In 1694 and 1697, she publishes *A Serious Proposal to the Ladies, Parts I and II. Wherein is a Method offer'd for the Improvement of their Minds.*

1667   Margaret is the first woman to attend a meeting at the Royal Society of London.

Margaret engages a correspondence with Joseph Glanvill.

1667   *The life of the thrice noble, high and puissant prince William Cavendishe, Duke, Marquess and Earl of Newcastle ... written by the thrice noble, illustrious and excellent princess, Margaret, Duchess of Newcastle, his wife* is published.

1668   *Grounds of natural philosophy divided into thirteen parts: with an appendix containing five parts / written by ... the Duchess of Newcastle* is published. This is a heavily revised version of the 1655 *Philosophical and Physical Opinions.*

1670   Princess Elisabeth of Bohemia provides sanctuary to Anna Maria van Schurman and other persecuted individuals.

1673   *An Essay to Revive the Antient Education of Gentlewomen* is published by Bathsua Makin.

Margaret Cavendish dies in Welbeck on December 15 and is laid to rest at Westminster Abbey. The inscription on her tomb, at the front (North Transept) entrance to the Abbey, reports: "This Dutches was a wise wittie & learned Lady, which her many Bookes do well testifie."

1676   William edits and publishes *Letters and Poems in Honour of the Incomparable Princess, Margaret, Dutchess of Newcastle*. William dies shortly thereafter.

*Note that some of the information in this chronology is from Eileen O'Neill (ed.), *Observations Upon Experimental Philosophy*, Cambridge UP (2001), xxxvii–xli; and Katie Whitaker, *Mad Madge, Mad Madge*, London: Chatto and Windus (2003).

EARLY MODERN TOPICS AND THEMES — FOR INSTRUCTORS AND STUDENTS

Below is a list of topics that are central to the philosophical debates of the seventeenth and eighteenth centuries, along with a cross-section of the corresponding Cavendish passages.

MATERIALIST VIEW OF MIND

Worlds Olio—"Fame makes a difference between Man and Beast"

Philosophical Letters—letter XXXV and XXXVI of section one; letters XV, XVI, XVIII, XXI, XXV, XXVIII, XXXI, and XXXII of section two; letters XXI and XLII of section three

Observations Upon Experimental Philosophy—sections XXI, XXXV

Further Observations Upon Experimental Philosophy—sections X, XX

Observations Upon the Opinions of Some Ancient Philosophers—section III.4

Appendix to Grounds of Natural Philosophy—chapters II and XI of the First Part

MATERIALIST VIEW OF NATURE

Philosophical Letters—letters VI, XVIII, XIX, XXXI, XXXII of section two; letter XLII of section three

Observations Upon Experimental Philosophy—section XXI

Further Observations Upon Experimental Philosophy—sections XX

Grounds of Natural Philosophy—chapter I of the First Part

MATTER AS ETERNAL

Worlds Olio—"Of Nature" / "The Opinions of Some
    Philosophers—Essay 128"
Philosophical and Physical Opinions—"Chapter 23: Of Annihilation"
Philosophical Letters—letter III of section one; letter III of section three;
    letter X of section four
Further Observations Upon Experimental Philosophy—section XI
*Observations Upon the Opinions of Some Ancient
    Philosophers*—section IV.5–6

NO EMPTY SPACE—THE UNIVERSE AS A CONTINUOUS PLENUM

Philosophical and Physical Opinions—"There is no Vacuity"
Philosophical Letters—letters II, XX, XXXI, and XXXII of section one
Observations Upon Experimental Philosophy—sections I, XIX, XXXI
Observations Upon the Opinions of Some Ancient Philosophers—sections
    III.4, IV.1
Poems and Fancies—"Of Vacuum"

THE CAUSAL INTERDEPENDENCE OF THE CONSTITUENTS OF THE PLENUM

Philosophical Letters—letter II of section one; letter II of section four
Observations Upon Experimental Philosophy—sections XV, XXXI

INDIVIDUATION

Philosophical Letters—letter XVII of section two; letter II of section three
Grounds of Natural Philosophy—chapter III of the Second Part

PRIMARY VS. SECONDARY QUALITIES

Observations Upon Experimental Philosophy—sections XXI, XXXV

MATTER AS PERCEPTIVE AND KNOWING

Worlds Olio—"Epistle"
Philosophical and Physical Opinions—"A Condemning Treatise of Atoms" /
    "Chapter 63: Whether motion is a thing, or nothing, or can be Annihilated" /
    "Chapter 65: Many Motions go to the producing of one thing, or to one end"
    / "Chapter 77: Of different knowledge in different figures"

Philosophical Letters—letters X, XI, and XXXVI of section one; letters IV, X, XIII, XV, and XVIII of section two; letter XXX of section four

Observations Upon Experimental Philosophy—sections XVII, XVII, and XXXV

Further Observations Upon Experimental Philosophy—sections XIII and XX

Observations Upon the Opinions of Some Ancient Philosophers—section IV.2–3

Grounds of Natural Philosophy—chapter VIII of the First Part; chapter IX of the Second Part; chapter V of the Fifth Part; chapter XII of the Thirteenth Part

Appendix to Grounds of Natural Philosophy—chapter VIII of the Third Part

DIFFERENT KINDS OF MATTER

Observations Upon Experimental Philosophy—section XXXVII

Further Observation Upon Experimental Philosophy—section VI

Grounds of Natural Philosophy—chapters III and V of the First Part; chapters X and XV of the Fifth Part

ARTIFACTS VS. NATURAL PRODUCTIONS

Worlds Olio—"The Power of Natural Works" / "Of Chymistry"

Philosophical and Physical Opinions—"Chapter 208: The Knowledge of Diseases"

Philosophical Letters—letter V, VII, and XV of section two; letter XXX of section three; letter XXX of section four

Observations Upon Experimental Philosophy—sections III, IX, XIV, XVIII, XXV, XXVI, XXXIV

Further Observations Upon Experimental Philosophy—sections II, VII

Grounds of Natural Philosophy—chapter IX of the Second Part; chapter XII of the Thirteenth Part

INTELLIGENCE IN ANIMALS, INSECTS, AND OTHER NON-HUMAN ORGANISMS

Worlds Olio—"Of Birds"

Philosophical and Physical Opinions—"Chapter 77: Of different knowledge in different figures"

Philosophical Letters—letters X, XXXV, and XXXVI of section one; letter XIII or section two

Philosophical Letters—letters I and XX of section one; letters II and III of section two; letter II of section three

Observations Upon Experimental Philosophy—section XXI

Appendix to Grounds of Natural Philosophy—chapters III, IV, and XI of the First Part

Worlds Olio—"The difference Betwixt Man and Beast"

KNOWLEDGE OF GOD'S EXISTENCE AND NATURE

Worlds Olio—"The difference Betwixt Man and Beast"

Philosophical Letters—letters I and XX of section one; letters I–III, XVIII, XXX, XXXIII of section two; letter XX of section three

Observations Upon Experimental Philosophy—section XIX, XXI, XXVII

Further Observations Upon Experimental Philosophy—sections X–XII

Appendix to Grounds of Natural Philosophy—chapters II–VI and XI of the First Part

THE RELATIONSHIP BETWEEN GOD AND THE CREATION

Worlds Olio—"The Opinions of Some Philosophers—Essay 128"

Philosophical Letters—letters II and III of section one

Further Observations Upon Experimental Philosophy—sections X, XX

Observations Upon the Opinions of Some Ancient Philosophers—sections IV.5, IV.6, V.1

Grounds of Natural Philosophy—Chapter V of the Sixth Part

Appendix to Grounds of Natural Philosophy—chapter IV of the First Part

IMMATERIAL FINITE SOUL / MIND

Philosophical Letters—letter XX of section one; letters XVIII, XXIX, and XXXII of section two

Observations Upon Experimental Philosophy—section XIX

Appendix to Grounds of Natural Philosophy—chapters II, III of the First Part

THE AFTERLIFE

Worlds Olio—"Fame makes a difference between Man and Beast" / "What the Desire of Fame proceeds from" / "Allegory 55"

Grounds of Natural Philosophy—chapter V of the Sixth Part

Appendix to Grounds of Natural Philosophy—chapter XI of the First Part; chapter VIII of the Third Part

SCRIPTURE

Worlds Olio—"Of Moderation"
Philosophical Letters—letter III of section I; letters III, XXXII, and XXXIII of section two; letter XX of section three; letter X of section four

FREE WILL

Philosophical and Physical Opinions—"Chapter 59: Of Fortune" / "The Agilenesse of innate Matter"
Philosophical Letters—letters VIII, XII, and XXIX of section one; letters VIII, XXIX and XXXI of section two; letters IV and VII of section two; letter XXIV of section three
Observations Upon Experimental Philosophy—sections XXVII, XXXI, and XXXV
Observations Upon the Opinions of Some Ancient Philosophers—section IV.5
Grounds of Natural Philosophy—chapters V, X, and XVIII of the First Part; chapter XII of the Sixth Part, chapter XII of the Seventh Part, chapter I of the Eighth Part
Appendix to Grounds of Natural Philosophy—chapters IV, V, VI, and VII of the First Part
Poems and Fancies, "The Fairies in the Braine, may be the causes of many Thoughts"

ORDER AND DISORDER

Worlds Olio—"Of Nature" / "Of the Predestination of Nature"
Philosophical and Physical Opinions—"A Condemning Treatise of Atoms"
Philosophical Letters—letter XI of section one; letters V and VII of section two; letters XXIII and XXIX of section three; letters IV and XXXIII of section four
Observations Upon Experimental Philosophy—section XV
Further Observations Upon Experimental Philosophy—section XX
Observations Upon the Opinions of Some Ancient Philosophers—section IV.2–3
Grounds of Natural Philosophy—chapter VIII of the First Part; chapter XII of the Sixth Part; and chapter I of the Eighth Part

Appendix to Grounds of Natural Philosophy—chapters IV and V of the First Part

CAUSE AND EFFECT

Worlds Olio—"Of the Predestination of Nature"
Philosophical and Physical Opinions—"Chapter 96: Of the Load-stone"
Grounds of Natural Philosophy—chapters XVI–XVIII of the First Part
Appendix to Grounds of Natural Philosophy—chapters VI and VII of the First Part
The She-Anchoret—pp. 224–225

GENDER

Worlds Olio—"The Preface" / "Of Noble Souls, and Strong Bodies"
Philosophical and Physical Opinions—"To the Two Universities"
Philosophical Letters—"A Preface to the Reader" and letter I of section four
Observations Upon Experimental Philosophy—"To the Reader"
Poems and Fancies—"To all Writing Ladies"
Bell in Campo—pp. 208–209

AGENCY AND AUTHORITY

Philosophical and Physical Opinions—"To the Two Universities"
Philosophical Letters—"A Preface to the Reader"
Observations Upon Experimental Philosophy—"To the Reader"
Poems and Fancies—"To all Writing Ladies"
Playes—"An Introduction"
Bell in Campo

HAPPINESS

Worlds Olio—"Of a Solitary Life" / "Of Moderation" / "Of the Happiness of a Farmer" / "Of the Vastness of Desires" / "The Nature of Man" / "Allegory 20" / "The difference Betwixt Man and Beast"
Poems and Fancies—"To Morall Philosophers" / "A Dialogue betwixt Man and Nature" / "Poets have most Pleasure in this Life"
The She-Anchoret—"The sixteenth sort of Visiters, were Poets"

POLITICS AND GOVERNMENT

Worlds Olio—"Clemency makes the best form of Government" / "The cause of Rebellion" / "Of Ceremony" / "Of a Civil-Warr"
Poems and Fancies—"A Dialogue betwixt Peace, and War"
Blazing World
Bell in Campo
The She-Anchoret—p. 226 and the discussion with "The Eighth sort of Visiters"

MORALITY AND VALUE—WHETHER OR NOT OBJECTIVE

Worlds Olio—"Of Imaginary Beauty"
Philosophical and Physical Opinions—"No Judge in Nature" / "Chapter 59: Of Fortune"
Philosophical Letters—letter XXIII of section three
Observations Upon the Opinions of Some Ancient Philosophers—section II
Grounds of Natural Philosophy—chapter XIV of the Thirteenth Part

ANIMAL CRUELTY

Poems and Fancies—"A Dialogue Betwixt Man, and Nature" / "A Morall Discourse betwixt Man, and Beast"

IMAGINATION AND ALTERNATIVE WORLDS

Philosophical and Physical Opinions—"Chapter 151: Of thoughts"
Grounds of Natural Philosophy—chapter IV of the Sixth Part
Poems and Fancies—"Similizing the Head of Man to the World"
Blazing World
Bell in Campo

IMAGINATION AS A SOURCE OF PLEASURE AND ESCAPE

Worlds Olio—"Allegory 20"
Philosophical and Physical Opinions—"Chapter 152: Of thinking, or thoughts"
Grounds of Natural Philosophy—chapter IV of the Sixth Part

EMPIRICISM

Worlds Olio—"Of the Senses and the Brain"
Observations Upon Experimental Philosophy—section XXXVI
Blazing World—"Epilogue to the Reader" / "To all Noble and Worthy Ladies"

KNOWLEDGE OF THE EXISTENCE OF THE EXTERNAL WORLD

Worlds Olio—"Of the Senses and Brain"
Philosophical and Physical Opinions—"Chapter 152: Of thinking, or thoughts" / "Chapter 153: Of Sleep and dreams"
Observations Upon Experimental Philosophy—section XXXVII
Further Observations Upon Experimental Philosophy—section IX
Grounds of Natural Philosophy—chapter X of the Fifth Part; chapter IV of the Sixth Part; chapter IV of the Seventh Part

THE LIMITS OF KNOWLEDGE

Worlds Olio—"Of Chymistry"
Philosophical and Physical Opinions—"Chapter 96: Of the Load-stone"
Philosophical Letters—letters XVI and XLIII of section three; letter XXVII of section four
Observations Upon Experimental Philosophy—sections XXV, XXVI, XXVII
Poems and Fancies—"Of many Worlds in this World" / "A Dialogue betwixt Man, and Nature"

PRACTICAL IMPORT OF PHILOSOPHY AND SCIENCE

Worlds Olio—"An Epistle to the Unbelieving Readers in Natural Philosophy" / "Of Philosophy" / "Of Physicians"
Philosophical and Physical Opinions—"Of the Motion of the Bodie"
Philosophical Letters—letter XXVII of section four

Introduction

Margaret Cavendish was a seventeenth-century philosopher, scientist, poet, essayist, and playwright who addressed a wide spectrum of perennial philosophical issues across a wide range of genres. Against Descartes and the Cartesian tradition, she argued that minds are material and that ideas are always imagistic pictures.[1] If God and supernatural souls cannot be depicted in an imagistic picture—and Cavendish thinks that they cannot—then we can have no ideas of such entities, and we need to be extremely restrained in the assertions that we might attempt to make about them. If we can form an idea of it, Cavendish might say, it is material, and if we cannot think about it, it is not thereby nothing, but nor is it a suitable subject matter for human inquiry.[2] Cavendish also argues that there is no vacuum and that the created universe is a contiguous plenum of bodies; since something cannot come from nothing, and nothing can reduce to nothing, the universe is also eternal. The universe is a contiguous plenum of bodies—indeed it is a single individual—and what we identify as smaller individuals are just regions of matter that preserve a regular proportion of motion.[3] Bodies are contiguous with other bodies, and each body depends for its properties, features, and structural integrity on the behavior of the bodies that surround it.[4] Bodies are also perceptive and intelligent: there could not exist the organization and order that we encounter in nature unless bodies were perceptive and intelligent, but Cavendish also argues that it is just *obvious* that

---

[1] See, for example, *Observations Upon Experimental Philosophy*, section XXI. Here and in the remaining footnotes of the Introduction, I refer to just one or two passages in which Cavendish articulates a particular view, though additional passages will of course be presented later in the volume.

[2] *Philosophical Letters*, letter XVII of section one.

[3] *Philosophical Letters*, letter XVII of section two; *Grounds of Natural Philosophy*, chapter III of the Second Part.

[4] *Observations Upon Experimental Philosophy*, section XV.

intelligence is ubiquitous in nature.[5] There is the skillful behavior of the ant, the bee, and the spider, all of which Cavendish celebrates in poetic verse:

> Mark but the little *Ant*, how she doth run,
> In what a busie *motion she* goeth on:
> As if she ordered all the *Worlds Affaires*;
> When tis but onely one small *Straw shee* beares.
> But when they find a *Flye*, which on the ground lyes dead,
> *Lord*, how they stir; so full is every *Head*.
> Some with their *Feet*, and *Mouths*, draw it along,
> Others their *Tailes*, and *Shoulders* thrust it on.
> And if a *Stranger Ant* comes on that way,
> *Shee* helpes them strait, nere asketh if *shee* may.
> Nor staies to ask *Rewardes*, but is well pleas'd:
> Thus paies her selfe with her owne *Paines*, their *Ease*.
> They live as the *Lacedemonians* did,
> All is in *Common, nothing* is forbid.
> No *Private Feast*, but altogether meet,
> *Wholesome*, though *Plaine*, in *Publick* do they eat.
> They have no *Envie*, all *Ambition's* downe,
> There is no *Superiority*, or *Clowne*.
> No *Stately Palaces* for *Pride* to dwell,
> Their *House* is *Common*, called the *Ants Hill*.
> All help to *build*, and keep it in *repaire*,
> No 'speciall *work-men*, all *Labourers* they are.[6]

There is the know-how and power that is exhibited in an organism's immune system; there is the embodied intelligence of our limbs when we walk without paying attention to how or where we go:

> [M]ost spend their time in talk rather then in thought; but there is a wise saying, think first, and speak after; and an old saying that many speak first, and think after; and doubtlesse many, if not most do so, for we do not alwayes think of our words we speak, for most commonly words flow out of the mouth, rather customarily then premeditately, just like actions of our walking, for we go by custome, force and strength, without a constant notice or observation; for though we designe our

---

[5] *Further Observations Upon Experimental Philosophy*, section XIII; *Poems and Fancies*, "Of the Ant."

[6] See "Of the Ant," in *Poems and Fancies*.

wayes, yet we do not ordinarily think of our pace, nor take notice of every several step; just so, most commonly we talk, for we seldom think of our words we speak, nor many times the sense they tend to; unlesse it be some affected person that would speak in fine phrases.[7]

The intelligence that is pervasive in nature is not necessarily conscious intelligence, according to Cavendish, but there is thinking of which a being is aware, she might say, and then there is the thinking itself. She offers these and numerous other theses throughout her corpus. The present volume is an attempt to display the central themes of her system and to motivate further understanding and study.

Cavendish is not a fixture of the philosophical canon, in part because her views and arguments were not picked up and made the subject of commentary in her own generation or in the generations that followed. However, she is a fascinating and penetrating thinker who puts forward original views and arguments, engages the work of her contemporaries, and anticipates ideas that are not advanced by more canonical philosophers until later. Her views on the contiguity and interdependence of the bodies of the plenum are an unacknowledged precursor to related views in Spinoza; her arguments concerning the sophistication (and she would say intelligence) of natural productions are similar to those of Hume in *Dialogues Concerning Natural Religion*; her views on agency and authority, and the ways in which these can be constrained by gender beliefs and other societal norms and expectations, anticipate de Beauvoir in *The Second Sex*. Cavendish also offers important objections to the views of the philosophers of her time—objections to Descartes's dualism; objections to the view in Hobbes (and later in Hume) that sensory perception is a matter of imprinting and impressions; objections to the view in Descartes, Henry More, Nicolas Malebranche, and others that matter is passive and not the source of its own motion; and objections to the Cartesian tradition generally that finite minds can have an idea of an infinite being. It is important to acknowledge that Cavendish engages a wide range of philosophical issues, but at the same time there is a danger in attempting to situate her in the canon by highlighting the respects in which she tackles normative canonical concerns. She does address a wide range of these: the mind-body problem, the nature of ideas, free will, God, the creation of the universe, the afterlife, external-world skepticism, individuation, autonomy, the nature and existence of empty space, the optimal form of government for human societies, and general issues surrounding human well-being. But Cavendish also focuses a significant amount of attention on issues about which her philosophical predecessors and contemporaries were largely

---

[7] *Worlds Olio*, "Epistle."

silent, yet about which many philosophers care a great deal. These include gender, social and political capital, animal cruelty, and the role of imagination in the context of human flourishing and social progress. The present volume includes excerpts from all of these categories of thought.

Margaret Lucas was born in 1623 in Colchester, Essex. She resided there for her first two decades of life, at St. John's Abbey, and then in 1643 joined the court of Queen Henrietta Maria at Oxford. Her presence at the court was in the early stages of what would become the English Civil War between the Parliamentarians and the Monarchists, with Charles I ultimately executed in 1649. The Lucas family had aligned itself with the monarchy before the time of Margaret's birth, and indeed, in 1642, her home at St. John's Abbey was sacked and looted by supporters of Parliament, who also desecrated the family tomb and vault. In 1644, Lucas would flee with Henrietta Maria to Paris, where she met and married William Cavendish in 1645. The couple relocated to Antwerp and made it their primary residence until 1660, although William was often away for reasons having to do with the war. Upon the restoration of Charles II (in 1660), they returned to England, residing at Welbeck Abbey in Nottinghamshire. Cavendish was named Duchess of Newcastle in 1665. She was an eccentric individual, expressing herself in ways that were outside of the mode—for example, in her work as a woman philosopher, writer, and scientist, and in her clothing and style—striving to fulfill what she in her autobiography identifies as a strong desire for singularity.[8] Over the course of her fifty years of life, Cavendish published twelve books and two collections of plays. She died in December 1673 and was laid to rest at Westminster Abbey.

Unlike the majority of her male philosophical counterparts, Cavendish had no formal training in philosophy. As she describes it herself, the scholarly education that she received in her youth was rather thin:

> As for tutors, although we had for all sorts of virtues, as singing, dancing, playing on music, reading, writing, and the like, yet we were not kept strictly thereto, they were rather for formality than benefit.[9]

Cavendish did have lengthy conversations in her youth with her university-educated brother, John, who later in life was a member (with Robert Boyle and others) of the Royal Society of London. As an adult she would have numerous scholarly interactions through the connections of her husband, William, even if her formal training remained minimal. Some of her philosophical texts indeed

[8] *A True Relation of my Birth, Breeding and Life*, 157. See also Katie Whitaker, *Mad Madge*, London: Chatto and Windus (2003), 300–301.

[9] *A True Relation of my Birth, Breeding and Life*, 157.

contain a large number of typos, which she wholly owns. For example, she writes in "Epistle" at the start of *Worlds Olio*,

> I find I live in a Carping age; for some find fault with my former Writings because they are not Grammar, nor good Orthography; and that all the last words are not matched with Rime; and that the Feet are not in just Numbers: As for the Orthography, the Printer should have rectified that; for I think it is against Nature for a Woman to spell right, for my part I confess I cannot.[10]

In the following chapters, there will be a consideration passages that bear on the question of whether Cavendish thinks that there is an intrinsic difference in the capacities of women and men. For now we might register that she was aware of her own scholarly limitations, and she expressed her intellectual creativity nonetheless. She also had a penchant for engaging in vivid episodes of imagination, and later in life—in her plays, poems, and stories—a penchant for putting them into print. She says in her autobiography,

> I was from childhood given to contemplation, being more taken with thoughts than in conversation with a society, insomuch as I would walk two or three hours, and never rest, in a musing, considering, contemplating manner, reasoning with myself of everything my senses did present.[11]

One of the prominent themes in her later writing is that individuals benefit enormously from crafting worlds of imagination in which they have control over how things unfold, and in which there is not the messiness and resistance that is so pervasive in the actual world. Cavendish inhabits numerous worlds of fancy herself, and she makes a record of them in print. She does so, she explains, in order to exist in the imagination of others—while she is alive and after she has died—and also to register that if the actual world were more like the reformed environments that we are able to inhabit in thought—for example, where a woman philosopher, scientist, physician, soldier, or merchant is taken seriously by the bulk of the contiguous plenum of bodies and minds—many individuals would have a much better chance of living a life with which they identify. Cavendish supposes that the actual-world plenum is more supportive and accommodating to some than to others, and that our mutual interdependence ought not go unstated. She also just supposes that, in the same way that we

[10] *Worlds Olio*, "Epistle."
[11] *A True Relation of my Birth, Breeding and Life*, 174.

can get lost in a good book or story, immersion in a world of imagination, especially one that is properly constructed, can be satisfying in its own right.

Another apparent reason for her retreat to imaginary worlds of fancy is that Cavendish was extremely shy in contexts that did not involve her immediate family. She remarks in her autobiography,

> This natural defect in me, if it be a defect, is rather a fear than a bashfulness, but whatsoever it is, I find it troublesome, for it hath many times obstructed the passages of my speech, and perturbed my natural actions, forcing a constrainedness or unusual motions.[12]
>
> My bashfulness is my nature, not for any crime, and though I have strived and reasoned with myself, yet that which is inbred I find is difficult to root out.[13]

When she applied to serve on the court of Queen Henrietta Maria in 1643, one of Cavendish's motivations was apparently to put herself into a context in which she would be forced to interact with a wide variety of unfamiliar individuals in ways that might help her to neutralize her shyness, at least to some extent. She was quickly overwhelmed, however, and she pleaded with her family to allow her to return home to Colchester. Her mother forbade it, out of fear that Henrietta Maria might be insulted in a way that would bring disgrace upon Margaret and the larger family. Cavendish would never overcome her shyness, although she would participate in social encounters while living at the Peter Paul Rubens house in Antwerp in the late 1640s and 1650s, and at Welbeck Abbey and on visits to London in the 1660s. She was also present at meetings of the "Cavendish Circle," organized by William, which over the years included such figures as Rene Descartes, Thomas Hobbes, Kenelm Digby, Marin Mersenne, Walter Charleton, and Pierre Gassendi, among others. William and his brother Charles, a mathematician, had both been tutored by Hobbes in their childhood, and they served as sources of intellectual engagement for Margaret as she absorbed a version of the education that was not made available to her formally. She was not an active participant at meetings of the Cavendish Circle, but it is difficult to measure the extent to which this was due to her shyness, to norms according to which public intellectual debate with women was unseemly, or perhaps to both.

Margaret published her first book in 1653, *Poems and Fancies*. In the eighteen years that follow there is an almost torrential output: *Philosophical Fancies* (1653), *Worlds Olio* (1655), *Philosophical and Physical Opinions* (1655), *A True*

---

[12] Ibid., 169.
[13] Ibid., 167.

Relation of My Birth, Breeding, and Life (1656), *Orations of Divers Sorts* (1662), *Playes* (1662), *Sociable Letters* (1664), *Philosophical Letters* (1664), *Observations Upon Experimental Philosophy* (1666), *Blazing World* (1666), *Grounds of Natural Philosophy* (1668), *Playes, Never Before Printed* (1668), and *Natures Picture* (1671). The theses that she advances are wide-ranging and numerous.

One of the central theses of the Cavendish corpus is that the matter that composes the natural universe is intelligent, perceptive, sophisticated, and skillful. She points to a number of considerations in favor of this view. One is that the bodies of the created universe exhibit a regular order in their interactions with each other—in cause and effect relationships, in the organized workings of an ecosystem, in the formation of species, in the workings of an immune system, in the pursuit of common goals—and that such behavior presupposes skill and intelligence. The world of natural bodies is not dead and stupid, Cavendish supposes, but something to appreciate and admire. She advances a separate but related view about human artifice and its limits: she argues that the elements that enter into an artifact do not have the same history of communication and integration as the elements that enter into more naturally occurring productions, and that the former are often thrown together too haphazardly to secure a rhythm. In the same way that a group of co-workers with a long history of familiarity and cooperation are likely to tackle a difficult project with more success and less clunkiness than a group of workers who have just met, the bodies that compose a human eye or any other extremely intricate production are likely to constitute a better product than an artificial version of it. The natural version is composed of very small bodies that are perceptive and contiguous; the human beings that create an artifact do not have such up-close perceptions of the elements that go into their productions, and they accordingly have much less guidance when it comes to the coordination of all the parts. Cavendish has harsh words for scientific instruments in particular—especially those that are advertised as the gateway to unlocking the secrets of nature. Indeed, she goes so far as to say that telescopes, microscopes, and other such tools are in most cases misleading and deceptive. We should *expect* them to be defective, given the difference between the dynamics of bodies that enter into artifacts and the dynamics of bodies that enter into natural productions, but she also supposes that experience bears out the same conclusion:

> [I]f the Picture of a young Beautiful Lady should be drawn according to the representation of the Microscope, or according to the various refraction and reflection of light through such like Glasses; it would be so far from being like her, as it would not be like a Humane face, but rather a Monster, then a picture of Nature. Wherefore those that invented Microscopes, and such like dioptrical Glasses, at first, did,

in my opinion, the World more injury then benefit; for this Art has intoxicated so many Mens brains, and wholly imployed their thoughts and bodily actions about Phaenomena, or the Exterior Figures of Objects, as all better Arts and Studies are laid aside; nay, those that are not as earnest and active in such imployments as they, are, by many of them, accounted unprofitable Subjects to the Commonwealth of Learning. . . . But, as Boys that play with watry Bubbles, or fling Dust into each others Eyes, or make a Hobby-horse of Snow, are worthy of reproof rather then praise, for wasting their time with useless sports; so those that addict themselves to unprofitable Arts, spend more time then they reap benefit thereby. . . . Wherefore the best Optick is a perfect natural Eye, and a regular sensitive Perception; and the best Judg, is Reason, and the best Study is Rational Contemplation joyned with the Observations of Regular Sense, but not deluding Arts; for Art is not onely gross in comparison to Nature, but, for the most part, deformed and defective, and at best produces mixt or hermaphroditical figures, that is, a third figure between Nature and Art: which proves, that natural Reason is above artificial Sense, as I may call it: wherefore those Arts are the best and surest Informers, that alter Nature least, and they the greatest deluders that alter Nature most.[14]

We can certainly make *some* artifacts that are functional, Cavendish allows, but only if we piggyback on the intricacy, know-how, and sophistication of bodies that are doing the most complicated and difficult work already. We can make a sword, she will argue, but we cannot make the metal; we can make healing remedies that know the body and can heal it, or that can put it in position to heal itself; we can make a baby, she might say, but only because all of the heavy lifting is being done by egg and sperm cells and by the uterus and placenta, and none of *that* is the result of artifice. On this issue the language in Cavendish articulates the views that we see later in Hume's *Dialogues Concerning Natural Religion*, where he argues that the causality that we encounter most often in nature is not the causality that is exhibited by conscious deliberative human beings—who might craft an artifact like a watch or a library, for example—but is instead the material causality of vegetation and generation.[15] Hume does not identify such causality as involving intelligence and perception—differing from Cavendish on that count—in part because he is friendly to the Cartesian view that thinking

---

[14] *Observations Upon Experimental Philosophy*, section III. Note also that microscopes and other scientific instruments were not of the same quality in the seventeenth century as they are today, and so Cavendish's report here would not be unusual.

[15] David Hume, *Dialogues Concerning Natural Religion*, 74–76.

and mentality always involve conscious awareness.[16] Cavendish herself identifies instances of behavior as intelligent that do not seem to involve conscious awareness at all.

A case in point is the skillful expert behavior of a human being. There appear to be instances in which we engage in an activity like walking or talking, and where our body makes all (or most) of the right sorts of intelligent adjustment, but without our conscious mind ever having to take notice. Cavendish indeed supposes that the highly conscious thinking that Descartes takes to be the essence of mind is not the only kind of intelligence that exists and that other kinds of intelligence are in fact the norm—in the knowledge and communication that is exhibited in cells (although she does not call them that); in the knowledge that is exhibited in spiders, crocodiles, bees, birds, and ants; and in the knowledge that is exhibited in goal-directed natural bodies more generally. Cavendish is here putting forward a view that is actually not so unusual in the seventeenth century. Although Descartes and other dualist philosophers argued that mentality is restricted to human beings, philosophers like Henry More and Ralph Cudworth argued that mentality is pervasive in nature.[17] Picking up on the Aristotelian view that one variety of cause in the natural world is the final cause (which is roughly the purpose or goal of an activity) and that another is the formal cause (which is roughly the idea or blueprint that guides that purposive activity), More and Cudworth argued that the order and organization that we observe in nature would not occur if passive and unintelligent matter were left to its own devices. But the order and organization that we observe in nature does occur, and so there is a need to posit the existence of immaterial entities that are attached to bodies and that help to guide them along. These entities are mind-like according to More and Cudworth (and Aristotle), given the sophistication and purposiveness that they exhibit, but they are not of the conscious and deliberative sort that we encounter in human beings. More and Cudworth would add that Descartes was correct that that sort of mentality takes place in human beings only. But that is not to suggest that there is no other sort of mentality, and it is not to suggest that the only sort of mentality that is featured in human behavior is of the Cartesian variety. Cavendish, More, and Cudworth highlight instances of human behavior that are guided by intelligence, know-how, and thought, but that are not accompanied by conscious thought. Presumably they highlight these instances of unconscious intelligence on the assumption that most of us

---

[16] This is perhaps controversial, but Hume's discussion of the origin of ideas, and our ability to notice the introspectable content of our ideas, is very suggestive. See, for example, *Enquiry Concerning Human Understanding*, section two, 96–100.

[17] For More, *The immortality of the soul*, III, xii, 1, 450; for Cudworth, see *True Intellectual System of the Universe*, 157, 162, 679.

will find the instances familiar and hence existent, even if we have no direct access to unconscious mentality that is exhibited anywhere else. Cavendish herself supposes that if conscious thinking is not the only kind of thinking, there might be additional kinds of thinking still: we do not know for certain what the cognition of other beings is like, and it is probable that thinking admits of a diversity and variety that is beyond us.[18]

Cavendish agrees with More and Cudworth that intelligence is pervasive in nature, but she disagrees with both philosophers (and also Descartes) about whether thinking is material. Matter *thinks*, according to Cavendish, and human beings are not especially different from other physical organisms. Cavendish indeed offers a number of arguments against the dualistic conception of thinking that was so common in the early modern period. One is a standard argument from mind-body interaction that other philosophers had expressed at the time, for example Princess Elisabeth of Bohemia and Pierre Gassendi. In their objections to Descartes, Elisabeth and Gassendi make note of the fact that immaterial minds and ideas appear to come into contact with bodies upon making them move—and presumably contact cannot occur without touch, and touch cannot occur except between bodies.[19] Cavendish herself offers a slew of arguments to the effect that mental entities have characteristics that are only had by material things, and that they must hence be material themselves. Our minds and ideas no doubt have a causal and interactive influence on our bodies—the views of Malebranche and Leibniz aside—but ideas have other features that are exclusive to material things as well. Cavendish offers, for example, an argument from the *motion* of ideas and minds. When we travel from one place to another, and we are thinking all the while, it would appear that our thinking is taking place at a location from beginning to end: but material things alone admit of location, and material things alone admit of motion, and so our minds are not the immaterial entities that the Cartesian tradition takes them to be. That tradition does allow that there are *metaphorical* descriptions that apply to minds and are in wholly physical terms—such as when Leibniz famously identifies monads as sometimes dizzy, and as perceiving from different spatial perspectives. Cavendish herself supposes that such language is descriptive precisely because it is not metaphorical. Minds do travel; they come into contact with bodies; their ideas admit of figure and dimension. Thought has features that only pertain to material things, and so thought is material itself.

---

[18] *Philosophical and Philosophical Opinions*, "Chapter 77: Of different knowledge in different figures"; *Further Observations Upon Experimental Philosophy*, section XIII; *Philosophical Letters*, letter XI of section one.

[19] Princess Elisabeth of Bohemia, "To Descartes, 16 May 1643," in *The Princess and the Philosopher*, 9–10; Pierre Gassendi, *Fifth Objections*, CSM 2:238–239.

Another tenet of the Cavendish corpus is that the material universe is a fully dense plenum and that what we identify as empty space is in every case a continuous stretch of body. We do not notice most of the material that lies in between macroscopic bodies, Cavendish supposes, and we do not notice the ways in which such material has regular causal effects. In her early *Poems and Fancies* (1653), she flirts with the view that the universe consists of indivisible atoms and void, but from 1655 she endorses the view that matter is inherently divisible and that void is nonexistent. There is no empty space, she argues, and a body is always identical with its "place."[20] Cavendish subscribes to the view that the universe is a plenum, and she then applies the view in ways that have implications for the rest of her system. For example, she argues that because each body is always surrounded by other bodies ad infinitum, all the bodies in nature depend for their properties and structural integrity on the bodies that immediately surround them, and on the bodies that surround those. She writes for example,

> I suppose some conceive Nature to be like a Granary or Store-house of Pinebarley, or the like; which if so, I would fain know in what grounds those Seeds should be sown to produce and increase: for no Seeds can produce of themselves if they be not assisted by some other matter; which proves, that Seeds are not the prime or principal Creatures in Nature, by reason they depend upon some other matter which helps them in their Productions: for if Seeds of Vegetables did lie never so long in a store-house, or any other place, they would never produce, until they were put into some proper and convenient ground: It is also an argument, that no Creature or part of Nature can subsist singly and divided from all the rest, but that all parts must live together; and since no part can subsist and live without the other, no part can also be called prime or principal.[21]

Cavendish embraces the view that creatures are causally dependent on the activity of the beings that surround them, and as the systematic thinker that she is, she explicitly connects the view with her conclusion that bodies exist side-by-side in a contiguous plenum.[22]

In some passages Cavendish also defends the view that for any event that occurs in nature, it has to occur exactly as it did, given its prior and contiguous causes.[23] At the same time, she is emphatic that the bodies of nature tend to be

---

[20] *Philosophical Letters*, letter XX of section one.
[21] *Observations Upon Experimental Philosophy*, section XV.
[22] Ibid., section XXXI.
[23] *Grounds of Natural Philosophy*, chapter XVIII of the First Part.

free, and so an interpretive issue arises about the nature of the freedom that she ascribes to creatures.[24] On the one hand, she allows that there are irregularities in nature, where these appear to be instances in which bodies spontaneously behave counter to the order that is exhibited as the norm. These would appear to be instances of libertarian freedom in which bodies are not necessitated to behave as they do—in which events *do not* have to occur exactly as they do, in their light of their prior and contiguous causes, and in which bodies retain a contra-causal "ability to do otherwise." On the other hand, Cavendish most often describes the freedom of creatures in terms of the agility and ease with which they achieve their ends, when they do not encounter interference or ob-struction.[25] She also says in a number of passages that strictly speaking there are no irregularities in nature and that what we identify as an irregularity is just any-thing that runs counter to our under-informed expectations and conceptions.[26] But on the *other* hand—she holds that the order and organization that we en-counter in nature requires that there be intelligence in play to keep bodies in line, and if she held that every event in nature has to occur exactly as it does in the light of its prior and contiguous causes, she would appear to be allowing that exception-less regularity can occur without the presence of mind. Perhaps she is contradicting herself here, or perhaps the order that she supposes to require intelligence is the goal-directed behavior of macroscopic bodies. There is such behavior, she insists, even if the goals and ends of a given macroscopic body do not always pan out, and even if there is a non-macroscopic level at which there are no irregularities at all. Here might be a good place to note that a critical issue of interpretation with respect to Cavendish is what we are to make of the texts in her corpus that appear to speak against each other. She says in some passages that there are irregularities in nature, but in other passages that there are no irregularities and that we identify things as irregular when they run afoul of our conceptions or expectations. As commentators, we would appear to have two interpretive options: we can count up the passages on both sides and see which of the two kinds is more predominant, or we can see if there is a way to reconcile the texts more directly such that the contradiction in question is only apparent. The same will apply in the case of Cavendish's view that we can have no idea or conception of God: in some texts she nonetheless makes assertions about God and God's nature, and indeed she will sometimes appeal to such assertions in the

[24] See, for example, Karen Detlefsen, "Reason and Freedom: Margaret Cavendish on the Order and Disorder of Nature," *Archiv fur Geschichte der Philosophie* 89 (2007), 157–191, and Lisa Sarasohn, "Leviathan and the Lady: Cavendish's Critique of Hobbes in the Philosophical Letters," in Line Cottegnies and Nancy Weitz (eds.), *Authorial Conquests: Essays on Genre in the Writings of Margaret Cavendish*, Madison: Fairleigh Dickinson UP (2003), 51.

[25] *Grounds of Natural Philosophy*, chapter V of the First Part.

[26] *Philosophical Letters*, letter XXIX of section three.

course of advancing a metaphysical argument. But she also will state that premises about God's nature have no place in a metaphysical argument and that she will not make use of such premises unless she is required to do so in responding to the views and arguments of her opponent.[27] In some cases, though, she will appeal to premises about God's nature when the views and arguments of her opponent are not under consideration. The interpretive debates in Cavendish are interesting and exciting, as they are in the case of any important philosopher of the seventeenth century, and as always, there remains much important work to be done in sorting them out.

Cavendish defends the view that the universe is a contiguous plenum, and she appeals to that view to generate a number of other views as well. One is that because there is no empty space, the larger universe is a single continuous individual and, strictly speaking, has no discrete parts. What we might identify as the parts of the plenum cannot in fact be plucked from it—if all bodies depend on each other for their features and their structural integrity—and Cavendish will argue indeed that a "part" exists only in our ways of conceiving, when we abstract from our thought of a body the information about its larger incubational context.[28] She speaks for example of the seed that only grows into a plant or tree if it has the support of surrounding ingredients as the soil, sun, rain, and air.[29] She supposes that the bodies of nature are dependent generally speaking—that no being is an island, as she might put it, and that not even an island is an island. She then extends the view into its social and political correlate. For an individual to have (what we might call) the property or feature of being a philosopher, or a scientist, or a priest, or the captain of a ship, much of his or her success will be a function of the makeup of the surrounding plenum—and in particular, of the beliefs and expectations of its inhabitants. A person might certainly call him- or herself a priest, but if they have no willing parishioners, and no authority bestowed upon them by a legitimating institution, there is a very important sense in which the person is not a priest, even if they make professions to the contrary. Cavendish herself had an extremely strong interest in metaphysical and scientific questions, and she was brilliant, but she was not in a position to receive the same sort of training as Descartes, Hobbes, and others; nor was she in a position to have students; nor was her written work in a position to be received by the philosophical community in a way that would get it a foothold. As she might put it, and with a playful amount of drama and poetical fancy, she was not going to become a faculty member at a university, and even if she did, her letters of recommendation would not carry the same kind weight for her graduate students

---

[27] *Philosophical Letters*, letter I of section one.
[28] *Philosophical Letters*, letter II of section four.
[29] *Observations Upon Experimental Philosophy*, section XV.

or post-docs, and so most would not have gone to the trouble to apply to be part of her (therefore non-existent) lab. The plenum is that thick, she would say, and it is unfailingly operative, even (and especially) in spaces that go unnoticed. Cavendish wrote numerous philosophical manuscripts, but her work was not the subject of critical commentary in the texts of the philosophers who came after her, and indeed her philosophical writing has not been studied in a way that is commensurate with her gravity as a thinker. A bibliography of the large amount of recent work on Cavendish is appended to the present volume, and a hope is that her thinking will be challenged further still. But women philosophers and scientists did not have a platform in the seventeenth century, and they did not have a platform from which to create a platform. To a large degree their voices were simply not heard.

Cavendish calls attention to the respects in which the plenum is supportive and accommodating to the aims and pursuits of some individuals, and dismissive and hostile toward the aims and pursuits of others. In her social and political philosophy—mostly by way of her fiction—she crafts alternative plena, or alternative possible worlds, in which the self-same individuals on seventeenth-century Earth are situated in alternative environments that grant them a much less hostile reception. In an actual-world climate in which the notion of a woman military general (or a woman philosopher or a woman scientist or a woman architect) is preposterous, there are not going to be military women in anything like the way or the numbers in which there are military men.[30] Cavendish accordingly uses her imagination to construct alternative worlds that shine a light on the respects in which all individuals depend on the details of the plenum that surrounds them. She is not suggesting that women depend for their social and political features on the structure of the plenum, and that men do not, but instead that men encounter a plenum that is more hospitable. She then uses her pen to make a record—to register how things could be different for women if the receptivity of their environment were different, and to register how things could be similarly different for men. In her thinking about education, for example, she argues that men and women are both up to the task of the highest levels of intellectual achievement, but that there are structures within the plenum that make the realization of a woman's potential almost impossible.[31] In *The Female*

[30] Cavendish would of course have to allow the rare exceptional case of someone like Queen Elizabeth of England, who had a very successful reign from 1558 to 1603. Part of what is tricky about this sort of case is that monarchs were regarded as having a kind of divine sanction, and so it was possible for English society to make a demarcation between a woman as monarch and the proper role of women in the remainder of social contexts. Elizabeth was also well-read in philosophy and other disciplines, but it was extremely unusual for these to be regarded as appropriate subjects for women generally.

[31] *Philosophical and Physical Opinions*, "To the Two Universities."

Academy, she paints a picture of an example—the women have found a way to successfully create a formal educational institution for themselves, but the men play trumpets outside the window, to make sure that the women are unable to concentrate.[32] Here Cavendish has us vividly imagine the prospect of women doing something that is not characteristically possible on seventeenth-century Earth: we vividly imagine women as intellectuals and scholars, without having to confront the prospect of the real thing, and we vividly imagine the obstacles that stand in their way. Another function of the alternative-world scenarios of Cavendish's fiction might accordingly be to ready the collective imagination for social change. Cavendish was a very conservative individual on questions of social change,[33] but her stories do allow us to entertain structural conditions to which a society might aspire, and without the threat of being required to adopt them right away. A reader today might regard these as thought experiments, and also as visions for reform.

A final benefit of documenting alternative fictional worlds, according to Cavendish, is to increase the chance that she and other aspiring individuals might live on in the minds of others, and with their achievements and failures depicted in context. Cavendish does not suppose that we can speak with any confidence of an immaterial afterlife—or that we can speak of immaterial matters at all—but she does think that the ideas that others have of us, which are in effect miniature imagistic versions of ourselves, can survive into future generations.[34] These versions of ourselves can capture what we were in the plenum while we inhabited it, and they can capture what we might have been able to achieve had the plenum been different. Cavendish also just supposes that we enjoy poetical fancies. We can fashion worlds of our own making—crafted to order—and the pleasures that we experience in these are often comparable to the pleasures that we experience in real life. If the actual-world plenum is largely hostile to our aims and pursuits, an imaginary fancy can even be preferable.

Cavendish defends the view that the plenum is a continuous stretch of bodies that are mutually interdependent, and she defends a number of related theses as well. One is that because something cannot come from nothing, and nothing can be reduced to nothing, the plenum of creatures is eternal. It does not come

---

[32] *The Female Academy*, in *Playes written by the thrice noble, illustrious and excellent princess, the Lady Marchioness of Newcastle*, London: Printed by A. Warren, for John Martyn, James Allestry, and Tho. Dicas et al., (1662), 653–679.

[33] See, for example, *Poems and Fancies*, "A Dialogue Betwixt Peace, and War," and also the terrific discussion in the introduction to Susan James, *Margaret Cavendish: Political Writings*, Cambridge: Cambridge UP (2003), ix–xxix.

[34] *Grounds of Natural Philosophy*, Chapter V of the Sixth Part. See also Deborah Boyle, "Fame, Virtue, and Government: Margaret Cavendish on Ethics and Politics," *Journal of the History of Ideas* 67 (2006), 251–289.

into existence, and it does not go out of existence; it has always been and it will always be.[35] To defend against the objection that her view here is heretical and that scripture says that creatures are not eternal, Cavendish will reply that she is only contending that the matter out of which things are made is eternal, and not those things themselves. Scripture does not treat such larger metaphysical issues, and indeed Cavendish will argue that we must be very cautious in our interpretations of scripture, especially with respect to conclusions that we draw in the course of doing philosophy.[36] And we must be cautious about theological matters more generally. Cavendish holds that matter is eternal, but she supposes that it is still a creature, which is to say that it depends for its existence on a being that is beyond nature.[37] She will be careful not to get into detail about the nature of this being, given that she supposes that we can have no idea or conception of it, but she does still want to posit that nature is a dependent. If it were not, it would be an eternal and infinite independent entity—a single individual, each of its parts in possession of knowledge of its contiguous surroundings, ad infinitum, constituting a being that is quite Godlike itself. Cavendish does not want to go as far as Spinoza in positing the view that God and Nature are one and the same, but in some passages, she comes close.[38] She approaches other Spinozistic positions as well. She argues that because there is no empty space into which the universe might expand, and because there can be no new matter—otherwise something would have to come from nothing—the infinitude of the universe is just its totality. She writes, for example, that

> it seems, *Pythagoras* understands by the World, no more then his senses can reach; so that beyond the Celestial Orbs, he supposes to be an infinite *Vacuum*; which is as much as to say, an infinite Nothing: and my Reason cannot apprehend how the World can breath and respire into Nothing, and out of Nothing.[39]

There do exist passages in which Cavendish speaks as though infinitude is more than this, however, and so once again there is much interpretive work to be done in deciphering the outlines of her ontology and in determining how these work to flesh out her larger system.

[35] *Philosophical Letters*, letter XXI of section one.

[36] *Philosophical Letters*, letter X of section four.

[37] *Observations Upon Experimental Philosophy*, section XXI.

[38] *Worlds Olio*, "The Opinions of some Philosophers—Essay 128."

[39] *Observations Upon the Opinions of Some Ancient Philosophers*, section III.4. See also *Grounds of Natural Philosophy*, chapter XII of the First Part, and *Observations Upon Experimental Philosophy*, section XXXV. For the view in Spinoza, see for example *Short Treatise on God, Man and His Well-Being*, I.ii, 40.

One further (and notorious) metaphysical issue of which Cavendish attempts to make sense is motion—and more specifically, the apparent transfer of motion from one body to the next when two bodies collide. Cavendish will admit that we certainly seem to encounter cases in which bodies pass along some of their motion, but she will argue that we have reason not to take these cases at face value. Many (if not most) of her contemporaries would agree with her on this, even if they offer their own (very different) analysis. For example, Nicolas Malebranche argues that although it appears to everyday common sense that bodies impart motion to other bodies, upon reflection we should recognize that God is the cause of all motion. There is always a necessary connection between a cause and its effect, Malebranche supposes, but there is never a necessary connection in the case of the interaction of two bodies: if there were, then God would not be able to intervene and stop the behavior, but God is omnipotent, and so that is absurd.[40] Cavendish herself takes a different approach to the question of motion—perhaps because she wants to refrain from incorporating into her philosophical arguments claims about God and God's nature, but also just because she supposes that another view is much more plausible. Motion is always the motion of the particular body that has it, she argues, and so a motion and its body cannot be separated. When a body *does* transmit motion to a second body, therefore, it must also contribute some of its substance along with it—namely, the substance from which the transmitted motion is inseparable. Motion does not hop from one body to another, she might say, but if a body does ever gain a new quantity of motion, it must also gain the corresponding amount of matter or substance:

> How can motion, being no substance, but onely a mode, quit one body, and pass into another? One body may either occasion, or imitate anothers motion, but it can neither give nor take away what belongs to its own or another bodies substance, no more then matter can quit its nature from being matter; and therefore my opinion is, that if motion doth go out of one body into another, then substance goes too; for motion, and substance or body, as afore-mentioned, are all one thing, and then all bodies that receive motion from other bodies, must needs increase in their substance and quantity, and those bodies which impart or transfer motion, must decrease as much as they increase.[41]

[40] Malebranche, *The Search After Truth*, VI.ii.3, 446–452.

[41] *Philosophical Letters*, letter XXX of section one. Note that in her view on the transfer of motion, and in her view on the vitality of bodies generally, Cavendish was likely influenced by the work of the ancient Stoic animists. Eileen O'Neill, "Margaret Cavendish, Stoic Antecedent Causes, and Early Modern Occasional Causes," *Revue philosophique de la France et de l'étranger* 3 (2013), 311–326.

There are many instances, no doubt, in which a body would appear to partake of new motions as a result of its interaction with another body, but without becoming larger or taking on any new substance. Here Cavendish responds that since there is never a transfer of motion without a corresponding transfer of substance, these are more accurately described as instances in which the second body moves by motions that are internal to it, but that were not overtly noticeable. In the present day, she might point to entities like electrons, which are quite active, and which are partly constitutive of the large-scale objects with which we are familiar, even if those large-scale objects would seem to us to be at rest. A body does not add motion to a second body without adding the substance from which that motion is inseparable, according to Cavendish, but a body can *redirect* the motions of a second body. One object or group of objects might dominate another, and sometimes the plenum can redirect motions to run counter to their initial aims and goals.[42] When a body does move, however, it does so by means of motions that it had already.

A final and related view to consider in the Cavendish corpus is the view that sensory perception is not a matter of imprinting, but instead is a matter of *patterning*, whereby sense organs utilize their own internal motions to make a pattern of the perceived external object. This is again a case where Cavendish supposes that competing views just do not make a lot of sense upon reflection. She already has up and running the view that bodies move by their own internal motions, and so the view that sense organs are passive, and the passive recipients of impressions, is for her a nonstarter. Furthermore, we sometimes perceive an object at a distance, and (she would insist) without intermediary bodies adding any motion to the bodies in between. If so, neither distant bodies nor intermediary bodies imprint themselves on passive sense organs, and another account is in order.[43] Nor do sense organs show any evidence of dents and dings, which we would find to be extremely common, Cavendish thinks, if we have waking perceptions on an almost moment-to-moment basis—and if our perceptions were formed by a process of stamping. We might object as in other contexts that the view that Cavendish is putting forward is a bit odd or unlikely, but she would no doubt respond that the view is unlikely only against the background of assumptions that have not been adequately examined. She would also be right to point out that almost any view of the early modern period will come across as odd if we do not read it in its larger and more systematic context. The views of

---

[42] *Philosophical Letters*, letter XXIX of section one and letter VIII of section two.

[43] *Philosophical Letters*, letter IV and XXIV of section one, and letter XVI of section two; *Observations Upon Experimental Philosophy*, section XXXVII, Q. 10.

philosophers like Descartes, Spinoza, Malebranche, and Leibniz merit that sort of global and rigorous attention, and arguably some of the views in Cavendish are more compelling still.[44]

Thus far we have considered a cross-section of the metaphysical views that Cavendish puts forward, but we must also address the epistemological question of how she thinks that we know that her (or any other) position is the right one. The short answer is that her epistemology tends to be fairly fallibilistic. She supposes that there are pressing questions in philosophy and science and that we have an investment in tackling them, but she also allows that we can only be so definitive in the answers that we provide. She advances axioms in support of the pillars of her metaphysical system—for example, the axiom that material things interact with material things only, in support of the view that thought is material—but she will often add qualifiers like that material-immaterial interaction is impossible "in my opinion," without offering any additional foundation or ground.[45] In another example, her view that thought is ubiquitous in nature carries along with it the supposition that material nature in fact exists, but she nowhere attempts to demonstrate *that*. She grants that we have dream perceptions that are indistinguishable from waking perceptions[46]—and that at any given moment we cannot be completely certain that our perceptions are veridical—but she does not suppose that that means that we should be skeptical of the existence of the external world. As best we can tell, our sensory perceptions are copies of entities that actually exist, and our ideas are copies of those, and the only way that we can make progress in such arenas as philosophy, science, politics, and medicine is if we proceed on the assumption that the world of bodies is for the most part as it seems. We do not have a proof of the existence of the external world, she thinks, and neither are we capable of a complete understanding of its workings. In a passage that reads as reminiscent of Hume, Malebranche, and Glanville—all of whom expressed the view only after she did—Cavendish remarks that if we had no experience of objects or events that are causally connected, we would never have the slightest idea or expectation that the second would follow the first. We feel that causal connections make sense because they are familiar to us, Cavendish supposes, but strictly speaking and on their own, they do not make sense at all. Instead, nature is intelligent and

---

[44] A terrific discussion of the work of Cavendish in the context of the work of her contemporaries is in Sarah Hutton, "In Dialogue with Thomas Hobbes: Margaret Cavendish's Natural Philosophy," *Women's Writing* 4 (1997), 421–432.

[45] *Philosophical Letters*, letter XXV of section two.

[46] *Philosophical and Physical Opinions*, chapter 153.

magical, and much of what transpires within it is a brute fact that does not admit of any further understanding or analysis:

> [A]nd as fire works upon several bodies after a different manner of way, according to the nature of the body it works on, producing divers effects; so for all I can perceive may the Load-stone; for certainly we do not know, nor never can come to that knowledge, as to perceive the several effects, that are produced from the least, or as we account the most inconsiderable creature made in nature; so that the Load-stone may work as variously upon several bodies, as fire, and produce as various effects, although nor to our sense, nor after the same manner of wayes, that fire doth, and as fire works variously upon various bodies, so there are fires, as several sorts, and those several sorts have several effects, yet one and the same kinde, but as the causes in nature are hid from us, so are most of the effects; but to conclude my discourse, we have onely found that effect of the Load-stone, as to draw iron to it; but the attracting motion is in obscurity, being invisible to the sense of man, so that his reason can onely discourse, & bring probabilities, to strengthen his arguments, having no perfect knowledge in that, nor in any thing else, besides that knowledge we have of several things, comes as it were by chance, or by experience, for certainly all the reason man hath, would never have found out that one effect of the Load-stone, as to draw iron, had not experience or chance presented it to us, nor the effect of the needle.... [S]o the Load-stone may work as various effects upon several subjects, as fire, but by reason we have not so much experience of one as the other, the strangenesse creates a wonder, for the old saying is, that ignorance is the mother of admiration, but fire which produceth greater effects by invisible motions, yet we stand not at such amaze as at the Load-stone, because these effects are familiar unto us.[47]

Thought is a basic feature of natural matter, for example, and there is nothing more there to explain, even if there is a whole lot there to admire.

Cavendish hoped that one day her philosophical views and arguments would re-appear in a climate that was willing to give them a fairer hearing.[48] It has been exciting to see that that is starting to happen, and given her views about fame and the afterlife, she would no doubt be excited as well.[49] There is, of course, a social

---

[47] *Philosophical and Physical Opinions*, chapter 96.

[48] *Philosophical and Physical Opinions*, "To the Two Universities."

[49] *Worlds Olio*, "Fame makes a difference between Man and Beast"; *Grounds of Natural Philosophy*, chapter V of the Sixth Part.

justice issue that arises with the exclusion of certain groups of individuals from the philosophical canon—if they were not able to live the same sort of engaged philosophical life as others because of the way that the plenum was differently responsive to them. There is a fairness issue here, but also an issue of self-interest, and as someone who took self-interest and self-love to be the primary motivators of human behavior,[50] Cavendish might say that we should be concerned to make sure that the creativity of all individuals is tapped and unleashed to deliver its maximum effect on the rest of us. We can think of examples of individuals like Emmy Noether, the brilliant mathematician of the early twentieth century who was not allowed to attend university as an undergraduate, and who only secured a paid teaching position very late in life, after encountering the full gamut of obstacles; or Harriet E. Wilson, the extraordinary the Civil War–era writer who might have published many books in addition to *Our Nig*, had she not been forced into domestic servitude, and if she had had an audience of readers that was differently receptive; or Japanese-Americans during World War II, who faced literal internment, but whose time before and after the war, in terms of business, academic, medical, scientific, legal, law enforcement, and other contexts, was spent in the same temporally contiguous plenum; and the descendants of enslaved African Americans and indigenous North Americans, who inhabited a temporally contiguous plenum as well. At a given point, two directions for a society are to dip down further into the mediocrity pool of the dominant group, or to tap the best of the strength and ingenuity of all creatures across the board. Self-interest might lean us in the direction of the latter—in terms of medical and scientific advancement, political insight, and philosophical clarity, to name just a few—but Cavendish would surely note that there is also self-interest involved in the feeling that one is superior merely by virtue of their membership in, or affiliation with, the group that is dominant. She enjoyed the benefits of her own social position, for example, and she also had a cautious view of the prospects for social change, in part because of the likely resistance of the beings of the plenum and in part because of her own experience in exile from the civil war in England.[51]

Cavendish invites a number of very interesting questions about how the plenum might be different and about how we might best attempt to alter it. One option is to resist the larger and more powerful regions that would oppose us, in ways that lead to pain and frustration. Alternately, we might allow the plenum to crush our will, and resign ourselves completely to the offerings that it makes available. Alternately again, we might take a stand on the lives with which we identify, even if we have to live some (or much) of them in our imagination. We might make a record of these lives and of the ways in which a large part of

---

[50] *Worlds Olio*, "Of Self-Love."

[51] Again, see James, "Introduction," ix–xxix.

what precludes them is the plenum and the beliefs and goals of its constituents. We might thereby nudge the imaginations of some individuals to become more open to behavior that the plenum blocks, in ways that amount to a gradual and eventual change in the plenum itself. We might also increase the chance that we live on in the minds of others, perhaps by our affiliation with imaginary worlds that finally come to be. Cavendish expresses a desire to be singular in many of her works. That is a desire that there is no doubt she fulfills.

CHAPTER 1

Worlds Olio

The Preface

It cannot be expected I should write so wisely or wittily as Men; being of the *Feminine* Sex, whose Brains Nature hath mix'd with the coldest and softest Elements: and to give some Reasons why we cannot be so wise as Men, I take leave, and ask Pardon of my own Sex, and present my Reasons to the Judgement of Truth. I believe all of my own Sex will be against me, out of partiality to themselves; and all Men will seem to be so too, out of a Complement to Women, or at least for quiet and ease sake; for they know, Womens Tongues to be like Stings of Bees; and what man would endure our *Feminine* Monarchy to swarm about his ears? For certainly he would be stung to death. So I shall be condemned of all sides; but Truth will help to defend me.

True it is, our Sex make great complaints, that men from their first Creation usurped a Supremacy to themselves, although we were made equal by Nature: which Tyrannical Government they have kept ever since; so that we could never come to be free, but rather more and more enslaved; using us either like Children, Fools, or Subjects, in flattering or threatening us, in alluring us or forcing us to obey; and will not let us divide the World equally with them; that is, to Govern and Command, to Direct and Dispose, as they do; which Slavery hath so dejected our spirits, that we are become so stupid, that Beasts being but a Degree below us, Men use us but a Degree above Beasts: Whereas in Nature we have as clear an understanding as Men, if we were bred in Schools to mature our Brains, and to manure our Understandings, that we might bring forth the Fruits of Knowledg.

To speak truth, Men have great Reason to give us no share in their Governments; for there is great difference betwixt the Masculine Brain and the Feminine; the Masculine Strength and the Feminine: for could we chuse, out of the world, two of the ablest Brains and strongest Bodies of each Sex, there would be great difference in the Understanding and Strength: for Nature hath made Man's Body more able to endure Labour, and Man's Brain more clear to understand and contrive, than those of Women; and as great a difference there is between them, as there is between the longest and strongest Willow, compared to the strongest and largest Oak. Though they be both Trees, yet the Willow is but a yielding Vegetable, not fit nor proper to build Houses and Ships, as the Oak, whose strength can grapple with the greatest Winds, and plow the Furrows in the Deep. It is true, the Willows may make fine Arbours and Bowers, winding and twisting its wreathy stalks about, to make a Shadow to eclipse the Light; or as a leight Shield to keep off the sharp Arrows of the Sun, which cannot wound deep, because they flye far before they touch the Earth. Men and Women may also be compared to the Black-Birds, where the Hen can never sing with so strong and loud a Voice, nor so clear and perfect Notes, as the Cock; her Breast being not made with that strength to strain so high: Even so Women can never have so strong Judgment, nor clear Understanding, nor so perfect Rhetorick, to speak Orations with that Eloquence, as to Perswade so forcibly, to Command so Powerfully, to Entice so subtilly, and to Insinuate so gently and softly into the Souls of men. . . . Women have no strength nor light of Understanding, but what is given them from Men.

This is the Reason why we are not Mathematicians, Arithmeticians, Logicians, Geometricians, Cosmographers, and the like. This is the Reason we are not Witty Poets, Eloquent Orators, Subtil Schoolmen, Excellent Chymists, Rare Musicians, Curious Limners. This is the reason we are not Navigators, Architects, Exact Surveyers, Inventive Artizans: This is the reason why we are not Skilful Souldiers, Politick Statists, Dispatchful Secretaries, or Conquering *Caesars*; and our Governments would be weak, had we not Masculine spirits and Counsellors to advise us.[1]

---

[1] There is an interpretive question about whether or not Cavendish is a kind of proto-feminist, or whether she holds that there are respects in which women are inherently inferior to men. The current passage from *Worlds Olio* is strongly suggestive of the latter view, but there are numerous passages elsewhere in her corpus in which Cavendish is clear that differences in the cognitive and other capacities of men and women have to do in large part with upbringing and education and with the willingness of men (and women) to take women seriously—as geometers, mathematicians, witty poets, navigators, soldiers, military strategists, philosophers, etc. See, for example, *Philosophical and Physical Opinions*, "To the Two Universities," which was published in the same year (1655) as *Worlds Olio*. See also "To all Writing Ladies," in *Poems and Fancies*; *Worlds Olio*, "Of Noble Souls, and Strong Bodies"; "To the Reader," in *Observations Upon Experimental Philosophy*; and *Philosophical Letters*, letter I of section four. In "Fiction," see *Blazing World*, the character of the Empress, *Bell in Campo*, the character of Lady Victoria, and *The She-Anchoret*, the character of the She-Anchoret; the latter three are women who function at an extremely high and impressive level, and are quite able to be Excellent Chymists, Skilful Souldiers, Eloquent Orators, and so on, as long as they are in environments that are not overtly hostile to the prospect of a woman occupying a position of authority. The 1655 *Worlds Olio* passage is over the top in its misogyny, and subsequent passages including "To the Two Universities" in *Philosophical and Physical Opinions* (1655) reflect the exact opposite view. In addition, if she had

What the Desire of Fame *proceeds from*

The desire of *Fame* proceeds from a doubt of an after-being. And *Fame* is a report that travels far, and many times lives long: and the older it groweth, the more it flourishes; and is more particularly a man's own, than the Child of his Loins.

Fame *makes a difference between Man and Beast*

For Beasts, when they are dead, the rest of the Beasts retain not their memory from one posterity to another, that we can perceive (and we study the natures of Beasts, and their way, so subtilly, as surely we should discover somewhat): But the difference betwixt Man and Beast (to speak naturally, and without any relation to Divine influence) is, that dead Men live in living Men; whereas beasts dye without Record of Beasts. So that those men that dye in Oblivion, are Beasts by nature: for the rational Soul in Man, is a work of nature, as well as the Body; and therefore ought to be taught by Nature to be as industrious to get a *Fame* to live to after-ages, as the Body to get food for present life: For, as Nature's Principles are created to produced some Effects, so the Soul to produce *Fame*.

Of the Senses *and* Brain

Some say, that there is such a nature in Man, that he would conceive and understand without the *Senses*, though not so clearly, if he had but Life, which is motion. Others say, There is nothing in the *Understanding*, that is not first in the *Senses*: which is more probable: for the *Senses* bring all the materials into the *Brain*; and then the *Brain* cuts and divides them, and gives them quite other forms than the *Senses* many times have presented; for of one Object, the brain makes thousands of several Figures; and these Figures are those things which are called *Imagination, Conception, Opinion, Understanding,* and *Knowledg,* which are the Children of the Brain. These put into action, are called *Arts* and *Sciences*; and every one of these, have a particular and proper Motion, Function, or Trade; as the Imagination and Conception, builds, squares, in-lays, grinds, moulds, and fashions all Opinions; carries, shows, and presents the Materials to the Conception and Imagination: Understanding distinguishes the several parcels,

meant the 1655 *Worlds Olio* passage as a sincere expression of her thinking, she presumably would have removed or revised it in the updated 1671 version of *Worlds Olio*, but she did not. She keeps the passage pretty much as is, and so another interpretive possibility is that in both versions the over-the-top language is meant to be ironic.

and puts them in right places. Knowledg is to make the proper use of them; and when the *Brain* works upon her own Materials, and at home, it is called *Poetry* and *Invention*: but when the *Brain* receives, and works journey-work, which is not of its own Materials, then it is called *Learning* and *Imitation*:[2] But Opinion makes great faction and disorder among them, disagreeing much with the Understanding, in presenting and bringing the wrong for the right; and many times with clamour and obstinacy carries it, especially when a strange opinion out of another *Brain*, comes and joyns with the other; and the *Brain* many times is so taken with his *Neighbor-Brain's* Figures, that he fills up his house so full of them, that he leaves no room for his own to work or abide in.

Epistle[3]

Some say as I heare, that my book of Poemes, and my book of Philosophical Fancies, was not my own; and that I had gathered my opinions from several Philosophers. To answer the first, I do protest, upon the grounds of Honour, honesty and Religion, they are my own, that is, my head was the forge, my thoughts the anvil to beat them out, and my industry shaped them and sent them forth to the use of the world. . . .

[M]ost spend their time in talk rather then in thought; but there is a wise saying, think first, and speak after; and an old saying that many speak first, and think after; and doubtlesse many, if not most do so, for we do not always think of our words we speak, for most commonly words flow out of the mouth, rather customarily then premeditately, just like actions of our walking, for we go by custome, force and strength, without a constant notice or observation;[4] for

---

[2] Here Cavendish appears to be supposing that when we have perceptions that are not the work of our own imaginative construction, those perceptions are veridical and "imitate" the outside world, making us "learn" from it. Nowhere in her corpus does Cavendish attempt to offer a proof that our sensory perceptions are veridical, even though there are passages in which she concedes that dream experience is sometimes indistinguishable from waking experience. (See, for example, *Philosophical and Physical Opinions*, chapters 152 and 153; and *Grounds of Natural Philosophy*, chapter IV of the Sixth Part, and chapter IV of the Seventh Part.) She appears to hold that our belief in the existence of the external world is a kind baseline assumption that cannot and need not be demonstrated.

[3] Note that this epistle is not included in the 1671 version of *Worlds Olio*, but was in the original version published in 1655.

[4] See also *Grounds of Natural Philosophy*, chapter XV of the Fifth Part. Note that Henry More and Ralph Cudworth also held that sophisticated behaviors like walking and talking often take place without conscious mentality to guide them along. (See More, *The Immortality of the Soul*, III. xii,1, 450, and Cudworth, *True Intellectual System of the Universe*, 157, 162, 679.) Cavendish agrees with More and Cudworth that sophisticated and orderly behavior is always guided by mind, and is often guided by unconscious mind, but she also holds (in opposition to More and Cudworth) that minds are material. (See also note 2 for *Philosophical and Physical Opinions*.) A very different view

though we designe our wayes, yet we do not ordinarily think of our pace, nor take notice of every several step; just so, most commonly we talk, for we seldom think of our words we speak, nor many times the sense they tend to; unlesse it be some affected person that would speak in fine phrases.

Of a Solitary Life

Certainly a *Solitary Life* is the happiest of all lives: I do not mean so *solitary*, as to live like an *Anchoret*, or not to be bound to inconveniences either of *Care* or *Fear*; or not to be tied to observance either to Parents, or Wedlock, or Superiors; or not to be troubled to the bringing up of their Children, and the care of bestowing them when brought up; but their Persons must be as free from all Bonds, as their Minds from all wandering desires: And as it is a great pleasure, so it is a great chance to find it; because the minde must be contracted into so round a compass, and so firm a *solitude*, that the thoughts must travel no further than home.

Of Moderation

The way to a Man's happiest condition of life in this World, and the way to the next, is, the straight way of *Moderation*; for the Extreams are to be shunn'd, even in Devotion; for the Holy Writ saith, *Turn not to the right hand, nor to the left, lest you go the wrong way*: For, Extreams in Devotion, run to Superstition and Idolatry; and the neglect in both, to *Atheisme*. But to keep the even way, is to obey God as he hath commanded, and not as we fancy by our wrong interpretation.

Of the Happiness of a Farmer

The *Farmer*, and his Wife, Sons, Daughters, and Servants, are happier than Kings, Nobles, or Gentry: for, a King hath more Cares to govern his Kingdom, than he receives Pleasure in the enjoyment. The *Farmer's* care is only to pay his Rent, which if he cannot do, he must have a very hard Bargain, or be a very ill Husband;

is in Descartes, who held that in order for an act to be attributed to us, it had to be caused by conscious mental states, as he held that mental states are always conscious and that a person's self is to be identified with the conscious "I" or ego. (See, for example, *Fourth Replies*, CSM 2:171; "To the Marquess of Newcastle, 23 November 1646," CSMK 302–304; and the Second Meditation, CSM 2:16–23.) Also noteworthy here is that the Marquess of Newcastle—to whom Descartes wrote the 23 November 1646 letter—is William Cavendish, the husband of Margaret, and with her a defender of the view that much of human [and other animal] behavior is guided by unconscious mentality. See also *Philosophical Letters*, letters X and XXXVI of section one; *Philosophical and Physical Opinions*, chapter 77; and note 35 for *Philosophical Letters*.

and he takes more pleasure in his Labour, than the Nobility in their Ease: His Labour gets a good Stomack, digests his Meat, provokes Sleep, quickens his Spirits, maintains Health, prolongs Life, and grows rich into the Bargain.

Of the Vastness of Desires

There are few, but *desire* to be absolute in the World, to be the singular work of nature, and to have the power over all her other Works. Although they may be more happy with lesse: yet Nature hath given men those *vast Desires*, that they can keep in no limits, be their beginning never so low and humble. As for example, A man that is very poor, and in great wants, desires only to have so much as will serve meer Necessity, and when he hath that, then he desireth Conveniences, then for Decency, after for Curiosity, and so for Glory, State, and Fame: and though *Desire* run several ways, yet they aim all at one end; if any end there were to those that will embrace all. But some say, that the Mind is the measure of Happiness: which is impossible, unless the Mind were reasonable: for, the Mind is not satisfied, though it had all, but requires more: so the Mind is like Eternity, always running, but never comes to an end.[5]

Of Atheism *and* Superstition

It is better to be an *Atheist*, than a *Superstitious man*: for, in *Atheism* there is Humanity and Civility from Man to Man; but *Superstition* regards no Humanity, but begets cruelty to all things, even to themselves.

Clemency *makes the greatest* Monarch.

He is the greatest *Monarch* that is most beloved of the Subject, because he hath not only the power over Men's bodies, but over their Minds; where he that is hated and feared, hath only a power of the Body; But the Mind is a rebel, and stands out against him. Thus Freedom makes Obedience, when Bondage and Slavery is but a forced Authority, because consent is not there; and there is more labour in Tyranny, with whipping the people into obedience, than the pleasure of being obeyed is.[6]

---

[5] See also *Worlds Olio*, "The Nature of Man," and *Poems and Fancies*, "A Dialogue betwixt Man, and Nature."

[6] See also *Appendix to Grounds of Natural Philosophy*, chapter XII of the First Part.

The cause of Rebellion.

There is nothing causeth *Rebellion,* so soon as the unequal living of the Subjects; as, when a Noble-man strives to live like his King, a Gentleman to live like a Noble-man, and a Peasant or a Citizen to live like a Gentleman; . . . And when a Noble-man seeth an Inferiour Person in as good or better Equipage than himself, it begets Envy, and Envy causeth Murmur; Murmur Faction, Faction Rebellion: and the Inferior sort living at the rate of the Nobler sort, begets Pride, Pride Ambition, Ambition Faction, Faction Rebellion. And thus the Nobler sort striving to keep up their Dignity; and the Inferior, through their Pride, out-braving the Noble, those of the same Degrees are tempted to live above their Abilities, even with their equals: Thus striving to out-brave one another, they run into Poverty; and being poor, they fear no loss: for, having little to maintain life, they set it at stake; either to lose all, or to get more: for in Civil-Wars, all is Fish that comes to Net; whereas every man living in his degree, Envy, Pride, and Luxury are abated; Neighbourly Love and Kindness bred, and Peace kept, and every one thrives in his Quality, and grows Rich by Frugality, and Riches beget Care, Care begets Fear: and modest Fear keeps Peace.

Of Ceremony

Ceremony is rather of Superstitious Shew, than a Substance; it lives in Formality, not in Reality: yet it is that which keeps up the Church, and is the life of Religion; it heightens and glories the Powers of Kings and States; it strikes such a reverence and respect in the beholders, that it begets fear and wonder, insomuch as it amazes the Spirits of Men to Humiliation and Adoration; and gives such a distance, that it deifies Human things.[7] *Ceremony* hath such a Majestical Form, that it becomes a kind of a god; for it creates such a Superstition, that it is not only served with earnest Endeavours, but many times with such a fury, that oft-times the Observer runs into Madness: But as it strikes Fear, so it begets Pride: And yet *Ceremony* is so necessary, that without it Commonwealths would run into a Confusion: for, it is the Officer to make way for Command and Obedience; which keeps Peace and creates Order; which Order is to place things in such Manner, Forms, and Times, as is needful.

---

[7] See also "Fiction," *Blazing World,* p. 194.

Of a Civil-Warr

The greatest storm that shipwrecks honest Education, good Laws, and decent Customs, is *Civil-Warrs*, which splits the Vessel of a Commonwealth, and buries it in the Waves of Ruin; And *Civil-Warrs* may be compared to a pair of Cards; which when they are made up in order, every several Suit is by it self, as from One, Two, and Three, and so to the Tenth Card, (which is like the Commons in several Degrees, in order) and the Coat-Cards by themselves, which are the Nobles: But Factions, which are like Gamesters when they play, setting life at the stake, shuffle them together, intermixing the Nobles and Commons, and so Loyalty is shuffled from the Crown, Duty from Parents, Tenderness from Children, Fidelity from Masters, Continence from Husbands and Wives, Truth from Friends; from Justice, Innocency; Charity from Misery. Chance plays, and Fortune draws the Stakes.

The Nature *of* Man

Man is more apt to take Dislike at all things, than to delight in any thing; but *Nature* hath given us no Pleasure but what ends in Pain; for the end of Pleasure is Grief: and Cruel *Nature* curbs us in with Fear, and yet spurrs us on with Desires; for, she hath made Man's mind to hunt more after Varieties by Desire, than she hath made Varieties to satisfie the Desire.

Of Imaginary Beauty

Some do *imagine*, That *Beauty* consists in the Opinions of Men, rather than in the Lineaments, Symmetry, and Motion of the Body, or the Colour of the Skin: for, what appeareth *beautiful* to one Nation, doth not so to another; witness the *Indians*, the *Ethiopians*, who think the blackest Skin, flattest Noses, and thickest Lips, the greatest *Beauties*; which seem Deformed and Monstrous to the *Europians*. The like of particular Persons in several Nations: for, what to one Person shall appear a *Beauty*, so much as to enamour his Soul with admiration; shall, to another, appear deformed, even to dislike: Which shews, that were there a Body never so exactly proportion'd, or its Motions never so graceful, or Colour never so Orient, yet it will not please all. I will not say, There is no such thing as a true *Beauty*; but, no such *Beauty* as appears to all Eyes alike; because there is not Variety enough in one *Beauty* to please the various Fancies of Mankind: for some fancy Black, some Brown, some Fair, some a Sad Countenance, some a Merry, some more Bashful, some a more Bold: and For Stature, some like a Tall, some a Low, some a Fat, some a Lean; and some Dislike some Motions, some others; some like grey Eyes, some black, some blew; and to make mixture of all these, is impossible. Therefore, although there may be as great, and as good a Harmony in *Beauty*, as in Musick; yet all Tunes please not all Ears, so all *Beauties* please not all Eyes.

Allegory 15[8]

The several Brains of men are like to several Governments or Kingdoms: the Monarchical Brain, is, where Reason rules as sole King, and is enthron'd in the Chair of Wisdom, which keeps the Vulgar Thoughts in Peace and Obedience, not daring to rise up in Rebellious Passions. But the Aristocratical Brain, is, where some Few, but strong Opinions govern all the Thoughts: these Governours, most commonly, are Tyrannical, executing their Authority by Obstinacy. But in the Democratical Brain, there is no certain Government, nor setled Governour: for, the Power lies among the Vulgar Thoughts, who are always Placing and Displacing; one while a vain Imagination is carried in the Chair of Ignorance, and cryed up with Applause by the idle and loose Thoughts; and, in a short time after, thrown out with Accusation and Exclamation, and afterwards executed upon the Block of Stupidity; and so Conceptions of all sorts are most commonly served with the same sauce; and if by chance they set up Reason or Truth, they fare no better; for the inconstant Multitude of Rude and Illiterate Thoughts displaces them again, and oft-times executes them upon the Scaffold of Injustice, with the sword of Falshood.

Allegory 20

The first best Poetical Brain, was as a Flint, and Fancy the Sparks that are struck by the Iron Senses, and all Modern Poets the Tinder that take fire from thence.

Fancies are tossed in the Brain, as a Ball against a Wall, where every Bound begets an Eccho: so from one Fancy arise more.

---

[8] Note that there is a point at which the numbering of the allegories in the 1671 version of *Worlds Olio* is different by one than the numbering in the 1655 version. Allegory 15 in the 1671 version (presented in this chapter) is Allegory 14 in the 1655 version, etc.

Phrase is the Painting, Number the Materials, and Fancy the Ground whereon the Poetical aery Castles are built. There is no such sweet and pleasing Companion as Fancy, in a Poetical head.[9]

Allegory 35

Imitations are like a flight of Wild Geese, which go each one after another: when Singularity is like a Phoenix, having no Companion or Competitor, which makes it the more admir'd. And though some Imitations are good, and those are to be commended that copy well an excellent Original; yet it expresseth want of Invention, that they cannot draw without a Pattern; and it is Weakness not to be able to go without the help of another.[10]

Allegory 39

The Mind is like a God, that governs all: The Imaginations, like Nature, that created all: the Brain, as the only Matter on which all Figurative Thoughts are printed and formed. Or the Mind is like an Infinite Nature, having no Dimension nor Extension; and the Thoughts are like Infinite Creatures therein.

---

[9] A theme that is predominant throughout the Cavendish corpus is that we can often benefit from inhabiting worlds of imaginary fancy, or worlds of imagination—and that our encounters with the objects of these worlds are sometimes more pleasant and fruitful than our engagement with the objects of the actual world. Cavendish suggests a number of reasons why imaginary worlds would be worth our time. One is that the external world often stands in the way of our leading the lives with which we identify, but we have more control over worlds of fancy, and can craft them to order. (See, for example, "Fiction," *Blazing World*, "The Epilogue to the Reader" and "To all Noble and Worthy Ladies;" and *Playes*, "The Lady Contemplation," 184, 229.) A second reason, although this is perhaps more speculative, is that a turn to imaginary worlds of fancy allows us to create for posterity a record of the world as we think it ought to be, if in the short term it is highly resistant to change. See, for example, *Worlds Olio*, "An Epistle to the Unbelieving Readers in Natural Philosophy," and *Philosophical and Physical Opinions*, "An Epistle to Condemning Readers."

[10] Cavendish speaks of her own desire to be singular, in her autobiography (*A True Relation of my Birth, Breeding, and Life*, 175). Perhaps this is from an interest in identifying with rational matter, which she distinguishes from sensitive matter and inanimate matter, where rational matter is the most creative, spontaneous, and agile of the three. (See, for example, *Observations Upon Experimental Philosophy*, section XXXVII, Q.3; and *Grounds of Natural Philosophy*, chapter V of the First Part.) Perhaps her desire to be singular also has to do with the benefits that come with being a creative and poetical mind, and with the increased likelihood of achieving fame for one who stands out as unusual. (See, for example, "Fame makes a difference between Man and Beast," in this chapter.)

Allegory 55

The Mind is like Nature, and the several Thoughts are the several Creatures it doth create: Forgetfulness is the Death, and Remembrance the Life.[11]

Of the Strength of Opinions—Essay 109

So strongly do men wedge or rivet Opinions with the Hammer of a confident belief, that it is, in many, impossible to remove them from them, though they are most ridiculous & foolish, but especially when they are begot of their own Brains, and all those that do not adhere to them shall be accounted as their Enemies; So much doth Opinion sway and rule in the mind of Man more than Truth doth; for though some Opinions jump upon Truth, yet it is a thousand to one when they meet.[12]

The Opinions of some Philosophers—Essay 128[13]

If it be, as some say, that the First Matter was from all Eternity, it is a Deity; and God, the Order of Nature from all Eternity: For what had no beginning, sure is a Deity. Thus Philosophers by their Arguments make three Deities, although they hold but one.

The difference Betwixt Man *and* Beast

Man strives after *Fame*, which *Beasts* do not. *Man* troubles himself with Heaven and Hell, which *Beasts* do not. *Man* is weary of what he hath, and torments his Life with various Desires. *Beasts* are contented with what they have. *Man*

---

[11] This is numbered as Allegory 51 in the original 1655 edition of *Worlds Olio*.

[12] This is numbered as Essay 127 in the 1655 edition. A recurring theme in the philosophical work of the early modern period is that if reality is quite different from how we normally tend to conceive it, and if we are tightly wedded to our own longstanding opinions, it is very unlikely that we would ever be able to appreciate the force of arguments for views on the opposing side. See, for example, Descartes, *Principles of Philosophy* I.71–75, CSM 1:218–221; Spinoza, *Treatise on the Emendation of the Intellect*, sections paragraphs 47–48, p. 13; Malebranche, Preface to *Elucidations of the Search After Truth*, 539–540, and *The Search After Truth*, III.i.2, 204; and Julian Offray de la Mettrie, "Preliminary Discourse," in *Machine Man and Other Writings*, ed. and trans. Ann Thomson, Cambridge: Cambridge UP (1996), 156. The theme makes its first appearance perhaps in Plato's "Allegory of the Cave."

[13] Note that "The Opinions of some Philosophers" appears in the 1655 edition of *Worlds Olio*, but not the 1671 edition.

repines at what is past, hates the present, and is affrighted with what is to come. *Beasts* content themselves with what is, and what must be. *Man* hates Ease, and yet is weary of Business. He is weary of Time, and yet repines that he hath not Enough. He loves himself, and yet doth all to hurt himself. But *Beasts* are wise only to their own good. *Man* makes himself a trouble; whereas *Beasts* strive to take away trouble. *Men* run into Dangers, *Beasts* avoid them. *Man* troubles himself with what the Sense is not capable of: But *Beasts* content themselves with their Senses, and seek no further than to what Nature directs them, with the just measure of the pleasure of their Senses.[14] *Beasts* seek not after Vain Desires or Impossibilities, but that which may be had; they do not back-bite or slander; they raise not false Reports; their Love is as plain as Nature taught; they have no seeming grief, make no Sacrifice to false Gods, nor promise Vows they never perform; they teach no Doctrine to delude, nor worship Gods they do not know.[15]

Of Birds

All *Birds* are full of Spirit, and have more ingenious Fancies than Beasts, as we may see by their curious building of their Nests, in providing for their Young, in avoiding great Storms, in chusing the best Seasons, by shifting their Habitation, and in their flying in a pointed Figure, which cuts or peirceth the Air, and makes the passage easie; and so in many other things of the like nature.

Of Self-Love

Self-Love is the ground from whence springs all Endeavours and Industry, Noble Qualities, Honourable Actions, Friendships, Charity, and Piety; and is the cause of all Passions, Affections, Vices, and Virtues; for we do nothing, nor think not of any thing, but hath a reference to our selves in one kind or other, either in things Divine, Humane, or Natural: for, if we part with Life, which is the chiefest good to Mankind, it is because we think in Death there is less pain than in Life: and if we endure Torment (which is worse than Death) for an Opinion, or anything else; it is because our Delight of what we suffer for, is beyond all Pains; which Delight proceeds from Self-love, and Self-love is the strongest Motion of the Mind; for it strives to attract all Delight, and gathers together, like the Sun-Beams, in one Point, as with a Glass, wherewith it sets all on fire. So,

---

[14] See also *Poems and Fancies*, "A Dialogue betwixt Man, and Nature."

[15] See also *Further Observations Upon Experimental Philosophy*, section XII; and *Philosophical Letters*, letter XX of section three.

Self-love enflames the *Mind*; which makes it subtil and active, and sometimes raging, violent and mad; and as it is the first that seizeth on us, so it is the last that parts from us: and though Reason should be the Judg of the Mind, yet Self-love is the Tyrant which makes the state of the Mind unhappy; for it is so partially Covetous, that it desires more than all, and is contented with nothing; which makes it many times grow furious, even to the ruin of its own Monarchy.

An Epistle to the Unbelieving Readers in Natural Philosophy[16]

Many say, That in Natural Philosophy nothing is to be known, not the Cause of any one thing; which I cannot perswade my self is Truth: for if we know Effects, we must needs know Causes, by reason Effects are the Causes of Effects; and if we can know but one Effect, it is a hundred to one but we shall know how to produce more Effects thereby.

Secondly, That Natural Philosophy is an endless Study, without any profitable Advantage: but I may answer, That there is no Art nor Science but is produced thereby; if we will, without Partiality, consider from whence they were derived.

Thirdly, That it is impossible that any thing should be known in Natural Philosophy, by reason it is so obscure, and hid from the knowledge of Mankind: I answer, That it is impossible that Nature should perfectly understand, and absolutely know her self, because she is Infinite, much less can any of her Works know her; yet it doth not follow, that nothing can be known; As for example, There are several parts of the World discovered, yet it is most likely, not all, nor maybe never shall be; yet most think, that all the World is found, because *Drake* and *Cavendish* went in a Circular Line, untill they came to that place from whence they set out at first;[17] and I am confident, that most of all Writers thought all the World was known unto them, before the *West-Indies* were discovered; and the Man that discovered it in his Brain, before he travelled on the Navigable Sea, and offered it to King *Henry* the Seventh, was slighted by him as a Foolish Fellow, nor his Intelligence believ'd; and no question there were many that laugh'd at him, as a Vain Fool; others pity'd him, as thinking him Mad. . . . But put the Case that many went to find that which can never be found, as they say Natural Philosophy is, yet they might find in the search, that they did not seek, nor expect, which might prove very beneficial to them. Or put the case ten thousand should go so

---

[16] Note that this epistle appears in the 1655 edition of *Worlds Olio*, but not in the 1671 edition.

[17] Thomas Cavendish (1560–1592) was a navigator and an ancestor of William Cavendish, Margaret's husband.

many waies to seek for a Cabinet of pretious Jewels, and all should miss of it but one, shall that one be scorn'd and laugh'd at for his Good Fortune, or Industry? This were a great Injustice: But Ignorance and Envy strive to take off the gloss of Truth, if they cannot wholly overthrow it. But I, and those that write, must arm our selves with Negligence against Censure; for my part, I do: for I verily believe, that Ignorance, and present Envy, will slight my Book; yet I make no question, when Envy is worn out by Time, but Understanding will remember me in after Ages, when I am changed from this Life: But I had rather live in a General Remembrance, than in a Particular Life.

Of Philosophy

[T]here are none that are more intemperate, than *Philosophers*; first, in their vain Imaginations of Nature; next, in the difficult and nice Rules of Morality: So that this kind of Study kills all the Industrious Inventions that are beneficial and easie for the Life of Man, and makes one fit only to *dye*, and not to *live*. Yet this kind of Study is not wholly to be neglected, but used so much as to ballast a Man, though not to fix him; for, *Natural Philosophy* is to be used as a Delight and Recreation in Mens Studies, as *Poetry* is, since they are both but Fictions, and not a fit Labour in Man's Life. Many Men make their Study their Grave, and bury themselves before they are dead. And the Precepts of *Moral Philosophy* are as airy and useless; I mean only that part that belongs to every particular Person, not the Politicks, that go to the framing of Commonwealths, as to make one Man live by another in Peace, without which no Man can enjoy any thing, or call any thing his own; for they would run into Hostility: but Community of Men will close into a Commonwealth for the Safety of each, as Bees and other Creatures do, that understand not *Moral Philosophy*, nor have they Grave and Learned Heads, to frame their Commonwealths.[18]

The Power of Natural Works

Although Nature hath made every thing Good, if it be rightly placed; yet she hath given her Works power of misplacing themselves, which produceth Evil Effects: for, that which corrupts Nature, is the disordered mixture. But about all her Works, Man hath entangled her ways by his Arts, which makes Nature seem Vicious; when, most commonly, Man's Curiosity causeth his Pain: for, there is

[18] See also Hume, *An Enquiry concerning Human Understanding*, section one, 89–91.

nothing that is purely made, and orderly set by Nature, that hath not a Virtue in it; but by her Creatures mis-applyings, produceth a Vice.[19]

Of going round the World

It is said, That *Drake, Cavendish*, and others, went round the World, because they set out of one place, and went till they came to the same place again, without turning. But yet, in my conceit, it doth not prove they went round the whole World: for, suppose there should be round Circle of a large Extent, and within this Circle many other Circles, and likewise without; so that if one of these inward or outward Circles be compass'd, shall we say it was the Circumference-Circle, when it may be it was the Center-Circle? But it may easily deceive the Understanding, since we can truly judge but according to what we find, and not to what we know not. But surely the World is bigger than Mens Compass or Embracing; and Man may make a Globe of what he knows, but he cannot make a Globe of what he knows not: So that the World may be bigger than Man can make Globes, for any thing he knoweth perfectly. This Globe Man makes for the whole World, is but an inward Circle; and that there may be many of them which we do not know, because not found out as yet.[20]

Of Nature

We find, that *Nature* hath a constant and setled course in all she doth; and what-soever she works, are but Patterns from her old Samplers. But the several Stiches, which are the several Motions; are the same; and the Stuff which she worketh

---

[19] In later works Cavendish will argue that most human-made artifacts lack the know-how and sophistication of productions that come about more naturally, and are to be used with great caution. Artifacts tend to be "hermaphroditical" composites of entities that do not regularly appear together and that do not have the long and methodical track record of communication and know-how that is found in non-human productions. See, for example, *Worlds Olio*, "Of Chymistry;" *Observations Upon Experimental Philosophy*, sections III, IX, XXV, and XXVI; *Further Observations Upon Experimental Philosophy*, section II; *Grounds of Natural Philosophy*, chapter XII of Part Thirteen; and *Philosophical Letters*, letter XV of section two, and letter XXX of section four.

[20] Note that Cavendish holds that there is no empty space and that the universe is a contiguous stretch of bodies, many of which we do not notice. (See *Observations Upon Experimental Philosophy*, sections I and XIX; *Observations Upon the Opinions of Some Ancient Philosophers*, section IV.1; and *Philosophical Letters*, letters II and XX of section one.) The universe is a dense continuum, for Cavendish, and the demarcation of individual finite bodies will have to do with the way in which smaller bodies work in unison to secure a regular pattern of motion and figure. (See *Philosophical Letters*, letter XVII of section two; and *Grounds of Natural Philosophy*, chapter III of the Second Part.)

upon (which is the Matter), is the same; and the Figures she makes, are after the same kind; and we find, through many ages since, that it is the same, as *Salomon* saith, *Nothing is new.*[21]

Of the Predestination *in* Nature

There is a *Predestination* in *Nature,* That whatsoever she gives Life to, she gives Death to; she hath also predestined such Effects from such Causes.[22]

Of Chymistry

Nature hath given such a Presumptuous Self-love to Mankind, and filled him with that Credulity of Powerful Art, that he thinks not only to learn Natures Ways, but to know her Means and Abilities, and become Lord of Nature, as to rule her, and bring her under his Subjection. But in this, Man seems rather to play, than work; to seek, rather than to find: for, Nature hath infinite Varieties of Motions to form Matters with, that Man knows not, nor can guess at;[23] and such Materials and Ingredients, as Man's gross Sense cannot find out: insomuch that we scarce see the Shadow of Nature's Works, but live in Twi-light; and have not always that, but sometimes we are in Utter Darkness; where the more we wander, the apter we are to break our Heads.

Of Physicians

It is almost impossible for all *Physicians* to know all Diseases, and their Remedies, as they profess to do by their general Practices: for we find, that to learn a mean Art, it is the study and Apprecentiship of Seven years; and certainly, it is much more difficult to know Diseases, which are (like Faces) not any one alike. Besides, Diseases lye so hid in the Body of an Animal, as they are never perfectly known, but guess'd at; and to know the Cure of a Disease, is as hard as to know the Disease; and indeed, we can never know a perfect Cure, unless we could know the undoubted Cause. But *Physicians* should watch Diseases

---

[21] See also *Philosophical Letters*, letter III of section one.

[22] See also *Grounds of Natural Philosophy*, chapter XVIII of the First Part; and *Appendix to Grounds of Natural Philosophy*, chapters VI and VII of the First Part.

[23] See also "Of going round the World," in this chapter, and *Observations Upon Experimental Philosophy*, sections XXV and XXVI.

(as *Philosophers* the Starrs) with Observations, and in time they may guess so well, as seldom to fail of a Remedy. Wherefore it were good, that every particular *Physician* should be bound by a Law to study only a single Disease, and the Cure thereof, and not to confound their Brains with Terms and Names of Diseases, and to kill the Patient, by being ignorant of the Causes of them. Let every Disease go to a proper *Physician*; and though there be a multitude of Diseases, yet there are more *Physicians*.

Of Noble Souls, *and Strong* Bodies

[But] I speak of Strength, to shew that Women who are bred, tender, idle and ignorant (as I have been) are not likely to have much Wit; nor is it fit they should be bred up to Masculine Actions, yet it were very fit and requisit they should be bred up to Masculine Understandings.

Philosophical and Physical Opinions

To the Two Universities

Most Famously learned,

I here present the sum of my works, not that I think wise School-men, and industrious, laborious students should value my book for any worth, but to receive it without a scorn, for the good incouragement of our sex, lest in time we should grow irrational as idiots, . . . through the carelesse neglects, and despisements of the masculine sex to the effeminate, thinking it impossible we should have either learning or understanding, wit or judgement, as if we had not rational souls as well as men, and we out of a custom of dejectednesse think so too, which makes us quit all industry towards profitable knowledge being imployed onely in loose, and pettie imployments, which takes away not onely our abilities towards arts, but higher capacities in speculations, so as we are become like worms that onely live in the dull earth of ignorance, winding our selves sometimes out, by the help of some refreshing rain of good educations which seldom is given us; for we are kept like birds in cages to hop up and down in our houses, not suffered to fly abroad to see the several changes of fortune, and the various humors, ordained and created by nature; thus wanting the experiences of nature, we must needs want the understanding and knowledge and so consequently prudence, and invention of men: thus by an opinion, which I hope is but an erronious one in men, we are shut out of all power, and Authority by reason we are never imployed either in civil nor marshall affaires, our counsels are despised, and laught at, the best of our actions are troden down with scorn, by the over-weaning conceit men have of themselves and through a dispisement of us.[1]

---

[1] See also *Worlds Olio*, "The Preface," and the corresponding note 1. See also *Bell in Campo*, pp. 208–209 in "Fiction."

But I considering with my self, that if a right judgement, and a true understanding, & a respectful civility live any where, it must be in learned Universities, where nature is best known, where truth is oftenest found, where civility is most practised, and if I finde not a resentment here, I am very confident I shall finde it no where, neither shall I think I deserve it, if you approve not of me, but if I desserve not Praise, I am sure to receive so much Courtship from this sage society, as to bury me in silence; thus I may have a quiet grave, since not worthy a famous memory; but to lie intombed under the dust of an University will be honour enough for me, and more then if I were worshipped by the vulgar as a Deity. . . . [A]nd who knows but after my honourable burial, I may have a glorious resurrection in following ages, since time brings strange and unusual things to passe, I mean unusual to men, though not in nature: and I hope this action of mine, is not unnatural, though unusual for a woman to present a Book to the University, nor impudence, for the action is honest, although it seem vainglorious, but if it be, I am to be pardoned, since there is little difference between man and beast, but what ambition and glory makes.

A Condemning Treatise of Atoms

I cannot think that the substance of infinite matter is onely a body of dust, such as small atoms, and that there is no solidity, but what they make, nor no degrees, but what they compose, nor no change and variety, but as they move, as onely by fleeing about as dust and ashes, that are blown about with winde, which me thinks should make such uncertainties, such disproportioned figures, and confused creations, as there would be an infinite and eternal disorder.[2] But surely such wandring and confused figures could never produce such infinite effects; such rare compositions, such various figures, such several kindes, such constant continuance of each kinde, such exact rules, such undissolvable Laws, such fixt decrees, such order, such method, such life, such sense, such faculties, such reason, such knowledge, such power, which makes me condemn the general opinions of atoms[3] . . . [B]ut this opinion of mine

---

[2] One of the recurring arguments throughout the Cavendish corpus is that bodies need to be intelligent, perceptive, and communicative in order to exhibit the order that they do. (See for example *Philosophical Letters*, letter XI of section one; letters IV and XIII of section two; and *Observations Upon Experimental Philosophy*, section XXXV.) She will also propose additional arguments for the view that matter thinks—from the motion and change of location of minds, from the interaction of mind and body, from the divisibility and deterioration of mind, and from the bounty of God's creation. See note 43 for *Philosophical Letters*.

[3] Cavendish did flirt with an atomist view of matter in some of her earliest poems; see, for example, *Poems and Fancies*, "A World made by Atomes" and "All things are govern'd by Atomes." One

is, if the infinite, and eternal matter are atoms, . . . then every atom must be of a living substance, that is innate matter, for else they could not move, but would be an infinite dull and immoving body, for figures cannot make motion, unlesse motion be in the matter, and it cannot be a motion that sets them at work without substance, for motion cannot be without substance or produced therefrom, and if motion proceeds from substance, that substance is moving innately.[4]

Chapter 8: No Judge in Nature

No *Intreaty,* nor *Petition* can perswade *Nature,* nor any Bribes can corrupt, or alter the course of nature. Justly there can be no complaints made against *Nature,* nor to *Nature. Nature* can give no redresse. There are no Appeals can be made, nor *Causes* determined, because *Nature* is infinite, and *eternal:* for *Infinite* cannot be confined, or prescribed, setled, rul'd, or dispos'd, because the *Effects* are [as] *infinite* as the *Causes.*[5]

of the many reasons that she ends up denying the existence of atoms is that she accepts that matter is inherently divisible (for example in *Observations Upon Experimental Philosophy*, section XXXI, and *Grounds of Natural Philosophy*, chapter V of the First Part).

[4] A puzzle in seventeenth-century philosophy and science was how motion was transmitted from one body to another, for example, in the case of a ricochet or collision. In the metaphysical views that were most common at the time, whatever exists was thought to be either a substance, on the one hand, or the property or mode of a substance, on the other. But if motion is to be understood as the property of a thing that moves, then a question arises about how we are to understand what happens when one body collides with another body and adds to its motion. Cavendish is suggesting here (and she develops the view in later texts) that if motion is always the property of the body that possesses it, there would appear to be no cases of transfer of motion that are not also cases of transfer of substance. (See also *Philosophical Letters*, letters XXIII and XXX of section one, and letter VI of section four.) In some passages Descartes does appear to state that the motion of a given body often transfers from one body to the next (for example in *Principles of Philosophy* Part II, sections 27, 36, and 45; CSM 1:234, 240, and 244), although he also articulates the view that motion never transfers from one body to another but that God is responsible for the motion of each and every body at each and every moment. See, for example, *Principles of Philosophy* II.36, CSM 1:240, and "The Third Meditation," CSM 2:33–34. See also Malebranche, *The Search After Truth*, VI.ii.3, 446–452.

[5] This passage might recall the similar passages in Hobbes and Spinoza in which qualities like goodness and badness are not regarded as inherent properties of actions or objects or states of affairs; instead, goodness and badness are reducible (in a very complicated way) to the attitudes and preferences of nature's inhabitants. See also *Philosophical Letters*, letter XXIII of section three; *Observations Upon the Opinions of Some Ancient Philosophers*, section II; and *Grounds of Natural Philosophy*, chapter XIV of the Thirteenth Part. For Spinoza, see *Ethics*, Part I, Appendix, pp. 238–243, and Part IV, Preface, pp. 320–322. For Hobbes, see *Leviathan*, I.xv.40, p. 100.

Chapter 12: There is no Vacuity

> In Nature if *Degrees* may equal be,
> All may be full, and no Vacuity.
> As Boxes small, and smaller may contain,
> So bigger, and bigger must there be again.
> Infinite may run contracting, and dilating,
> Still, still, by degrees without a separating.[6]

Chapter 18: Of War, and no absolute *Power*

The Reason that all things make War upon one another, is, the several *Degrees* of *matter*, the contradiction of *motion*, and the Degrees, and the *advantage* of *the shapes* of *Figures* always striving.

Chapter 19: Of Power

There is no *absolute* Power, because *Power* is *infinite*, and the *infinitenesse* hinders the absolutenesse: for if there were an *absolute power*, there would be no dispute: . . . but because there is no *absolute power*, therefore there be Disputes, and will be eternally: for the several degrees of *matter*, *motion*, and *Figure* strive for Superiority.

Chapter 20: Similsing the spirits, or Innate Matter

This *innate matter* is a kinde of *god* or *gods* to the *dull part of matter*, having power to form it, as it please, and why may not every degree of *Innate matter* be as several *gods*, and so a *strong motion* be a god to the *weaker*, and so have an *infinite*, and *Eternal Government*? As we will compare *motions* to *Officers*, or *Magistrates*. The *Constable* rules the *Parish*, the *Mayor*, the Constable, the King the Mayor, and some *Higher power* the *King*: thus *infinite powers* rule *Eternity*. Or again thus,

---

[6] Here Cavendish is floating the idea (although her title for the chapter is more definitive) that there may be no such thing as empty space and that instead the physical universe is a plenum of contiguous matter. In other texts she embraces the view wholeheartedly; see note 20 for *Worlds Olio*. Note that a similar view appears in Descartes, *Principles of Philosophy*, II.10–22, CSM 1: 227–232.

the *Constable* rules the *Hundred*, the *Major* rules the *City*, the *King* the *kingdom*, and *Caesar* the *world*.

> Thus may *dull matter* over others rule,
> According as 'tis shap'd by *motions Tool.*
> So *Innate matter* Governs by degree,
> According as the *stronger motions* be.[7]

Chapter 22: Natural, or Sensitive War

All *Natural War* is caused either by a *Sympathetical motion*, or an *Antepathetical motion*. For *Natural War*, and *Peace* proceed from Self-preservation, which belongs only to the *Figure*; for nothing is annihilated in *Nature*, but the particular prints, or *several shapes* that *motion* makes of *matter*; which *motion* in every *Figure* strives to maintain what they have created: for when some *Figures* destroy others, it is for the maintenance or security of themselves: and when the destruction is for Food, it is *Sympathetical motion*, which makes a particular Appetite, or nourishment from some *Creatures* to others; but an *Antipathetical motion* that makes the *Destruction*.[8]

Chapter 23: Of Annihilation

There can be no *Annihilation* in *Nature*: nor particular *motions*, and *Figures*, because the *matter* remains that was the *Cause* of those *Motions* and *Figures*. As for *particular figures*, although every *part* is separated that made such a *figure*, yet it

---

[7] Although Cavendish insists that motion is never transferred from one body to another (unless the first body also transfers the corresponding amount of its matter or substance), she does allow that a body can still influence the motions of a second body. Here she indicates that one body can have 'stronger motions' than another, and elsewhere she allows that bodies in many cases 'alter the motion' of other bodies, for example, in *Philosophical Letters*, letters IV and VIII of section two. See also *Philosophical and Physical Opinions*, chapters 18 and 19; and *Grounds of Natural Philosophy*, chapter I of the Eighth Part. A body cannot transfer its motion to a second body, but it can affect the direction of the motion that the second body contains already.

[8] See also *Grounds of Natural Philosophy*, chapter XVII of the First Part. Note that Cavendish speaks of the antipathies and sympathies of bodies, but she does not appear to hold that these are anything in addition to the more basic qualities of matter like figure, motion, perception, and vitality. (See for example *Philosophical Letters*, letter VI of section two.) Instead, what it is for a body to act in antipathy to another body is for it to struggle against that body in the course of striving to maintain its own existence.

is not *Annihilated*; because *those parts remain* that *made it.*[9] So as it is not impossible but the same particular Figures may be erected by the same *motions*, that joyned those parts, and in the *matter* may repeat the same *motion eternally so by succession*: and the same *matter* in a *figure* may be erected and dispersed eternally. Thus the dispersing of the *matter* into particular figures by an *Alteration of motion*, we call *Death*; and the joyning of parts to create a *Figure*, we call life. *Death* is a *Separation, life* is a *Contraction*.

Chapter 45: Of Matter, Motion, and Knowledge, or Understanding

Whatsoever hath an *innate motion, hath knowledge*; and what matter soever hath this *innate motion*, is *knowing*, but according to the several motions, are several knowledges made; for *knowledge* lives in *motion*, as motion lives in *matter*: for though the kind of *matter* never alters, yet the manner of *motions* alters in that *matter*: and as *motions* alter, so *knowledge* differs, which makes the several *motions* in several *figures* to give several knowledges. And where there is a likenesse of *motion*, there is a likeness of *knowledge*: As the *Appetite* of *Sensitive spirits*, and the desire of *rational spirits* are alike motions in several degrees of matter. And the *touch* in the heel, or any part of the body else, is the like *motion*, as the *thought* thereof in the head; the one is the *motion* of the *sensitive* spirits, the other in the rational *spirits*.

Chapter 46: Of the Animal Figure

[W]ho knows, but *Vegetables* and *Minerals* may have some of those *rational spirits*, which is a *minde* or *soul* in in them, as well as *man*? Onely they want that *Figure* (with such kinde of motion proper thereunto) to expresse *knowledge* that way. For had *Vegetables* and *Minerals* the same shape, made by such *motions*, as the sensitive spirits create; then there might be wooden *men*, and *iron beasts*; for though marks do not come in the same way, yet the same *marks* may come in, and be made by the same *motion*; for the spirits are so subtle, as they can pass and repass through the solidest matter. Thus there may be as many several and various motions in *Vegetables* and *Minerals*, as in *Animals*; and as many internal *figures* made by the *rational spirits*; only they want the *Animal*, to express it the *Animal* way. And

[9] See also *Philosophical Letters*, letter III of section one, letter III of section three, letter X of section four; *Further Observations Upon Experimental Philosophy*, section XI; *Observations Upon the Opinions of Some Ancient Philosophers*, IV.6; and *Worlds Olio*, "The Opinions of some Philosophers—Essay 128."

if their knowledge be not the same knowledge, but different from the *knowledge of Animals*, by reason of their different *figures*, made by other kinde of *motion* on other tempered matter, yet it is *knowledge*. For shall we say, A *man* doth not know, because he doth not know what another man knows, or some higher power?

AN EPISTLE TO CONDEMNING READERS

[T]hough in natural Philosophy there may be many touches found out by experiences, and experiments, yet the Study is onely conjecturally, and built upon probabilities, and until probabilities be condemned by absolute and known truth, let them have a place amongst the rest of probabilities, and be not so partial to contradict, as to be unjust to me, take not away the right of my place because young; for though age ought to have respect, yet not so as to do youth wrong, but I hope my new born opinions will be nourished in Noble and learned Schools, and bred up with industrious Students; but howsoever, I delight my self, for next to the finding out of truthes, the greatest pleasure in Study, is, to finde out probabilities. I make no question but after Ages will esteem this work of mine, but what soever is new, is not received at the first with that good acceptation, by reason it is utterly unknown unto them, and a newnesse, and an unacquaintednesse makes the ignorance, but when time hath made acquaintance, and a right understanding, a right understanding will make a friendship betwixt Fame and my Book.

Chapter 59: Of Fortune

Matter, Figure, and Motions, are the gods that Create fortune; For fortune is nothing in it self but various motions gathered, or drawn to a point, which point man onely thinks it fixt upon him, but he is deceived, for it fixes upon all other things; for if any thing comes, and rubs off the bark of a tree, or breaks the tree, it is a miss-fortune to that tree, and if a house be built in such a place, as to shelter a tree from great storms, or cold weather, it were good fortune to that tree, and if a beast be hurt it is a miss-fortune to that beast, or bird, and when a beast, or bird, is brought up for pleasure, or delight, and not to work or be imprisoned, it is a good fortune to that beast, or bird; but as I said before fortune is onely various motions, drawn to a point, and that point that comes from crosse motions, we call bad fortune, and those that come from Sympathetical motions we call good fortune,[10] and there must needs be Antipathetical Motions as well as Sympathetical Motions, since Motions are so various.

[10] See also "No Judge in Nature," in this chapter, and *Philosophical Letters*, letter XXIII of section three.

But man, and for all that I know, all other things, are governed by outward Objects, they rule, and we obey; for we do not rule and they Obey, but every thing is led like dogs in a string, by a stronger power, but the outward power being invisible, makes us think, we set the rules, and not the outward Causes, so that we are governed by that which is without us, not that which is within us; for man hath no power over himself.[11]

Chapter 63: Whether motion is a thing, or nothing, or can be Annihilated

Some have the opinion that Motion is nothing, but to my reason it is a thing; for if matter, is a substance, a substance is a thing, and the motion, and matter being unseparablely united, makes it but one thing.

For as there could be no motion without such a degree, or extract of matter so there could be no such degree or extract of matter without motion, thus motion is a thing. But by reason particular motions leave moving in such matters and figures, shall we say they are deceased, dead, or become nothing; but say some, motions are accidents, and accidents are nothing; but I say, all accidents live in substance, as all effects in the causes, say some, when a man for example shakes his hand, and when he leaves shaking, whether is that motion gone (say others) no where, for that particular motion ceaseth to be, say they. I answer, that my reason tells me, it is neither fled away, nor ceased to be, for it remains in the hand, and in that matter that created the hand, that is in that, and the like innated matter, that is in the hand. But some will say, the hand never moves so again, but I say the motion is never the lesse there,[12] they may as well say, when they have seen a Chest full of Gold, or the like, and when their eyes are shut, or that they never see it more, that the Gold doth not lie in the Chest, although the Gold may lie there eternally, or if they should see it again, say it is not the same Gold. . . .

---

[11] There is an interpretive question about whether or not Cavendish holds that creatures have libertarian freedom, according which they exhibit a contra-causal "ability to do otherwise," or if instead she accepts a compatibilist view, according to which the behavior of a creature is free when it is fully determined by prior motions, but is agile and nimble and in accord with the creature's preferences and aims. For some of the different passages, see *Philosophical and Physical Opinions*, "The Agilenesse of innate Matter"; *Philosophical Letters*, letters VIII and XXIX of section one, and letters IV and VII of section two; *Observations Upon Experimental Philosophy*, sections XXVII, XXXI, and XXXV; *Observations Upon the Opinions of Some Ancient Philosophers*, section IV.5; *Grounds of Natural Philosophy*, chapters V, X, and XVIII of the First Part, chapter XII of the Sixth Part, chapter XII of the Seventh Part, and chapter I of the Eighth Part; and *Appendix to Grounds of Natural Philosophy*, chapter IV, V, and VII of the First Part.

[12] Here we might consider that a "stationary" object like a table or chair nonetheless has a tremendous amount of activity that is taking place in it at the atomic level.

But particular motion, as the vessels, or hand is but used, not annihilated, for particular motions can be no more annihilated, then particular figures that are dissolved, and how in reason can we say particular figures are Annihilated, when every part and parcel, grain, and atome, remains in infinite matter, but some will say, when a house: for example, is pull'd down, by taking asunder the materials, that very figure of that house is annihilated; but my opinion is, that it is not, for that very figure of that house remains in those materials, and shal do eternally although those materials were dissolved into Atoms, and every Atome in a several place, part, or figure & though infinite figures should be made by those materials by several dissolutions and Creations, yet those infinites would remain in those particular materials eternally, and was there from all eternity;[13] And if any of those figures be rebuilt, or Created again, it is the same figure it was.

So likewise the motion of the hand which I said for example, if the same hand moves after the same manner, it is the same motion that moved the hand before; so it may make infinite repetitions; thus one and the same motion may move eternally, and rest from moving, and yet have a being.

Chapter 65: Many motions go to the producing of one thing, or to one end

[A]s there are infinite changes of motions, amongst the sensitive innated matter, working on the dull parts of matter, so there are infinite changes of motions in the rational innated matter, making infinite kinds of knowledge, and degrees of knowledge, and understanding, and as there are infinite changes of motion, so there are infinite effects, and every produced effect, is a producing effect, and effects which effect produce effects, and the onely matter is the cause of all effects, for the several degrees of onely matter, is the effect of onely matter, and motion is the effect of some sorts of the degrees of onely matter, and varieties

---

[13] Cavendish might be thinking here that since bodies are intelligent and perceptive insofar as they work toward the ends that they seek—for example, in striving to become a full-grown plant—the ideas of such ends must remain in existence even if the particular figures that are the realization of those ends do not; otherwise, those ends would no longer be possible objects of pursuit. More generally, Cavendish supposes that the intelligent bodies of nature behave with an eye to aims and goals. (See also chapter 65 of *Philosophical and Physical Opinions*, especially the title.) This is not an uncommon view in the history of philosophy of course. Aristotle famously offered a four-fold categorization of causes and argued that one sort of cause that is essential to the bringing about of any production is a final cause or purpose. See, for example *Physics*, Book II, chapters 7–8, in J. L. Ackrill, *A New Aristotle Reader* (Princeton, NJ: Princeton UP, 1987), 105–109. A related view is in the work of the seventeenth-century philosophers Henry More and Ralph Cudworth; see also note 4 for *Worlds Olio*.

are the effects of matter and motion, and life is the effect of innate matter; and knowledge the effect of life.

Chapter 70: The creations of Figures, and the difference of Motions

Those motions that are proper to create figures, are different from those motions that dissolve them, so that sympathetical internal motions, do not onely assist one another, but Sympathetical external Motions, and Sympathetical figures; this is the reason that from two figures, a third, or more is created, by the way of procreation; yet all figures are created, after one and the same kinde of way; yet not after one and the same manner of way, as Vegetables, Minerals, and some sorts of Animals, as such as are bred from that we call corruption, as some sorts of worms, and some sorts of flies, and the like; Yet are they created by the procreation of the heat, and moisture, the same way are plants that grow wilde produced, but those that are sown or set, although they are after one and the same kinde of way, yet not after the same manner; for the young vegetables, were produced from the seeds, and the earth, which were sowed, or set together, and in grafts is when two different plants produce seed of mixt nature, as a Mule is produced, or the like creature, from two different Animals, which make them of mixt nature; for As there is a Sympathetical conjunction in one, and the same kinde of figure, so there is a Sympathetical conjunction in some sorts of figures; but not in all, nor to all, for that would make such a confusion in nature, as there would be no distinction, of kindes; besides, it were impossible for some kinde of figures, to make a conjunction with other kindes, being such a difference betwixt them, some from the nature of the figures, others from the shape of the figures.

And Minerals are produced by the Conjunction of such Elements, which were begot by such motions, as make heat, and drought, and cold and dry. Thus all figures are created from different motions, and different degrees, of infinite onely matter; for onely matter joyns, and divides it self by self motions, and hath done so, and will do so, or must do so eternally, being its nature, yet the divisions, and subtractions, joynings, and creations, are not alike, nor do they continue, or dissolve, with the like measure of time, which time is onely as in a reference to several motions.

But as I have said, there can be nothing lost in nature, Although there be infinite changes, and their changes never repeated. For say a man dies, and his figure dissolves into dust, as smal as Atoms, and is disperst so, as never to meet, and every Atome goeth to the making of several figures, and so changes infinitely, from figure, to figure, yet the figures of all these changes lie in those parts, and those parts in onely matter; so likewise several motions may cease as figures dissolve, but still those motions lies in innated matter, and each particular figure, in the generality of matter and motion, which is on the dull part, and innated part of onely matter.

Chapter 71: The Agilenesse of innate Matter

Innated matter seems much nimbler in some works, then in other, as making Elements, and their several changes, being more porous then Animals, Vegetables, and Minerals, which are more contracted, and not so easily metamorphosed, and on the thin part of dull matter, they seem much nimbler, and agil, then when they work on the grosse part of dull matter; for though the innated matter can work, but according to the strength, yet not alwayes according to that strength; for their burthens are not alwayes equal to their strength; for we see in light thin dull matter, their motions to be more swift, having lesse incumbrances, and lighter burthens, unlesse it be oposed, and stopped by the innated matter, that works in the more solid, or thicker part of dull matter, or move solid and united figures, yet many times the innated matter, that works on the thin part of dull matter, or in more porous figures, will make way through solid and thick bodies, and have the power on those that work on more grosse matter, for the innate matter that works on grosse matter, cannot resist so well, having greater burthens, nor act with that facility as the others can, whose matter is lighter, or figures more pourous; for we see many times water to passe through great rocks, and mountains, piercing and dividing their strengths, by the frequent assaults thereon, or to.

Chapter 77: Of different knowledge in different figures

Man may have a different knowledge from beasts, birds, fish, worms, and the like, and yet be no wiser, or knowing then they; For different wayes in knowledge makes not knowledge more or lesse, no more then different paths inlarge one compasse of ground; nor no more then several words for one and the same thing, for the thing is the same, onely the words differ; so if a man hath different knowledge from a fish, yet the fish may be as knowing as man, but man hath not a fishes knowledge, nor a fish a mans knowledge.[14]

[14] See also *Philosophical Letters*, letters X and XI of section one; and also note 4 for *Worlds Olio*, and note 2 in this chapter.

And as there is different Knowledge, and different Kinds, and several sorts, so there is different Knowledge in different senses, in one and the same creature; for what man hath seen the interior biting motion of Gold, and burning motions of heat? Yet feels them we may imagine by the touch, the interior nature of fire to be composed of sharp points, yet our sight hath no Knowledge thereof, so our sight hath the Knowledge of light; but the rest of our senses are utterly ignorant thereof; our ears have the Knowledge of sound, but our eyes are ignorant of the Knowledge thereof; thus, though our ears may be as Knowing as our eyes, and our eyes as Knowing as our ears, yet they may be ignorant of each other, I say Knowledge, for sense is Knowledg, as well as reason, onely reason is a degree above sense, or sense, a degree beneath reason.

Chapter 96: Of the Load-stone

[A]nd as fire works upon several bodies after a different manner of way, according to the nature of the body it works on, producing divers effects; so for all I can perceive may the Load-stone; for certainly we do not know, nor never can come to that knowledge, as to perceive the several effects, that are produced from the least, or as we account the most inconsiderable creature made in nature; so that the Load-stone may work as variously upon several bodies, as fire, and produce as various effects, although nor to our sense, nor after the same manner of wayes, that fire doth, and as fire works variously upon various bodies, so there are fires, as several sorts, and those several sorts have several effects, yet one and the same kinde, but as the causes in nature are hid from us, so are most of the effects; but to conclude my discourse, we have onely found that effect of the Load-stone, as to draw iron to it; but the attracting motion is in obscurity, being invisible to the sense of man, so that his reason can onely discourse, & bring probabilities, to strengthen his arguments, having no perfect knowledge in that, nor in any thing else, besides that knowledge we have of several things, comes as it were by chance, or by experience, for certainly all the reason man hath, would never have found out that one effect of the Load-stone, as to draw iron, had not experience or chance presented it to us, nor the effect of the needle.... [S]o the Load-stone may work as various effects upon several subjects, as fire, but by reason we have not so much experience of one as the other, the strangenesse creates a wonder, for the old saying is, that ignorance is the mother of admiration, but fire which produceth greater effects by invisible motions, yet we stand not at such amaze as at the Load-stone, because these effects are familiar unto us.[15]

---

[15] This passage calls to mind the similar thinking in Hume, *An Enquiry Concerning Human Understanding*, section four, part one, 108–113. Hume famously argues that there is no intelligible

Chapter 141: Of the Motion of the Bodie

Physitians should study the motions of the body, as naturall Philosophers, study the motions of the heavens, for several diseases have several motions, and if they were well watched, and weighed, and observed, they might easily be found out severally; and as they take compass of the heaven, and stand upon the earth, so they may take the degrees of the disease, although they dissect not the body. Thus natural Physitians may know, when the sun of health will be eclipsed by the shaddow of melancholly, which gets betwixt the body and health; and natural physitians may come to know the thoughts, as they the stars, by studying the humors of men, & may know what influences they may have upon the body; and may know the severall changes of their humor, as they the several changes of the moon, that the several changes of the humor, causeth the blood to ebb and to flow, as the Tides of the Sea; thus they may make an Almanack of the body, for to shew what weather and seasons there will be, as great tempests and stormes of wind-collick; whether there will fall upon the Lungs, great rheumes, as showers of rain, or whether there may be great and hot fevers, or whether there will be earthquakes of shaking Agues, or cold, and dumb-palsies, or whether there will be dearths of flesh, and so leave bones bare, by the droughts of heated fevers, or whether the over-flowing of moisture, which causeth dropsies; thus if we could finde the several motions in several diseases in a body, as surely might be done by observations, and study, and could finde out the several motions by the several operations in physick, we might surely so apply them together, as to make animals, though not live eternally, yet very long; and truly I think this both of philosophical opinions, may give a great light to this study.[16]

connection between a cause and its effect and that the reason why it comes to seem normal and reasonable to us that a given effect would follow from its cause is that their connection is extremely familiar. There is similar language in Joseph Glanvill, *The Vanity of Dogmatizing*, London: Printed by E.C. for Henry Eversden (1661), chapter XX, 189–193; and Malebranche *Elucidations of the Search After Truth*, 657–685. *Philosophical and Physical Opinions* is from 1655. It is tempting to think that some of these philosophers might have read or heard about the views and arguments in the Cavendish text, but this is difficult to confirm. For example, *Philosophical and Physical Opinions* was available at a library to which Hume had access at the University of Edinburgh, but borrowing records only go back to the 1750s. Hume's *Treatise* was first published in 1739–40, and his *Enquiry* in 1748.

[16] Cavendish says some very negative things about artifice and medicine, and about our ability to create instruments that unlock the secrets of nature, but she does allow that if we are patient and focused and meticulous, and if we piggyback on the perceptivity and sophistication of nonhuman creatures, we can make important interventions. See note 19 for *Worlds Olio*; *Worlds Olio*, "The Power of Natural Works"; *Philosophical and Physical Opinions*, chapter 208; *Philosophical Letters*, letters V, VII, and XV of section two; *Observations Upon Experimental Philosophy*, sections III, XIV, XVIII, XXV and XXVI; and *Grounds of Natural Philosophy*, chapter IX of the Second Part.

Chapter 151: Of thoughts

Many wonder what Thoughts are, and how such millions can be within so little a compasse as the brain.

I answer, that a little quantity of the rational innate matter, may make millions of figures, which figures are thoughts.

As for example, from eight notes, millions of tunes are made, and from twenty four letters millions of several Languages may be made.

Likewise one lump of clay may be molded, and formed into millions of several figures; and like Pictures many figures may be drawn in one piece, and every figure in a several posture; Likewise a little picture will represent so great an Army, as would take up many acres of land, were it in a pitched field.

Again, a Globe no bigger then a Head, will present the whole world.

Chapter 152: Of thinking, or thoughts

Thoughts are more pleasant to the minde, then the appetite to the senses, and the minde feeds as greatly on thoughts, as a hungry stomacke doth upon meat; and as some meat breeds good nourishment, and some bad nourishment, causing either health and strength, or diseases and pain; so doth thoughts, for displeasing thoughts of grief, and all sad remembrances cause the minde to be dull, and melancholly, . . . and discontented; and pleasing thoughts cause the minde to be chearful, pleasant, and delightful. Besides, the minde is like chewing of the cud, for what the senses bring in, and are fed with outward objects; those swallowed objects, the thoughts of the minde chews over again; thus the minde is alwayes feeding; besides, the senses have no longer pleasure, or pain then the objects remain; but the minde is as much grieved, or delighted when the object is removed, as when they are present; As for example, a man is as much grieved when he hears his friend is dead, or kill'd, as if he saw him die, or slaine; for the dead friend lives in the minde, not the minde in the dead friend, and if a man have a fine house, or great riches, or an excellent rare race of horses, or the like, whereupon the minde takes as great delight in thinking of his fine house, as if it dwelt in the house, and as great delight in thinking of his riches, or what he could do with the use of his riches; for the minde doth not so much dwell in the house, as the house in the minde,[17] nor

---

[17] Here Cavendish is reflecting her view that in both waking veridical experience and in imaginary contemplation, the object of our attention is a mental image (for example, "Chapter 153: Of Sleep and dreams," just below), and she is also positing that in some cases bouts of poetical imagination can be at least as satisfying as our encounters with objects in the actual world. See also *Worlds Olio*, "Allegory 20"; *Grounds of Natural Philosophy*, chapter IV of the Sixth Part; and in "Fiction," *Blazing World*, "The Epilogue to the Reader."

the minde doth not take so much delight in the use of the riches, as the use to be in the minde, and the remembrance of the curious horses is as much in the minde, as when those horses were in the eye; for when the sense is filled, the minde can but think, and the minde may as well think when the objects are gone, as when they are present, and the minde may take as much delight, in thinking what the senses have enjoyed, as what they are to injoy, or desire to enjoy; for thoughts are the fruition of the minde, as objects the fruition of the senses; for the minde takes as much delight (if not more) in thinking of an absolute power, as when the commands of an absolute power is obeyed, for obedience dwells no more in the minde when it is acted, then it did before it was acted, or by the imagination that it is acted; thus the minde receives no more by action, then it doth by contemplation, onely when the pleasure of the senses are joyned with delightful thoughts, may be said to be more happy, though I beleeve the pleasure of senses draws the delight from the thoughts; for the more at rest the body is, the more busie the minde is imployed, and as torments of the minde are beyond the torments of the body, or at least the displeasure of the senses; so the delight of the minde is beyond the ease or rest of the body, or the pleasure of the senses.

Chapter 153: Of Sleep and dreams

Dreaming is when [rational matter] moves in figures, making such figures as these objects, which have presented to them by the sensitive motions, which are onely pictures, or copies of the Original objects, which we call remembrance, for remembrance is nothing but a waking dream, and a dream is nothing but a sleeping remembrance, but if the sensitive innated matter moves in the same manner, on the same place, as printing and drawing such figures or objects in the optick nerve . . . without the presence of the outward objects; then we see hear, taste, smell, touch, as strong as if we were awake, if their motions be as strong and industrious; but many times we have in sleep those objects but in part, and not in whole, the reason is, that either the sensitive innated matter is slow, or else they are not so perfect Artists to work without a sampler, working by misplacing, and mistaking, or else works by halves, according to their skil, or as appetite moves them, make a hogpog, or gallimophry of many several pieces or draughts, into one figure or picture, which make extravagant dreams; by reason they work not in a methodical manner, and the rational innated matter, moving in the same manner makes a mixt resemblance, but the sensitive innate having not the outward objects in sleep to work by, seldom works perfect, or plain, and working imperfectly they move disorderly. . . . [A]nd when the sensitive innated matter works perfectly, and the rational innate matter moves justly, we have as much knowledge, and understanding of what we dream of, and as much satisfaction from our senses, as if we were awake, and the real objects presented to us.[18]

Chapter 160: Of Sight

[W]hen we hear of a deity, we say in words it is an incorporeal thing; but we cannot conceive it so in thought,[19] we say we do, but we cannot prove we do; Tis true, the minde may be in a maze, and so have no fixt thought of any particular thing; yet that amaze hath a figurative ground, although not subscribed; as for example, my eyes may see the sea, or air, yet not the compasse, and so the earth, or heavens; so likewise my eye may see a long pole, yet not the two ends, these are but the parts of these figures, but I see not the circumference to the uttermost extention, so the mind in amaze, or the amaze of thinking cuts not out a whole and distinct figurative thought,[20] but doth as it were spread upon a flat, without a circumference, and though there are not such figures in the brain, as it brought through the opticks, yet such figures as the minde creates; for the minde is innate matter, and innate matter is self-motion, and self-motion, is always moving, and working, which working is figuring; thus the sensitives innated matter prints figures in the brain, and the rational innated matter creates figures in the brain after its own invention, which are imagination and conception, wherein are made imaginary worlds, without the materials of outward objects: and perchance these motions may create such a figure as this world, and such several figures, as the several creatures therein, although not so solid and lasting, because those motions want those grosse materials, of which they should create it withal.

[I]t is not the outward objects that make the sense, but the innate matter, which is self motion, which is the sense and knowledge, and the different motions therein, and therefrom, make the differences thereof.[21]

[18] See also note 2 for *Worlds Olio*.

[19] Cavendish argues in a number of passages that because ideas are imagistic pictures, we can have no ideas of immaterials, and hence no idea of God. See, for example, *Philosophical Letters*, letter XX of section one, and letter II of section two; *Observations Upon Experimental Philosophy*, section XXI; and *Appendix to Grounds of Natural Philosophy*, chapters III and XI of the First Part.

[20] See also the exchange between Descartes and Gassendi on whether ideas are always imagistic pictures and whether there are instances in which an idea does not have any imagistic content but is still an idea of something. This is at *Fifth Objections*, CSM 2: 229–230, and *Fifth Replies*, CSM 2:264. See also *Philosophical Letters*, letter XX of section one.

[21] Here Cavendish is referencing a view that she will develop and then express much more prominently in later work—the view that, in sense perception, external bodies do not imprint themselves on our sense organs, but instead our sense organs use their own motions to *pattern* images of external bodies. Part of Cavendish's motivation of course is her doctrine that bodies always move by their own

Chapter 182: Musick may cure mad folks

There is great reason why Musick should cure madnesse; for this sort of madnesse is no other but the spirits that are in the brain and heart put out of their natural motion, and the spirits having a natural sympathy with Musick, may be composed into their right order; but it must be such Musick, as the number of the notes must goe in such order as the natural motion of the brain, though every brain hath not one and the same motion, but are set like notes to several tunes: wherefore if it were possible, to set notes to the natural motion of the heart, or that brain that is distempered, it might be perfectly cured, but as some notes do compose the brain by a sympathy to the natural motion, so others do make a discord or antipathy, and discompose it, putting the natural motions out of tune.[22]

Chapter 208: The knowledge of diseases

[A] man buyes a horse, and he having onely an old saddle, that he was accustomed to ride with on a horse he formerly had, put it on his new horses back, yet although his horse is of the same Country, or sort of horses, as his former horse was, yet the saddle may not be fit for the new horse, but may be either too big or too little, and by the unfitnesse may gall his horse so sore, and corrupt the flesh so much, as he may be a scald back jade, as long as he lives, if it festers not as to kill him; so in diseases medicines may be too strong, or too weak, or they may evacuate too much or too little, if they do not know the just dimension, and extention of the disease. Again, one the same sort of horses may be so dull, as hardly to move out of his pace with the spur, although it should prick so deep, as to make his sides to bleed, when another horse of the same sort, shall run away, over hedg, and ditch, against trees, and stones, untill he hurt himself, and flings his rider, or at least flings, and leaps, and snorts, and stamps; and grows into a furious heat; so diseases, some must be handled gently, others more roughly, for

---

self-motion, but she offers other reasons as well—for example, that we sometimes perceive things at a distance. See, for example, *Philosophical Letters*, letters IV, XXII, and XXIV of section one, and letter XVI of section two; *Observations Upon Experimental Philosophy*, section XXXVII, Q. 10; and *Grounds of Natural Philosophy*, chapter IX of the Fifth Part.

[22] This is perhaps not the most pragmatic suggestion for curing mental illness, but according to Cavendish's materialist view of mind, ideas are literally imagistic pictures, and if "mad" people are moved by false representations of the outside world, perhaps there are material causes (of the musical variety) that could put their ideas back into line. For Cavendish's materialist view of mind, see, for example, *Philosophical Letters*, letters XV, XVIII, and XXI of section two; *Observations Upon Experimental Philosophy*, section XXI; and note 43 for *Philosophical Letters*.

in diseases you must learn the disposition of the disease, as well of what kinde, sort, or breed it is; so likewise it is not enough for a physitian to know what drugs will purge choler, what flegme, and what melancholy, or the like; but they should study to know the several motions, which work in them, or else their op-erations will be as their imploiments are, which is chance-medly; for otherwise a Physitian neither applies his medicines knowingly, nor skilfully, but custom-arily, because they are usually given in such diseases, whereof some do mend, others do die with them; but certain if Physitians would take pains to study the several motions of the diseases, and also of the drugs, and medicines they give, and would do as skilful musitians, which make a consort, where although every one plaies upon a several instrument, yet they all make their notes agree, there would follow a harmony of health in the body, as well as a harmony of musick in these consorts.

Chapter 210: The diatical Centers

Although infinite matter and motion was from all eternity; yet that infinite moving matter is disposed by an infinite Deity, which hath power to order that moving matter, as that Deity pleaseth, by reason there is nothing greater then it self, therefore there is nothing that can oppose its will.

Likewise this Deity is as the center of infinite moving matter, for though there can be no center in infinites, by reason there is no circumference, yet in respect the matter is infinite every way from, and to this Deity; we may say the Deity is the center of infinite matter, and by reason, the infinite moving matter, flowes as much to this diatical, center, as from it, it doth as it were present it self, or rather is forced to be ordered, by its infinite wisdom, which otherwise it would run into an infinite confusion, with which there would be an infinite, horrid and eternal war in nature; and though this Deity is as the center to infinite matter, yet this Deity in it self is as infinite matter, for its wisdom is as infinite as matter, and its knowledge as infinite as its wisdom, and its power as infinite as both, and the effects of these attributes run with infinite matter, like infinite paralel lines, even and straight, not crossing, nor obstructing, nor can they circumference or circle in each other, the matter and the Deity being both infinite neither is the matter or Deity finite to, or in themselves, for infinite matter hath no end, or period, neither can the infinite Deity comprehend it self, so as it is a god to it self, as well, or as much as to matter; for this Deity is no wayes finite, neither to its self, nor matter, its knowledge being as infinite as its power, and its wisdom as infinite its knowledge, and its power as infinit as both, and being infinit, its wisdom cannot be above its power, nor its power beyond its wisdom, neither can its knowledge comprehend its power, or the wayes of its wisdom being all infinite and eternal.

And though nature is infinit matter, motion and figure creating all things out of its self, for of matter they are made, and by motion they are formed into several and particular figures, yet this Deity orders and disposes of all natures works.

> Great God, from thee all infinites do flow;
> And by thy power from thence effects do grow;
> Thou orderest all degrees of matter, just
> As t'is thy will and pleasure move it must,
> And by thy knowledge orderd'st all the best,
> For in thy knowledge doth thy wisdom rest;
> And wisdom cannot order things amiss,
> For where disorder is, no wisdom is.
> Besides, great God, thy will is just, for why?
> Thy will still on thy wisdom doth rely.
> O pardon Lord, for what, I now hear speak
> Upon a guesse, my knowledge is but weak;
> But thou hast made such creatures as mankinde,
> And gav'st them somthing which we cal a mind,
> Always in motion, never quiet lies,
> Untill the figure, of his body dies,
> His several thoughts, which several motions are
> Do raise up love, hope, joyes, doubts and feare;
> As love doth raise up hope, so fear doth doubt,
> which makes him seek to find the great God out:
> Self love doth make him seek to finde, if he
> Came from, or shall last to eternity;
> But motion being slow, makes knowledge weak,
> And then his thoughts 'gainst ignorance doth beat,
> As fluid waters 'gainst hard rocks do flow,
> Break their soft streams, & so they backward go:
> Just so do thoughts, & then they backward slide,
> Unto the place, where first they did abide;
> And there in gentle murmurs, do complain,
> That all their care and labour is in vain;
> But since none knows, the great Creator must,
> Man seek no more, but in his greatness trust.[23]

FINIS.

[23] Although Cavendish holds that human beings (and all other creatures) have no idea of God, in some passages (as here) Cavendish still wants to speak of God, suggesting that we can refer to God in at least some manner. See also note 19, in this chapter, and note 3 for *Philosophical Letters*.

CHAPTER 3

Philosophical Letters

"A Preface to the Reader"

I desire so much favour, or rather Justice of you, *Worthy Readers*, as not to interpret my objections or answers any other ways then against several opinions in Philosophy; for I am confident there is not any body, that doth esteem, respect and honour learned and ingenious Persons more then I do: Wherefore judg me neither to be of a contradicting humor, nor of a vain-glorious mind for dissenting from other mens opinions, but rather that it is done out of love to Truth, and to make my own opinions the more intelligible, which cannot better be done then by arguing and comparing other mens opinions with them. The Authors whose opinions I mention, I have read, as I found them printed, in my native Language, except *DesCartes*, who being in Latine, I had some few places translated to me out of his works; and I must confess, that since I have read the works of these learned men, I understand the names and terms of Art a little better then I did before....

But I cannot conceive why it should be a disgrace to any man to maintain his own or others opinions against a woman, so it be done with respect and civility; but to become a cheat by dissembling, and quit the Breeches for a Petticoat, meerly out of spight and malice, is base, and not fit for the honour of a man, or the masculine sex.

Section 1

I

MADAM,

You have been pleased to send me the Works of four Famous and Learned Authors, to wit, of two most Famous Philosophers of our Age, *DesCartes*, and *Hobbs*, and of that Learned Philosopher and Divine Dr. *More*, as also of that

Famous Physician and Chymist *Van Helmont.* Which Works you have sent me not onely to peruse, but also to give my judgment of them, and to send you word by the usual way of our Correspondence, which is by Letters, how far, and wherein I do dissent from these Famous Authors, their Opinions in *Natural Philosophy.* To tell you truly, *Madam,* your Commands did at first much affright me, for it did appear, as if you had commanded me to get upon a high Rock, and fling my self into the Sea, where neither a Ship, nor a Plank, nor any kind of help was near to rescue me, and save my life; but that I was forced to sink, by reason I cannot swim: So I having no Learning nor Art to assist me in this dangerous undertaking, thought, I must of necessity perish under the rough censures of my Readers, and be not onely accounted a fool for my labour, but a vain and presumptuous person, to undertake things surpassing the ability of my performance; but on the other side I considered first, that those Worthy Authors, were they my censurers, would not deny me the same liberty they take themselves; which is, that I may dissent from their Opinions, as well as they dissent from others, and from amongst themselves: And if I should express more Vanity then Wit, more Ignorance then Knowledg, more Folly then Discretion, it being according to the Nature of our Sex, I hoped that my Masculine Readers would civilly excuse me, and my Female Readers could not justly condemn me. . . .

[S]ince neither the strength of my Body, nor of my understanding, or wit, is able to mark every line, or every word of their works, and to argue upon them, I shall onely pick out the ground Opinions of the aforementioned Authors, and those which do directly dissent from mine, upon which I intend to make some few Reflections, according to the ability of my Reason; and I shall meerly go upon the bare Ground of *Natural Philosophy,* and not mix Divinity with it, as many Philosophers use to do, except it be in those places, where I am forced by the Authors Arguments to reflect upon it, which yet shall be rather with an expression of my ignorance, then a positive declaration of my opinion or judgment thereof; for I think it not onely an absurdity, but an injury to the holy Profession of Divinity to draw her to the Proofs in *Natural Philosophy;* wherefore I shall strictly follow the Guidance of *Natural Reason,* and keep to my own ground and Principles as much as I can.[1]

---

[1] Here Cavendish says that in *Philosophical Letters* she will not appeal to premises about God or God's nature in the course of offering philosophical arguments, unless she is responding to an argument that one of her opponents puts forward that appeals to such a premise. Given that she holds that we have no idea of God—see for example *Philosophical and Physical Opinions,* chapter 160, and the corresponding note 19—this is probably a good thing, but note that there are passages outside of *Philosophical Letters* in which Cavendish advances claims about God's nature. See, for example, *Worlds Olio,* "Of Moderation"; *Observations Upon Experimental Philosophy,* sections XIX, XXI, and XXVII; and *Appendix to Grounds of Natural Philosophy,* chapters III–VI of Part I.

II

[A] Body of a continued quantity may be divided and severed into so many Parts either actually, or mentally in our Conceptions or thoughts; besides nature is one continued Body, for there is no such *Vacuum* in Nature, as if her Parts did hang together like a linked Chain; nor can any of her Parts subsist single and by it self,[2] but all the Parts of Infinite Nature, although they are in one continued Piece, yet are they several and discerned from each other by their several Figures. . . . [Y]ou will say perhaps, if I attribute an Infinite Wisdom, Strength, Power, Knowledge, &c. to Nature; then Nature is in all coequal with God, for God has the same Attributes: I answer, Not at all; for I desire you to understand me rightly, when I speak of Infinite Nature, and when I speak of the Infinite Deity, for there is great difference between them, for it is one thing a Deitical or Divine Infinite, and another a Natural Infinite; You know, that God is a Spirit, and not a bodily substance, again that Nature is a Body, and not a Spirit, and therefore none of these Infinites can obstruct or hinder each other, as being different in their kinds, for a Spirit being no Body, requires no place, Place being an attribute which onely belongs to a Body, and therefore when I call Nature Infinite, I mean an Infinite extension of Body, containing an Infinite number of Parts; but what doth an Infinite extension of Body hinder the Infiniteness of God, as an Immaterial Spiritual being? Next, when I do attribute an Infinite Power, Wisdom, Knowledge, &c. to Nature, I do not understand a Divine, but a Natural Infinite Wisdom and Power, that is, such as properly belongs to Nature, and not a supernatural, as is in God; For Nature having Infinite parts of Infinite degrees, must also have an Infinite natural wisdom to order her natural Infinite parts and actions, and consequently an Infinite natural power to put her wisdom into act; and so of the rest of her attributes, which are all natural: But Gods Attributes being supernatural, transcend much these natural infinite attributes;[3] for God, being the God of Nature, has not onely Natures Infinite Wisdom and Power, but besides, a Supernatural and Incomprehensible Infinite Wisdom and Power; which in no wayes do hinder each other, but may very well subsist together. . . . And the disparity between the Natural and Divine Infinite is such, as they cannot joyn, mix, and work together, unless you believe that Divine Actions can have allay. . . .

---

[2] See also letter II of section four, in this chapter, and *Observations Upon Experimental Philosophy*, section XV.

[3] Cavendish grants that many (and indeed she argues that all) creatures believe in the existence of God, but she specifies that the content of our belief when we believe in the existence of God is that there is a being that is beyond nature and apart from it. See, for example, letter II of section two, in this chapter; *Observations Upon Experimental Philosophy*, section XXI; and *Further Observations Upon Experimental Philosophy*, section X.

But in my opinion, Nature is material, and not any thing in Nature, what belongs to her, is immaterial; but whatsoever is Immaterial, is Supernatural, Therefore Motions, Forms, Thoughts, Ideas, Conceptions, Sympathies, Antipathies, Accidents, Qualities, as also Natural Life, and Soul, are all Material.

III

But as for *Nature*, that it cannot be Eternal without beginning, because God is the Creator and Cause of it, and that the Creator must be before the Creature, as the Cause before the Effect, so, that it is impossible for *Nature* to be without a beginning; if you will speak naturally, as human reason guides you, and bring an Argument concluding from the Priority of the *Cause* before the *Effect*, give me leave to tell you, that God is not tied to Natural Rules, but that he can do beyond our Understanding, and therefore he is neither bound up to time, as to be before, for if we will do this, we must not allow, that the Eternal Son of God is Coeternal with the Father, because nature requires a Father to exist before the Son, but in God is no time, but all Eternity; and if you allow, that God hath made some Creatures, as Supernatural Spirits, to live Eternally, why should he not as well have made a Creature from all Eternity? For Gods making is not our making, he needs no Priority of Time. But you may say, the Comparison of the Eternal Generation of the Son of God is Mystical and Divine, and not to be applied to natural things: I answer, The action by which God created the World or made Nature, was it natural of supernatural? Surely you will say it was a Supernatural and God-like action, why then will you apply Natural Rules to a God-like and Supernatural Action? For what Man knows, how and when God created Nature? You will say, the Scripture doth teach us that, for it is not Six thousand years, when God created this World. I answer, the holy Scripture informs us onely of the Creation of this Visible World, but not of Nature and natural Matter; for I firmly believe according to the Word of God, that this World has been Created, as is described by *Moses*, but what is that to natural Matter?[4]

IV

I have chosen, in the first place, the Work of that famous Philosopher *Hobbs*, called *Leviathan*, wherein I find he sayes, *That the cause of sense or sensitive*

[4] Spinoza also held that creatures are co-eternal with God, and that creatures are in a sense caused by God, but he took creatures to be modifications of God (for example in *Ethics*, Part II, corollary to proposition 10), and Cavendish does not appear to be willing to go that far. See, for example, *Appendix to Grounds of Natural Philosophy*, chapter IV of the First Part; but also see *Worlds Olio*, "The Opinions of some Philosophers—Essay 128."

perception is the external body or Object, which presses the Organ proper to each Sense.[5] To which I answer, according to the ground of my own *Philosophical Opinions,* That all things, and therefore outward objects as well as sensitive organs, have both Sense and Reason, yet neither the objects nor the organs are the cause of them; for Perception is but the effect of the Sensitive and rational Motions, and not the Motions of the Perception; neither doth the pressure of parts upon parts make Perception; for although Matter by the power of self-motion is as much composeable as divideable, and parts do joyn to parts, yet that doth not make perception; nay, the several parts, be-twixt which the Perception is made, may be at such a distance, as not capable to press:[6] As for example, Two men may see or hear each other at a distance, and yet there may be other bodies between them, that do not move to those perceptions, so that no pressure can be made, for all pressures are by some constraint and force; wherefore, according to my Opinion, the Sensitive and Rational free Motions, do pattern out each others object, as Figure and Voice in each others Eye and Ear; for Life and Knowledge, which I name Rational and Sensitive Matter, are in every Creature, and in all parts of every Creature, and make all perceptions in Nature, because they are the self-moving parts of Nature, and according as those Corporeal, Rational, and Sensitive Motions move, such or such perceptions are made.

VIII

And as for his *Train of Thoughts,* I must confess, that Thoughts for the most part are made orderly, but yet they do not follow each other like Geese, for surely, man has sometimes very different thoughts; as for Example, a man sometime is very sad for the death of his Friend, and thinks of his own death, and imme-diately thinks of a wanton Mistress, which later thought, surely, the thought of Death did not draw in; wherefore, though some thought may be the Ring-leader of others, yet many are made without leaders.[7]

---

[5] This is from Hobbes, *Leviathan,* I.i.4, 6.

[6] One of Cavendish's reasons for thinking that external bodies do not impress themselves on our sense organs when we have a sense perception is that, like all bodies, the bodies that compose a sense organ move by their own motions, and not by motion that is transferred to them; another reason is that she supposes that sense organs would be damaged and dinged if external objects were so im-posing (for example, in *Philosophical Letters,* letter XXII of section one, and letter XVI of section two); a third reason that she is putting forward here (in letter IV) is that perception often occurs at a dis-tance and without intervening bodies pressing upon and dinging each other, and of course without transferring motion. See also letter XXIV of section I.

[7] See also note 11 for *Philosophical and Physical Opinions.*

X

[Y]our *Author* says, *That Man doth excel all other Animals in this faculty, that when he conceives any thing whatsoever, he is apt to enquire the Consequences of it, and what effects he can do with it: Besides this* (says he) *Man hath an other degree of Excellence, that he can by Words reduce the Consequences he finds to General Rules called Theoremes or Aphorisms, that is, he can reason or reckon not onely in Number, but in all other things, whereof one may be added unto, or subtracted from an other.*[8] To which I answer, That according to my Reason I cannot perceive, but that all Creatures may do as much; but by reason they do it not after the same manner or way as Man, Man denies, they can do it at all; which is very hard; for what man knows, whether Fish do not Know more of the nature of Water, and ebbing and flowing, and the saltness of the Sea? Or whether Birds do not know more of the nature and degrees of Air, or the cause of Tempests? Or whether Worms do not know more of the nature of Earth, and how Plants are produced? Or Bees of the several sorts of juices of Flowers, then Men?[9] And whether they do not make there Aphorismes and Theoremes by their manner of Intelligence? For, though they have not the speech of Man, yet thence doth not follow, that they have no Intelligence at all. But the Ignorance of Men concerning other Creatures is the cause of despising other Creatures, imagining themselves as petty Gods in Nature, when as *Nature* is not capable to make one God, much less so many as Mankind; and were it not for Mans supernatural Soul, Man would not be more Supreme, then other Creatures in Nature.

XI

I grant, some other Creatures appear to have more Knowledg when new born then others; as for example, a young Foal has more knowledg than a young Child, because a Child cannot run and play; besides a Foal knows his own Dam, and can tell where to take his food, as to run and suck his Dam, when as an Infant cannot do so, nor all beasts, though most of them can, but yet this doth not prove, that a Child hath no reason at all; Neither can I perceive that man is a Monopoler of all Reason, or Animals of all Sense, but that Sense and Reason are in other Creatures as well as in Man and Animals; for example, Drugs, as Vegetables and Minerals, although they cannot slice, pound or infuse, as man can, yet they can work upon man more subtilly, wisely, and as sensibly either by purging, vomiting, spitting, or any other way, as man by mincing, pounding and

[8] This is from Hobbes, *Leviathan*, I.v.6, 24.

[9] See also letter XXXVI of section one, in this chapter; *Philosophical and Physical Opinions*, chapter 77; *Observations Upon Experimental Philosophy*, section XIV; *Further Observations Upon Experimental Philosophy*, section XIII; *Poems and Fancies*, "Of the Ant"; and note 4 for *Worlds Olio*.

infusing them, and Vegetables will as wisely nourish Men, as Men can nourish Vegetables; Also some Vegetables are as malicious and mischievous to Man, as Man is to one another, witness Hemlock, Nightshade, and many more; and a little Poppy will as soon, nay sooner cause a Man to sleep, though silently, then a Nurse a Child with singing and rocking; But because they do not act in such manner or way as Man, Man judgeth them to be without sense and reason; and because they do not prate and talk as Man, Man believes they have not so much wit as he hath; and because they cannot run and go, Man thinks they are not industrious; the like for Infants concerning Reason. But certainly, it is not local motion or speech that makes sense and reason, but sense and reason makes them; neither is sense and reason bound onely to the actions of Man, but it is free to the actions, forms, figures and proprieties of all Creatures; for if none but Man had reason, and none but Animals sense, the World could not be so exact, and so well in order as it is.[10]

XII

Whereof in short I give you my opinion, first concerning Vital Motions, that it appears improbable if not impossible to me, that Generation should be the cause and beginning of Life, because Life must of necessity be the cause of Generation, life being the Generator of all things, for without life motion could not be, and without motion not any thing could be begun, increased, perfected, or dissolved. Next, that Imagination is not necessary to Vital Motions, it is probable it may not, but yet there is required Knowledg, which I name Reason; for if there were not Knowledg in all Generations or Productions, there could not any distinct Creature be made or produced, for then all Generations would be confusedly mixt, neither would there be any distinct kinds or sorts of Creatures, nor no different Faculties, Proprieties, and the like. Thirdly, concerning *Animal Motions,* which your *Author* names *Voluntary Motions, as to go, to speak, to move any of our limbs, in such manner as is first fancied in our minds, and that they depend upon a precedent thought of whither, which way, and what, and that Imagination is the first Internal beginning of them;*[11] I think, by your *Authors* leave, it doth imply

---

[10] See also *Further Observations Upon Experimental Philosophy,* section XX; *Observations Upon the Opinions of Some Ancient Philosophers,* section IV.2–3; and *Grounds of Natural Philosophy,* chapter VIII of the First Part.

[11] Hobbes, *Leviathan,* I.vi.1. Note that at the end of the first (the 1666) edition of *Observations Upon Experimental Philosophy,* Cavendish offers a number of notes of clarification about passages in her earlier works, and one such note is about the current passage in letter XII. She writes, "When, contradicting the opinion of Mr. *Hobbes* concerning voluntary motions, who says, *That voluntary motions, as going, speaking, moving our lips, depend upon a precedent thought of whither, which way, and what, &c.* I answer, that it implies a contradiction, to call them Voluntary Motions, and yet say they depend on our imagination; for if the imagination draws them this or that way, how can they

a contradiction, to call them Voluntary Motions, and yet to say they are caused and depend upon our Imagination; for if the Imagination draws them this way, or that way, how can they be voluntary motions, being in a manner forced and necessitated to move according to Fancy or Imagination?

XX

Some perhaps will question the truth or probability of my saying, that Light is a Body, objecting that if light were a body, when the Sun is absent or retires under our Horizon, its light would leave an empty place, or if there were no empty place but all full, the light of the Sun at its return would not have room to display it self, especially in so great a compass as it doth, for two bodies cannot be in one place at one time. *I answer*, all bodies carry their places along with them, for body and place go together and are inseparable, and when the light of the Sun is gone, darkness succeeds, and when darkness is gone, light succeeds, so that it is with light and darkness as with all Creatures else; For you cannot believe, that if the whole World were removed, there would be a place of the world left, for there cannot be an empty nothing, no more then there can be an empty something; but if the world were annihilated, the place would be annihilated too, place and body being one and the same thing; and therefore in my opinion, there be no more places then there are bodies, nor no more bodies then there are places.[12]

[W] hen the mind or the rational matter conceives any thing that hath not such an exact figure, or is not so perceptible by our senses; then the mind uses art, and makes such figures, which stand like to that; as for example, to express infinite to it self, it dilates it parts without alteration, and without limitation or circumference; Likewise, when it will conceive a constant succession of Time, it draws out its parts into the figure of a line; and if eternity, it figures a line without beginning and end: But as for Immaterial, no mind can conceive that,

be voluntary? My meaning is not as if those actions were not self-actions, nor as if there were no voluntary actions at all; for to make a balance between Natures actions, there are voluntary, as well as occasioned actions, both in sense and reason; but because Mr *Hobbs* says, that those actions are depending upon Imagination and Fancy, and that Imagination is the first internal beginning of them, which sets them a going, as the prime wheel of a Watch does the rest: My opinion is, that after this rate they cannot properly be called voluntary, but are rather necessitated, at least occasioned by the Mind or Fancy; for I oppose voluntary actions to those that are occasioned or forced; which voluntary actions are made by the self-moving parts by rote, and of their own accord; but occasioned actions are made by imitation, although they are all self-actions, that is, move by their own inherent self-motion."

[12] See also, in this chapter, letters XXXI and XXXII of section one; and note 20 for *Worlds Olio*.

for it cannot put it self into nothing, although it can dilate and rarifie it self to an higher degree, but must stay within the circle of natural bodies.[13]

XXI

[N]ot that I mean there is any new Creation in nature, of any thing that was not before in nature; for nature is not God, to make new beings out of nothing, but any thing may be called new, when it is altered from one figure into another.

XXII

The Generation of sound, according to your worthy *Authors* opinion, is as follows: *As Vision,* says he, *so hearing is Generated by the medium, but not in the same manner; for sight is from pressure, that is, from an endeavour, in which there is no perceptible progression of any of the parts of the medium, but one part urging or thrusting on another, propagateth that action successively to any distance whatsoever; where as the motion of the medium, by which sound is made, is a stroke; for when we hear, the drum of the Ear, which is the first organ of hearing, is strucken, and the drum being stricken, the* Pia Mater *is also shaken, and with it the arteries inserted into it, by which the action propagated to the heart it self, by the reaction of the heart a Phantasme is made which we call Sound.*[14] Thus far your *Author:* To which give me leave to reply, that I fear, if the Ear was bound to hear any loud Musick, or another sound a good while, it would soundly be beaten, and grow sore and bruised with so many strokes; but since a pleasant sound would be rendred very unpleasant in this manner, my opinion is, that like as in the Eye, so in the Ear the corporeal sensitive motions do pattern out as many several figures, as sounds are presented to them. . . . But to prove it is not the outward object of sound with its striking or pressing motion, nor the medium, that causes this perception of sense, if there be a great solid body, as a wall, or any other partition betwixt two rooms, parting the object and the sensitive organ, so, as the sound is not able to press it, nevertheless the perception will be made.[15]

---

[13] See also *Philosophical and Physical Opinions,* chapter 160. A tricky question for Cavendish is how an idea would be able to successfully represent infinity (or eternity) if it is along the imagisic and pictorial lines that she specifies here.

[14] This is from Thomas Hobbes, *Elements of Philosophy the first section, concerning body,* chapter XXIX, 362.

[15] See also letters IV and XXIV of section one, in this chapter, and note 21 for *Philosophical and Physical Opinions.*

XXIII

I ask, whether the motion that moves the Instrument, be the Instruments, or the Hands? Perchance you will say the Hands; but I answer, how can it be the Hands motion, if it be in the Instrument? You will say, perhaps, the motion of the hand is transferred out of the hand into the instrument, and so from the instrument into the carved figure; but give me leave to ask you, was this motion of the hand, that was transferred, Corporeal or Incorporeal? If you say, Corporeal, then the hand must become less and weak, but if Incorporeal, I ask you, how a bodiless motion can have force and strength to carve and cut? But put an Impossible proposition, as that there is an Immaterial motion, and that this Incorporeal motion could be transferred out of one body into another; then I ask you, when the hand and instrument cease to move, what is become of the motion? Perhaps you will say, the motion perishes or is annihilated, and when the hand and the instrument do move again, to the carving or cutting of the figure, then a new Incorporeal Motion is created; Truly then there will be a perpetual creation and annihilation of Incorporeal motions, that is, of that which naturally is nothing; for an Incorporeal being is as much as a natural No-thing, for Natural reason cannot know nor have naturally any perception or Idea of an Incorporeal being: besides, if the motion be Incorporeal, then it must needs be a supernatural Spirit, for there is not any thing else Immaterial but they, and then it will be either an Angel or a Devil, or the Immortal Soul of man; but if you say it is the supernatural Soul, truly I cannot be perswaded that the supernatural Soul should not have any other imployment then to carve or cut prints, or figures, or move in the hands, or heels, or legs, or arms of a Man; for other animals have the same kind of Motions, and then they might have a Supernatural Soul as well as Man, which moves in them. But if you say, that these transferrable motions are material, then every action whereby the hand moves to the making or moving of some other body, would lessen the number of the motions in the hand, and weaken it, so that in the writing of one letter, the hand would not be able to write a second letter, at least not a third. But I pray, *Madam*, consider rationally, that though the Artificer or Workman be the occasion of the motions of the carved body, yet the motions of the body that is carved, are they which put themselves into such or such a figure, or give themselves such or such a print as the Artificer intended; for a Watch, although the Artist or Watch-maker be the occasional cause that the Watch moves in such or such an artificial figure, as the figure of a Watch, yet it is the Watches own motion by which it moves. . . . Wherefore I say that some things may be Occasional causes of other things, but not the Prime or Principal causes; and this distinction is very well to be considered, for there are no frequenter mistakes then to confound these two different causes, which make so many confusions in natural Philosophy.[16]

XXIV

[Y]ou will ask me, whether the glass takes the copy of the face, or the face prints its copy on the glass, or whether it be the *medium* of light and air that makes it? I answer, although many Learned men say, that as all perception, so also the seeing of ones face in a Looking-glass, and Eccho, are made by impression and reaction; yet I cannot in my simplicity conceive it, how bodies that come not near, or touch each other, can make a figure by impression and reaction: They say it proceeds from the motions of the *Medium* of light, or air, or both, *viz.* that the *Medium* is like a long stick with two ends, whereof one touches the object, the other the organ of sense, and that one end of it moving, the other moves also at the same point of Time, by which motions it may make many several figures; But I cannot conceive, how this motion of pressing forward and backward should make so many figures, wherein there is so much variety and curiosity. But, say light and air are as one figure, and like as a seal do print another body; I answer, if any thing could print, yet it is not probable, that so soft and rare bodies as light and air, could print such solid bodies as glass, nor could air by reverberation make such a sound as Eccho. But mistake me not, for, *I do not say*, that the Corporeal motions of light or air, cannot, or do not pencil, copie, or pattern out any figure, for both light and air are very active in such sorts of Motions, but I say, they cannot do it on any other bodies but their own. But to cut off tedious and unnecessary disputes, I return to the expressing of my own opinion, and believe, that the glass in its own substance doth figure out the copy of the face, or the like, and from that copy the sensitive motions in the eyes take another copy, and so the rational from the sensitive; and in this manner is made both rational and sensitive perception, sight and knowledg. The same with Ecchoes; for the air patterns out the copy of the sound, and then the sensitive corporeal motions in the ear pattern again this copy from the air, and so do make the perception and sense of hearing.[17] You may ask me, *Madam,* if it be so, that the glass and the air copy out the figure of the face and of sound, whether the Glass may be said to see and the Air to speak? I answer, I cannot tell that; for though I say, that the air

[16] See also *Grounds of Natural Philosophy*, chapter IX of the Fifth Part; and note 4 for *Philosophical and Physical Opinions*.

[17] Here, and also at the end of the same letter, Cavendish is suggesting that in cases of action at a distance, intervening bodies pattern and copy each other's motions all the way from the distant body to the affected body. See also *Observations Upon Experimental Philosophy*, section XXXVII, Q. 10.

repeats the words, and the glass represents the face, yet I cannot guess what their perceptions are, onely this I may say, that the air hath an elemental, and the glass a mineral,[18] but not an animal perception. . . .

[I]f one body did give another body motion, it must needs give it also substance, for motion is either something or nothing, body or no body, substance or no substance; if nothing, it cannot enter into another body; if something, it must lessen the bulk of the body it quits, and increase the bulk of the body it enters, and so the Sun and Fire with giving light and heat, would become less, for they cannot both give and keep at once, for this is as impossible, as for a man to give to another creature his human Nature, and yet to keep it still. Wherefore my opinion is for heat, that when many men stand round about a fire, and are heated and warmed by it, the fire doth not give them any thing, nor do they receive something from the fire, but the sensitive motions in their bodies pattern out the object of the fires heat, and so they become more or less hot according as their patterns are numerous or perfect; And as for air, it patterns out the light of the Sun, and the sensitive motions in the eyes of animals pattern out the light in the air. The like for Ecchoes, or any other sound, and for the figures which are presented in a Looking-glass. And thus millions of parts or creatures may make patterns of one or more objects, and the objects neither give nor loose any thing.

XXIX

Next your *Author* sayes, *He hath already clearly enough demonstrated, that there can be no beginning of motion, but from an external and moved body, and that heavy bodies being once cast upwards cannot be cast down again, but by external motion.*[19] Truly, *Madam*, I will not speak of your *Authors* demonstrations, for it is done most by art, which I have no knowledg in, but I think I have probably declared, that all the actions of nature are not forced by one part, driving, pressing, or shoving another, as a man doth a wheel-barrow, or a whip a horse; nor by reactions, as if men were at foot-ball or cuffs, or as men with carts meeting each other in a narrow lane. But to prove there is no self-motion in nature, he goes on and says; *To attribute to created bodies the power to move themselves, what is it else, then to say that there be creatures which have no dependance upon the Creator?* To which I answer, That if man (who is but a single part of nature) hath given him by God the power and a free will of moving himself, why should not God give it to Nature? Neither can I see, how it can take off the dependance upon God, more then Eternity; for if there be an Eternal Creator, there is also an Eternal

---

[18] See also *Observations Upon Experimental Philosophy*, section III.

[19] This is from Thomas Hobbes, *Elements of Philosophy the first section, concerning body*, chapter XXX, 379.

Creature, and if an Eternal Master, an Eternal Servant, which is Nature; and yet Nature is subject to Gods Command, and depends upon him; and if all Gods Attributes be Infinite, then his Bounty is Infinite also, which cannot be exercised but by an Infinite Gift, but a Gift doth not cause a less dependance. I do not say, That man hath an absolute Free-will, or power to move, according to his desire; for it is not conceived, that a part can have an absolute power: nevertheless his motion both of body and mind is a free and self-motion, and such a self-motion hath every thing in Nature according to its figure or shape; for motion and figure, being inherent in matter, matter moves figuratively. Yet do I not say, That there is no hindrance, obstruction and opposition in nature; but as there is no particular Creature, that hath an absolute power of self-moving; so that Creature which hath the advantage of strength, subtilty, or policy, shape, or figure, and the like, may oppose and over-power another which is inferior to it, in all this; yet this hinderance and opposition doth not take away self-motion.[20] But I perceive your *Author* is much for necessitation, and against free-will, which I leave to Moral Philosophers and Divines.

XXX

I am reading now the works of that Famous and most Renowned *Author, DesCartes*, out of which I intend to pick out onely those discourses which I like best, and not to examine his opinions, as they go along from the beginning to the end of his books; And in order to this, I have chosen in the first place, his discourse of motion, and do not assent to his opinion, when he defines *Motion to be onely a Mode of a thing, and not the thing or body it selfe;*[21] for, in my opinion, there can be no abstraction made of motion from body, neither really, nor in the manner of our conception, for how can I conceive that which is not, nor cannot be in nature, that is, to conceive motion without body? Wherefore Motion is but one thing with body, without any separation or abstraction soever. Neither doth it agree with my reason, that *one body can give or transfer motion into another body; and as much motion it gives or transfers into that body, as much loses it: As for example, in two hard bodies thrown against one another, where one, that is thrown with greater force, takes the other along with it, and loses as much motion as it gives it.*[22] For how can motion, being no substance, but onely a mode, quit one body, and pass into another? One body may either occasion, or imitate anothers motion, but it can neither give nor take away what belongs to its own or another bodies substance, no more then matter can quit its nature from being

---

[20] See also *Philosophical and Physical Opinions*, chapter XXII.
[21] This is from *Principles of Philosophy* II.27, CSM 1:234.
[22] This is from *Principles of Philosophy* II.40, CSM 1:242.

matter; and therefore my opinion is, that if motion doth go out of one body into another, then substance goes too; for motion, and substance or body, as afore-mentioned, are all one thing, and then all bodies that receive motion from other bodies, must needs increase in their substance and quantity, and those bodies which impart or transfer motion, must decrease as much as they increase: Truly, *Madam*, that neither Motion nor Figure should subsist by themselves, and yet be transferrable into other bodies, is very strange, and as much as to prove them to be nothing, and yet to say they are something. The like may be said of all others, which they call accidents, as skill, learning, knowledge, &c. saying, they are no bodies, because they have no extension, but inherent in bodies or substances as in their subjects; for although the body may subsist without them, yet they being always with the body, body and they are all one thing: And so is power and body, for body cannot quit power, nor power the body, being all one thing. But to return to Motion, my opinion is, That all matter is partly animate, and partly inanimate, and all matter is moving and moved, and that there is no part of Nature that hath not life and knowledg, for there is no Part that has not a comixture of animate and inanimate matter; and though the inanimate matter has no motion, nor life and knowledg of it self, as the animate has, neverthe-less being both so closely joyned and commixed as in one body, the inanimate moves as well as the animate, although not in the same manner; for the animate moves of it self, and the inanimate moves by the help of the animate, and thus the animate is moving and the inanimate moved; not that the animate matter transfers, infuses, or communicates its own motion to the inanimate; for this is impossible, by reason it cannot part with its own nature, nor alter the nature of inanimate matter, but each retains its own nature; for the inanimate matter remains inanimate, that is, without self-motion, and the animate loses nothing of its self-motion, which otherwise it would, if it should impart or transferr its motion into the inanimate matter; but onely as I said heretofore, the inanimate works or moves with the animate, because of their close union and commixture; for the animate forces or causes the inanimate matter to work with her; and thus one is moving, the other moved, and consequently there is life and knowledg in all parts of nature, by reason in all parts of nature there is a commixture of ani-mate and inanimate matter: and this Life and Knowledg is sense and reason, or sensitive and rational corporeal motions, which are all one thing with animate matter without any distinction or abstraction, and can no more quit matter, then matter can quit motion.[23]

---

[23] The language here in letter XXX calls to mind the similar view in Descartes, *Principles of Philosophy* I.62 (CSM 1:214), that there are features of substances that are distinct in thought— or rationally distinct—but that are not distinct in reality. See also *Observations Upon Experimental Philosophy*, section XXXV.

XXXI

I believe not that there is any more place then body; as for example, Water being mix'd with Earth, the water doth not take the Earths place, but as their parts intermix, so do their places, and as their parts change, so do their places, so that there is no more place, then there is water and earth; the same may be said of Air and Water, or Air and Earth, or did they all mix together; for as their bodies join, so do their places, and as they are separated from each other, so are their places. Say a man travels a hundred miles, and so a hundred thousand paces; but yet this man has not been in a hundred thousand places, for he never had any other place but his own, he hath joined and separated himselfe from a hundred thousand, nay millions of parts, but he has left no places behind him. You will say, if he travel the same way back again, then he is said to travel thorow the same places. I answer, It may be the vulgar way of expression, or the common phrase; but to speak properly, after a Philosophical way, and according to the truth in nature, he cannot be said to go back again thorow the same places he went, because he left none behind him. . . . 'Tis true, a man may return to the same adjoining bodies, where he was before, but then he brings his place with him again, and as his body, so his place returnes also, and if a mans arm be cut off, you may say, there was an arm heretofore, but you cannot say properly, this is the place where the arm was.

XXXII

In my last, I hope, I have sufficiently declared my opinion, That to one body belongs but one place, and that no body can leave a place behind it, but wheresoever is body, there is place also. Now give me leave to examine this question: when a bodies figure is printed on snow, or any other fluid or soft matter, as air, water, and the like; whether it be the body, that prints its own figure upon the snow, or whether it be the snow, that patterns the figure of the body? My answer is, That it is not the body, which prints its figure upon the snow, but the snow that patterns out the figure of the body; for if a seal be printed upon wax, 'tis true, it is the figure of the seal, which is printed on the wax, but yet the seal doth not give the wax the print of its own figure, but it is the wax that takes the print or pattern from the seal, and patterns or copies it out in its own substance, just as the sensitive motions in the eye do pattern out the figure of an object, as I have declared heretofore.

XXXV

That the Mind, according to your Authors opinion, is a substance really distinct from the body, and may be actually separated from it and subsist without it. [24] . . . Neither can I apprehend, that the Mind's or Soul's seat should be in the *Glandula* or kernel[25] of the Brain, and there sit like a Spider in a Cobweb, to whom the least motion of the Cobweb gives intelligence of a Flye, which he is ready to assault, and that the Brain should get intelligence by the animal spirits as his servants, which run to and fro like Ants to inform it; or that the Mind should, according to others opinions, be a light, and imbroidered all with Ideas, like a Heraulds Coat; and that the sensitive organs should have no knowledg in themselves, but serve onely like peepingholes for the mind, or barn-dores to receive bundles of pressures, like sheaves of Corn; For there being a thorow mixture of animate, rational and sensitive, and inanimate matter, we canot assign a certain seat or place to the rational, another to the sensitive, and another to the inanimate, but they are diffused and intermixt throughout all the body; And this is the reason, that sense and knowledg cannot be bound onely to the head or brain: But although they are mixt together, nevertheless they do not lose their interior natures by this mixture, nor their purity and subtilty, nor their proper motions or actions, but each moves according to its nature and substance, without confusion; The actions of the rational part in Man, which is the Mind or Soul, are called Thoughts, or thoughtful perceptions, which are numerous, and so are the sensitive perceptions; for though Man, or any other animal hath but five exterior sensitive organs, yet there be numerous perceptions made in these sensitive organs, and in all the body; nay, every several Pore of the flesh is a sensitive organ, as well as the Eye, or the Ear.

XXXVI

That all other animals, besides man, want reason, your *Author* endeavours to prove in his *discourse of method*, where his chief argument is, That other animals cannot express their mind, thoughts or conceptions, either by speech or any other signs, as man can do: For, sayes he, *it is not for want of the organs belonging to the framing of words, as we may observe in Parrats and Pies, which are apt enough to express words they are taught, but understand nothing of them.*[26] My answer is, That one man expressing his mind by speech or words to an other, doth not declare by it his excellency and supremacy above all other Creatures, but for the most part more folly, for a talking man is not so wise as a contemplating man.

---

[24] This is from *Principles of Philosophy* I.60, CSM 1:213, but see also the Sixth Meditation, CSM 2:54–55.

[25] Descartes famously held that the mind is connected to the brain at the pineal gland (*The World, or Treatise on Light*, CSM 1:100–107).

[26] This is from *Discourse on the Method*, CSM 1:140–141.

But by reason other Creatures cannot speak or discourse with each other as men, or make certain signs, whereby to express themselves as dumb and deaf men do, should we conclude, they have neither knowledge, sense, reason, or intelligence? Certainly, this is a very weak argument; for one part of a mans body, as one hand, is not less sensible then the other, nor the heel less sensible then the heart, nor the legg less sensible then the head, but each part hath its sense and reason, and so consequently its sensitive and rational knowledge.[27]

Section 2

I

Being come now to the Perusal of the Works of that learned *Author* Dr. *Moor*, I find that the onely design of his Book called *Antidote*, is *to prove the Existence of a God*, and to refute, or rather convert Atheists; which I wonder very much at, considering, he says himself, That *there is no man under the cope of Heaven but believes a God;*[28] which if so, what needs there to make so many arguments to no purpose? Unless it be to shew Learning and wit; In my opinion, it were better to convert Pagans to be Christians, or to reform irregular Christians to a more pious life, then to prove that, which all men believe, which is the way to bring it into question. For certainly, according to the natural Light of Reason, there is a God, and no man, I believe, doth doubt it; for though there may be many vain words, yet I think there is no such atheistical belief amongst man-kind, nay, not onely amongst men, but also, amongst all other creatures, for if nature believes a God, all her parts, especially the sensitive and rational, which are the living and knowing parts, and are in all natural creatures, do the like, and therefore all parts and creatures in nature do adore and worship God, for any thing man can know to the contrary; for no question, but natures soule adores and worships God as well as man's soule; and why may not God be worshipped by all sorts and kinds of creatures as well, as by one kind or sort? I will not say the same way, but I believe there is a general worship and adoration of God; for as God is an Infinite Deity, so certainly he has an Infinite Worship and Adoration, and there is not any part of nature, but adores and worships the only omnipotent God, to whom belongs Praise and Glory from and to all eternity: For it is very improbable, that God should be worshipped onely in part, and not in whole, and that all creatures were made to obey man, and not to worship God, onely for man's sake, and not for God's worship, for man's use, and not God's adoration, for mans spoil and not God's blessing.

[27] See also *Worlds Olio*, "Epistle."
[28] This is in Henry More, *An Antidote against Atheism*, I.x, 31–32.

II

Since I spake in my last of the adoration and worship of God, you would faine know, whether we can have an Idea of God? I answer, That naturally we may, and really have a knowledge of the existence of God, as I proved in my former letter, to wit, that there is a God, and that he is the *Author* of all things, who rules and governs all things, and is also the God of Nature: but I dare not think, that naturally we can have an Idea of the essence of God, so as to know what God is in his very nature and essence; for how can there be a finite Idea of an Infinite God? You may say, As well as of Infinite space. I answer, Space is relative, or has respect to body, but there is not any thing that can be compared to God; for the Idea of Infinite nature is material, as being a material creature of Infinite material Nature. You will say, How can a finite part have an Idea of infinite nature? I answer, Very well, by reason the Idea is part of Infinite Nature, and so of the same kind, as material; but God being an Eternal, Infinite, Immaterial, Individable Being, no natural creature can have an Idea of him.[29]

III

God being an Infinite Deity, there is required an Infinite capacity to conceive him; nay, Nature her self although Infinite, yet cannot posibly have an exact notion of God, by reason of the disparity between God and her self; and therefore it is not probable, if the Infinite servant of God is not able to conceive him, that a finite part or creature of nature, of what kind or sort soever, whether Spiritual, as your *Author* is pleased to name it, or Corporeal, should comprehend God. Concerning my belief of God, I submit wholly to the Church, and believe as I have bin informed out of the *Athanasian* Creed, that the Father is Incomprehensible, the Sonne Incomprehensible, and the Holy Ghost Incomprehensible; and that there are not three, but one Incomprehensible God; Wherefore if any man can prove (as I do verily believe he cannot) that God is not Incomprehensible, he must of necessity be more knowing then the whole Church, however he must needs dissent from the Church. But perchance your *Author* may say, I raise new and prejudicial opinions, in saying that matter is eternal.[30] I answer, The Holy Writ doth not mention Matter to be created, but onely Particular Creatures, as this Visible World, with all its Parts, as the history or description of the Creation of the World in *Genesis* plainly shews; For *God said, Let it be Light, and there was Light; Let there be a Firmament in the midst of the Waters, and let it divide the Waters from the Waters; and Let the Waters under the Heaven be gathered together*

---

[29] See also *Philosophical and Physical Opinions*, chapter 160.
[30] See also *Philosophical and Physical Opinions*, chapter 23.

unto one place, and let the dry Land appear; and let the Earth bring forth Grass, the Herb yielding Seed, and the Fruit-tree yielding Fruit after his kind; and let there be Lights in the Firmament of the Heaven, to divide the Day from the Night, &c. Which proves, that all creatures and figures were made and produced out of that rude and desolate heap or chaos which the Scripture mentions, which is nothing else but matter, by the powerful Word and Command of God, executed by his Eternal Servant, Nature; as I have heretofore declared it in a Letter I sent you in the beginning concerning Infinite Nature. But lest I seem to encroach too much upon Divinity, I submit this Interpretation to the Church; However, I think it not against the ground of our Faith; for I am so far from maintaining any thing either against Church or State, as I am submitting to both in all duty, and shall do so as long as I live, and rest.

IV

[T]hough Nature is a self-moving substance, and by self-motion divides and composes her self several manners or ways into several forms and figures, yet being a knowing, as well as a living substance, she knows how to order her parts and actions wisely; for as she hath an Infinite body or substance, so she has an Infinite life and knowledg; and as she hath an Infinite life and knowledg, so she hath an infinite wisdom: But mistake me not, *Madam*; I do not mean an Infinite Divine Wisdom, but an Infinite Natural Wisdom, given her by the Infinite bounty of the Omnipotent God; but yet this Infinite Wisdom, Life and Knowledg in Nature make but one Infinite. And as Nature hath degrees of matter, so she has also degrees and variety of corporeal motions; for some parts of matter are self-moving, and some are moved by these self-moving parts of matter; and all these parts, both the moving and moved, are so intermixed, that none is without the other, no not in any the least Creature or part of Nature we can conceive; for there is no Creature or part of Nature, but has a comixture of those mentioned parts of animate and inanimate matter, and all the motions are so ordered by Natures wisdom, as not any thing in Nature can be otherwise, unless by a Supernatural Command and Power of God; for no part of corporeal matter and motion can either perish, or but rest; one part may cause another part to alter its motions, but not to quit motion, no more then one part of matter can annihilate or destroy another; and therefore matter is not meerly Passive, but always Active, by reason of the thorow mixture of animate and inanimate matter; for although the animate matter is onely active in its nature, and the in-animate passive, yet because they are so closely united and mixed together that they make but one body, the parts of the animate or self-moving matter do bear up and cause the inanimate parts to move and work with them; and thus there is an activity in all parts of matter moving and working as one body, without any fixation or rest, for all is moveable, moving and moved.

V

I Cannot well conceive what your *Author* means by the *Common Laws of Nature*;[31] But if you desire my opinion how many Laws Nature hath, and what they are; I say Nature hath but One Law, which is a wise Law, *viz.* to keep Infinite matter in order, and to keep so much Peace, as not to disturb the Foundation of her Government: for though Natures actions are various, and so many times opposite, which would seem to make wars between several Parts, yet those active Parts, being united into one Infinite body, cannot break Natures general Peace; for that which Man names War, Sickness, Sleep, Death, and the like, are but various particular actions of the onely matter; not, as your *Author* imagines, in a confusion, like Bullets, or such like things juggled together in a mans Hat, but very orderly and methodical. Concerning the Preeminence and Prerogative of *Man*, whom your *Author* calls *The flower and chief of all the products of nature upon this Globe of the earth*;[32] I answer, That Man cannot well be judged of himself, because he is a Party, and so may be Partial; But if we observe well, we shall find that the Elemental Creatures are as excellent as Man, and as able to be a friend or foe to Man, as Man to them, and so the rest of all Creatures; so that I cannot perceive more abilities in Man then in the rest of natural Creatures; for though he can build a stately House, yet he cannot make a Honey-comb; and though he can plant a Slip, yet he cannot make a Tree; though he can make a Sword, or Knife, yet he cannot make the Mettal.[33] And as Man makes use of other Creatures, so other Creatures make use of Man, as far as he is good for any thing: But Man is not so useful to his neighbour or fellow-creatures, as his neighbour or fellow-creatures to him, being not so profitable for use, as apt to make spoil. And so leaving him, I rest.

[31] This is in *An Antidote against Atheism*, II.i, 46–47.

[32] This is in *An Antidote against Atheism*, II.iii, 54.

[33] Cavendish supposes that human beings often seek way too much credit for the creations that they produce: these come to fruition only because (or mostly because) of the sophistication and know-how of the smaller bodies out of which they are built. In an extreme case, we might say that we are responsible for producing a child, when in fact it is remarkable items like the placenta, egg and sperm cells, and other bodily parts that do all of the real and meticulous work. One of the criticisms that Cavendish levels against human artifacts is they tend to bypass and shortcut this level of natural know-how and sophistication, and hence should not be expected to function very well. See, for example, *Worlds Olio*, "The Power of Natural Works," and the corresponding note 19.

VI

[I]f you conceive Matter to be one thing, Figure another, and Motion a third, several, distinct and dividable from each other, it will produce gross errors, for, matter, motion, and figure, are but one thing.[34] ... [T]here is nothing in Nature but what is material; but he that thinks it absurd to say, the World is composed of meer self-moving Matter, may consider, that it is more absurd to believe Immaterial substances or spirits in Nature, as also a spirit of Nature,[35] which is the Vicarious power of God upon Matter; For why should it not be as probable, that God did give Matter a selfmoving power to her self, as to have made another Creature to govern her? For Nature is not a Babe, or Child, to need such a Spiritual Nurse, to teach her to go, or to move; neither is she so young a Lady as to have need of a Governess, for surely she can govern her self.

VII

[T]he General actions of Nature are both life and knowledg, which are the architects of all Creatures, and know better how to frame all kinds and sorts of Creatures then man can conceive; and the several parts of Matter have a more easie way of communication, then Mans head hath with his hand, or his hand with pen, ink, and paper, when he is going to write. ... But give me leave, *Madam*, to tell you, That self-moving Matter may sometimes erre and move irregularly, and in some parts not move so strong, curious, or subtil at sometimes, as in other parts, for Nature delights in variety; Nevertheless she is more wise then any Particular Creature or part can conceive, which is the cause that Man thinks Nature's wise, subtil and lively actions, are as his own gross actions, conceiving them to be constrained and turbulent, not free and easie, as well as wise and knowing; Whereas Nature's Creating, Generating and Producing actions are by an easie connexion of parts to parts, without Counterbuffs, Joggs and Jolts, producing a particular figure by degrees, and in order and method, as humane sense and reason may well perceive: And why may not the sensitive and rational part of Matter know better how to make a Bee, then a Bee doth how to make Honey and Wax? or have a better communication betwixt them, then Bees that fly several ways, meeting and joyning to make their Combes in their Hives?

---

[34] See also note 23, in this chapter.

[35] More held that, in addition to bodies, the created universe also contains an immaterial spirit of nature that serves as the source of motion for bodies and helps them to behave in an orderly manner. See, for example, *The Immortality of the Soul*, I.xi–xii, 75–89. One of the reasons for thinking that Cavendish holds that much of the mentality in nature is unconscious is that a central component of More's philosophy is that unconscious mentality (the "spirit of nature") is pervasive in nature, and Cavendish never once takes issue with that view in *Philosophical Letters*, even though she makes sure to object to More on possible points of disagreement at every turn.

VIII

Your *Author* is pleased to say, that *Matter is a Principle purely passive, and no otherwise moved or modified, then as some other thing moves or modifies it, but cannot move it self at all; which is most demonstrable to them that contend for sense and perception in it: For if it had any such perception, it would, by vertue of its self-motion withdraw it self from under the knocks of hammers, or fury of the fire, or of its own accord approach to such things as are most agreeable to it.* [36] ... By his leave, *Madam,* I must tell you, I see no consequence in this argument; Because some parts of matter cannot withdraw themselves from the force and power of other parts, therefore they have neither sense, reason, nor perception: For put the case, a man should be overpowr'd by some other men, truly he would be force to suffer, and no Immaterial Spirits, I think, would assist him. The very same may be said of other Creatures or parts of Nature; for some may over-power others, as the fire, hammer and hand doth over-power a Horse-shoe, which cannot prevail over so much odds of power and strength; And so likewise it is with sickness and health, life and death; for example, some corporeal motions in the body turning Rebels, by moving contrary to the health of an animal Creature, it must become sick; for not every particular creature hath an absolute power, the power being in the Infinite whole, and not in single divided parts.

X

[S]ince man is not able to know perfectly all those proprieties which belong to animals, much less will he be able to know and judg of those that are in Vegetables, Minerals and Elements; and yet these Creatures, for any thing Man knows, may be as knowing, understanding, and wise as he; and each as knowing of its kind or sort, as man is of his. . . . But to conclude: some of our modern Philosophers think they do God good service, when they endeavour to prove Nature, as Gods good Servant, to be stupid, ignorant, foolish and mad, or any thing rather then wise, and yet they believe themselves wise, as if they were no part of Nature; but I cannot imagine any reason why they should rail on her, except Nature had not given them as great a share or portion, as she hath given to others; for children in this case do often rail at their Parents, for leaving their Brothers and Sisters more then themselves. However, Nature can do more then any of her Creatures: and if Man can Paint, Imbroider, Carve, Ingrave curiously; why may not Nature have more Ingenuity, Wit and Wisdom then any of her particular Creatures? The same may be said of her Government.[37]

---

[36] This is in *The Immortality of the Soul,* I.ii.7, 81.
[37] See also *Philosophical and Physical Opinions,* chapter 77.

XIII

That Matter is uncapable of Sense, your *Author* proves by the example of dead Carcasses; *For,* says he, *Motion and Sense being really one and the same thing, it must needs follow, that where there is motion, there is also sense and perception; but on the contrary, there is Reaction in dead Carkasses, and yet no Sense.*[38] I answer shortly, That it is no consequence, because there is no animal sense nor exterior perceptible local motion in a dead Carcass, therefore there is no sense at all in it; for though it has not animal sense, yet it may nevertheless have sense according to the nature of that figure, into which it did change from being an animal. . . . Though [a] Bell hath not an animal knowledg, yet it may have a mineral life and knowledg, and the Bow, and the Jack-in-a-box a vegetable knowledg; for the shape and form of the Bell, Bow, and Jack-in-a-box, is artificial; nevertheless each in its own kind may have as much knowledg as an animal in his kind; onely they are different according to the different proprieties of their Figures: And who can prove the contrary that they have not? For certainly Man cannot prove what he cannot know; but Mans nature is so, that knowing but little of other Creatures, he presently judges there is no more knowledg in Nature, then what Man, at least Animals, have; and confines all sense onely to Animal sense, and all knowledg to Animal knowledge.[39]

XV

[T]his is to be observed, That all rational perceptions or cogitations, are not so perspicuous and clear as if they were Mathematical Demonstrations, but there is some obscurity, more or less in them, at least they are not so well perceivable without comparing several figures together, which proves, they are not made by an individable, immaterial Spirit, but by dividable corporeal parts: As for example, Man writes oftentimes false, and seldom so exact, but he is forced to mend his hand, and correct his opinions, and sometimes quite to alter them, according as the figures continue or are dissolved and altered by change of motion, and according as the actions are quick or slow in these alterations, the humane mind is setled or wavering; and as figures are made, or dissolved and transformed, Opinions, Conceptions, Imaginations, Understanding, and the like, are more or less[40] . . . [T]he curious actions of the purest rational matter are neither rude nor rough; but although this matter is so subtil and pure, as not subject to exterior human senses and organs, yet certainly it is dividable, not

---

[38] This is in *The Immortality of the Soul*, II.ii.1, 124.
[39] See also *Appendix to Grounds of Natural Philosophy*, chapter VIII of the Third Part.
[40] See also Hume's *A Treatise of Human Nature*, I.ii.iv, 45.

onely in several Creatures, but in the several parts of one and the same Creature, as well as the sensitive, which is the Life of Nature, as the other is the Soul; not the Divine, but natural Soul; neither is this Soul Immaterial, but Corporeal; not composed of raggs and shreds, but it is the purest, simplest and subtillest matter in Nature. But to conclude, I desire you to remember, *Madam*, that this rational and sensitive Matter in one united and finite Figure or particular Creature, has both common and particular actions; for as there are several kinds and sorts of Creatures, and particulars in every kind and sort: so the like for the actions of the rational and sensitive matter in one particular Creature. Also it is to be noted, That the Parts of rational matter, can more suddenly give and take Intelligence to and from each other, then the sensitive; nevertheless, all Parts in Nature, at least adjoyning parts, have Intelligence between each other,[41] more or less, because all parts make but one body; for it is not with the parts of Matter, as with several Constables in several Hundreds, or several Parishes, which are a great way distant from each other, but they may be as close as the combs of Bees, and yet as partable and as active as Bees.

XVI

[I]t is well to be observed, That all Motions are not Impressions, neither do all Impressions make such dents, as to disturb the adjoyning Parts: Wherefore those, in my opinion, understand *Nature* best, which say, that Sensation and Perception are really one and the same; but they are out, that say, there can be no communication at a distance, unless by pressing and crowding; for the patterning of an outward object, may be done without any inforcement or disturbance, jogging or crowding, as I have declared heretofore;[42] for the sensitive and rational motions in the sensitive and rational parts of matter in one creature, observing the exterior motions in outward objects, move accordingly, either regularly or irregularly in patterns; and if they have no exterior objects, as in dreams, they work by rote. And so to conclude, I am absolutely of their opinion, who believe, that there is nothing existent in Nature, but what is purely Corporeal, for this seems most probable in sense and reason to me.

[41] See also note 19 for *Worlds Olio*. Note the similarity between the materialism of Cavendish and the (*prima facie* opposite) view of Anne Conway that matter does not exist and that everything in nature is instead spirit. Conway holds that spirit has extension, partakes of motion, and is divisible, but she argues that because matter is by definition inactive and dead, no such thing as matter in fact exists. See *Principles of the Most Ancient and Modern Philosophy*, chapter VII, pp. 41–55.

[42] See also, in this chapter, letters IV and XXIV of section one.

XVII

[F]or every Creature, if regularly made, hath particular motions proper to its figure; for natural Matters wisdom makes distinctions by her distinct corporeal motions, giving every particular Creature their due Portion and Proportion according to the nature of their figures, and to the rules of her actions.

XVIII

[I]n my opinion, Fancy and Reason are not made in the Brain, as there is a Brain, but as there is sensitive and rational matter, which makes not onely the Brain, but all Thoughts, Conceptions, Imaginations, Fancy, Understanding, Memory, Remembrance, and whatsoever motions are in the Head, or Brain: neither doth this sensitive and rational matter remain or act in one place of the Brain, but in every part thereof; and not onely in every part of the Brain, but in every part of the Body; nay, not onely in every part of a Mans Body, but in every part of Nature. But, *Madam*, I would ask those, that say the Brain has neither sense, reason, nor self-motion, and therefore no Perception; but that all proceeds from an Immaterial Principle, as an Incorporeal Spirit, distinct from the body, which moveth and actuates corporeal matter; I would fain ask them, I say, where their Immaterial Ideas reside, in what part or place of the Body? and whether they be little or great? . . . if [the mind] have no dimension, how can it be confined in a material body?[43] Wherefore when your *Author* says, the mind is a substance, it is to my reason very probable; but not when he says, it is an immaterial substance, which will never agree with my sense and reason; for it must be either something, or nothing, there being no *medium* between, in Nature. But pray mistake me not, *Madam*, when I say Immaterial is nothing; for I mean nothing Natural, or so as to be a part of Nature;[44] for God forbid, I should deny, that God is a Spiritual Immaterial substance, or Being; neither do I deny that we can have an Idea, notion, conception, or thought of the Existence of God; for I am of your *Authors* opinion, That there is no Man under the cope of Heaven, that doth not by the light of Nature, know, and believe there is a God; but that we should have such a perfect Idea of God, as of

[43] A regular refrain in the Cavendish corpus is that features like figure, shape, and motion are had by corporeal entities only and hence that if minds have such features, they must be corporeal as well. See letters XXI and XLII of section three, in this chapter; *Further Observations Upon Experimental Philosophy*, section XX; *Observations Upon the Opinions of Some Ancient Philosophers*, section III.4; and *Appendix to Grounds of Natural Philosophy*, chapters III and XI of the First Part.

[44] Note that Cavendish denies that immaterial entities exist in nature, and she holds that we cannot detect or conceive or come into contact with them (for example in *Appendix to Grounds of Natural Philosophy*, chapter III of the First Part), but she does not thereby deny that they exist.

any thing else in the World, or as of our selves, as your *Author* says, I cannot in sense and reason conceive to be true or possible. Neither am I against those Spirits, which the holy Scripture mentions, as Angels and Devils, and the divine Soul of Man;[45] but I say onely, that no Immaterial Spirit belongs to Nature, so as to be a part thereof; for Nature is Material, or Corporeal; and whatsoever is not composed of matter or body, belongs not to Nature; nevertheless, Immaterial Spirits may be in Nature, although not parts of Nature. But there can neither be an Immaterial Nature, nor a Natural Immaterial; Nay, our very thoughts and conceptions of Immaterial are Material, as made of self-moving Matter. Wherefore to conclude, these opinions in Men proceed from a Vain-glory, as to have found out something that is not in Nature; to which I leave them, and their natural Immaterial Substances, like so many Hobgoblins to fright Children withal.

XXI

[A]ll that is a substance in Nature, is a body, and what has a body, is corporeal; for though there be several degrees of matter, as in purity, rarity, subtilty, activity; yet there is no degree so pure, rare and subtil, that can go beyond its nature, and change from corporeal to incorporeal, except it could change from being something to nothing, which is impossible in Nature. Next, there is no substance in Nature that is not divisible; for all that is a body, or a bodily substance, hath extension, and all extension hath parts, and what has parts, is divisible. As for self-motion, contraction and dilation, these are actions onely of Natural Matter; for Matter by the Power of God is self-moving, and all sorts of motions, as contraction, dilation, alteration, penetration, &c. do properly belong to Matter; so that natural Matter stands in no need to have some Immaterial or Incorporeal substance to move, rule, guide and govern her, but she is able enough to do it all her self, by the free Gift of the Omnipotent God; for why should we trouble our selves to invent or frame other unconceivable substances, when there is no need for it, but Matter can act, and move as well without them and of it self? Is not God able to give such power to Matter, as to an other Incorporeal substance? ... Spirit and Body are things of contrary Natures. In fine, I cannot conceive, how a Spirit should fill up a place or space, having no body, nor how it can have the effects of a body, being none it self; for the effects flow from the cause; and as the cause is, so are its effects.

[45] But see also *Appendix to Grounds of Natural Philosophy*, chapter II of the First Part, in which Cavendish says that there is at most one immaterial being, which is God.

XXV

[I]t is, in my opinion, more probable, that one material should act upon another material, or one immaterial upon another immaterial, then that an immaterial should act upon a material or corporeal.[46] Thus the consideration or contemplation of immaterial natural Spirits puts me always into doubts, and raises so many contradictions in my sense and reason, as I know not, nor am not able to reconcile them.

XXVIII

I cannot imagine why God should make an Immaterial Spirit to be the Proxy or Vice-gerent of his Power, or the *Quarter-master General of his Divine Providence*,[47] as your *Author* is pleased to style it, when he is able to effect it without any Under-Officers, and in a more easie and compendious way, as to impart immediately such self-moving power to Natural Matter, which man attributes to an Incorporeal Spirit.

XXIX

[A]ll that I have writ hitherto to you of the Soul, concerns the natural Soul of Man, which is material, and not the supernatural or divine Soul; neither do I contradict any thing concerning this divine soul, but I am onely against those opinions, which make the natural soul of man an immaterial natural spirit, and confound supernatural Creatures with natural, believing those spirits to be as well natural Creatures and parts of Nature, as material and corporeal beings are; when as there is great difference betwixt them, and nothing in Nature to be found, but what is corporeal. Upon this account I take all their relations of Daemons, of the Genii, and of the Souls after the departure from humane Bodies, their Vehicles, Shapes, Habitations, Converses, Conferences, Entertainments, Exercises, Pleasures, Pastimes, Governments, Orders, Laws, Magistrates, Officers, Executioners, Punishments, and the like, rather for Poetical Fictions, then Rational Probabilities; containing more Fancy, then Truth and Reason, whether they concern the divine or natural Soul: for as for the divine Soul, the Scripture makes no other mention of it, but that immediately after her departure out of this natural life, she goeth either to Heaven or Hell, either to enjoy Reward, or to suffer Punishment, according to man's actions in this life. But as for the Natural Soul, she being material, has no need of any Vehicles, neither

---

[46] See also letter XVIII of section two, and letter XXXII, in this chapter.
[47] This is in *The Immortality of the Soul*, III.xiii.9, 469.

is natural death any thing else but an alteration of the rational and sensitive motions, which from the dissolution of one figure go to the formation or production of another.[48] Thus the natural soul is not like a Traveller, going out of one body into another, neither is air her lodging; for certainly, if the natural humane soul should travel through the airy regions, she would at last grow weary, it being so great a journey, except she did meet with the soul of a Horse, and so ease her self with riding on Horseback.

XXX

For what Man would be so senceless as to deny a God? Wherefore to prove either a God, or the Immortality of the Soul, is to make a man doubt of either: for as Physicians and Surgeons apply strengthening Medicines onely to those parts of the body which they suppose the weakest, so it is with proofs and arguments, those being for the most part used in such subjects, the truth of which is most questionable. But in things Divine, Disputes do rather weaken Faith, then prove Truth, and breed several strange opinions; for Man being naturally ambitious, and endeavouring to excel each other, will not content himself with what God has been pleased to reveal in his holy Word; but invents and adds something of his own; and hence arise so many monstrous expressions and opinions, that a simple man is puzzled, not knowing which to adhere to; which is the cause of so many schismes, sects, and divisions in Religion: Hence it comes also, that some pretend to know the very nature and essence of God, his divine Counsels, all his Actions, Designs, Rules, Decrees, Power, Attributes, nay, his Motions, Affections, and Passions, as if the Omnipotent Infinite God were of a humane shape; so that there are already more divisions then Religions, which disturb the peace and quiet both of mind and body; when as the ground of our belief consists but in some few and short Articles, which clearly explained, and the moral part of Divinity well pressed upon the People, would do more good, then unnecessary and tedious disputes, which rather confound Religion, then advance it: but if man had a mind to shew Learning, and exercise his Wit, certainly there are other subjects, wherein he can do it with more profit, and less danger, then by proving Christian Religion by Natural Philosophy, which is the way to destroy them both. . . . And I hope they will not take any offence at the maintaining and publishing my opinions concerning Nature and Natural effects, for they are as harmless, and as little prejudicial to them, as my designs; for my onely and chief design is, and ever hath been to understand Nature rightly, obey the Church exactly, Believe undoubtedly, Pray zealously, Live vertuously, and Wish earnestly, that both Church and Schools may increase and flourish in the

---

[48] See also *Appendix to Grounds of Natural Philosophy*, chapter VIII of the Third Part.

sacred knowledge of the true Word of God, and that each one may live peaceable and happily in this world, die quietly, and rise blessedly and gloriously to everlasting Life and happiness.

XXXI

I Will leave the Controversie of Free-Will and Necessity, which your *Author* is discoursing of,[49] to Divines to decide it, onely I say this, that Nature hath a natural Free-will and power of self-moving, and is not necessitated; but yet that this Free-will proceeds from God, who hath given her both will and power to act freely. But as for the question,[50] whether there be nothing in the Universe, but meer body? I answer, My opinion is not, that there is nothing in the world but meer Body; but that Nature is purely material or corporeal, and that there is no part of Nature, or natural Creature, which is not Matter, or Body, or made of Matter; also, that there is not any thing else mixt with body, as a copartner in natural actions, which is distinct from Body or Matter; nevertheless, there may be supernatural spiritual beings or substances in Nature, without any hinderance to Matter or corporeal Nature. The same I may say of the natural material, and the divine and supernatural Soul; for though the divine Soul is in a natural body, and both their powers and actions be different, yet they cause no ruine or disturbance to each other, but do in many cases agree with each other, without incroachment upon each others powers or actions.... [T]he divine Soul is not a part of Nature, but supernatural, as a supernatural Gift from God onely to Man, and to no other Creature: and although in this respect it may be called a part of Man, yet it is no natural or material part of Man; neither doth this supernatural Gift disturb Nature or natural Matter, or natural Matter this supernatural Gift.

XXXII

[T]hough I believe that there is a Devil, as the Word of God and the Church inform me, yet I am not of the opinion, that God should suffer him to have such a familiar conjunction, and make such contracts with Man, as to impower him to do mischief and hurt to others, or to foretell things to come, and the like; for I believe that all things Immaterial, as Spirits, Angels, Devils, and the divine Soul of Man, are no parts of Nature, but Supernatural, Nature knowing of no Creature that belongs to her, but what is material; and since incorporeal Creatures are no parts of Nature, they neither have natural actions, nor are they concerned as copartners or co-agents in the actions of Nature and natural

---

[49] See *The Immortality of the Soul*, I.iii.2, 17.
[50] See *The Immortality of the Soul*, II.i, 109–122.

Creatures; but as their substances, so their actions are supernatural, and beyond our conceivement. As for Fairies, I will not say, but there may be such Creatures in Nature, and have airy bodies, and be of a humane shape, and have humane actions, as I have described in my Book of Poems;[51] for there are many things in Nature, whereof Man hath no knowledg at all, and it would be a great folly for any one to deny what he doth not see, or to ascribe all the unusual effects in Nature to Immaterial Spirits; for Nature is so full of variety, that she can and doth present sometimes such figures to our exterior senses, as are not familiar to us, so as we need not to take our refuge to Immaterial Spirits: nay, even those that are so much for Incorporeal Spirits, must confess, that they cannot be seen in their own natures, as being Invisible, and therefore have need to take vehicles of some grosser bodies to manifest themselves to men: and if Spirits cannot appear without bodies, the neerest way is to ascribe such unusual effects or apparitions, as happen sometimes, rather to matter that is already corporeal, and not to go so far as to draw Immaterial Spirits to Natural actions, and to make those Spirits take vehicles fit for their purposes.

XXXIII

As for the Natural Soul, humane sense and reason may perceive, that it consists of Matter, as being Material; but as for the Divine Soul, being not material, no humane sense and reason is able naturally to conceive it; for there cannot possibly be so much as an Idea of a natural nothing, or an immaterial being, neither can sense and reason naturally conceive the Creation of an Immaterial substance. . . . Concerning *the Key of Divine Providence*, I believe God did never give or lend it to any man; for surely, God, who is infinitely Wise, would never intrust so frail and foolish a Creature as Man, with it, as to let him know his secret Counsels, Acts, and Decrees. But setting aside Pride and Presumption, Sense and Reason may easily perceive, that Man, though counted the best of Creatures, is not made with such infinite Excellence, as to pierce into the least secrets of God; Wherefore I am in a maze when I hear of such men, which pretend to know so much, as if they had plundered the Celestial Cabinet of the Omnipotent God; for certainly, had they done it, they could not pretend to more knowledg then they do. But I, *Madam*, confess my Ignorance, as having neither divine Inspirations, nor extraordinary Visions, nor any divine or humane learning, but what Nature has been pleased to bestow upon me.

[51] See also *Poems and Fancies*, "To all Writing Ladies," "Of small Creatures, such as we call Fairies," and "The Fairies in the Braine, may be the causes of many thoughts."

Section 3

I

I have discharged my duty thus far, that in obedience to your commands, I have given you my answers to the opinions of three of those famous and learned *Authors* you sent me, *viz. Hobbes, Descartes*, and *More*, and explained my own opinions by examining theirs; My onely task shall be now to proceed in the same manner with that famous Philosopher and Chymist, *Van Helmont*; But him I find more difficult to be understood then any of the forementioned, not onely by reason of the Art of Chymistry, which I confess my self not versed in, but especially, that he has such strange terms and unusual expressions as may puzle any body to apprehend the sense and meaning of them.

II

It is no wonder, your *Author* has so many odd and strange opinions in Philosophy (here specifically in his chapter the Fiction of Elementary Complexions and Mixtures), since they do not onely proceed from strange Visions, Apparitions, and Dreams, but are built upon so strange grounds and principles as *Ideas, Archeus, Gas, Blas, Ferment*, and the like,[52] the names of which sound so harsh and terrifying, as they might put any body easily into a fright, like so many Hobgoblins or Immaterial spirits; but the best is, they can do no great harm, except it be to trouble the brains of them, that love to maintain those opinions; for though they are thought to be powerful beings, yet being not corporeal substances, I cannot imagine wherein their power should consist; for Nothing can do nothing.

[N]ot that I think a Part can really subsist single and by it self, but it is onely considered so in the manner of our Conception, by reason of the difference and variousness of natural Creatures: for these being different from each other in their figures, and not all alike, so that we can make a distinction betwixt them; this difference and distinction causes us to conceive every part of a different figure by it self: but properly and according to the Truth of Nature, there is no part by it self subsisting; for all parts are to be considered, not onely as parts of the whole, but as parts of other parts, all parts being joyned in Infinite Nature, and tied by an inseparable tie one way or other, although we do not altogether perceive it.

---

[52] See, for example, Van Helmont, chapter XVII, "The Fiction of Elementary Complexions an Mixtures," 110.

V

Neither can I admit in reason that the Elements should be called, first, pure, and simple beings; we might as well call all other creatures, first, pure, and simple beings: for although the word Element sounds as much as Principle, yet they are in my reason no more Principles of Nature, then other Creatures are, there being but one Principle in Nature, out of which all things are composed, *viz.* the onely matter, which is a pure and simple corporeal substance; and what Man names impure dregs and filths, these are onely irregular and cross motions of that matter, in respect to the nature of such or such a figure; or such motions as are not agreeable and sympathetical to our Passions, Humors, Appetites, and the like.

XV

For in some subjects, Sympathy requires a certain distance; as for example, in Iron and the Loadstone; for if the Iron be too far off, the Loadstone cannot exercise its power, when as in other subjects, there is no need of any such certain distance, as betwixt the Needle and the North-pole, as also the Weapon-salve; for the Needle will turn it self towards the North, whether it be near or far off from the North-pole; and so, be the Weapon which inflicted the wound, never so far from the wounded Person, as they say, yet it will nevertheless do its effect: But yet there must withal be some conjunction with the blood; for as your *Author* mentions, the Weapon shall be in vain anointed with the Unguent, unless it be made bloody, and the same blood be first dried on the same Weapon. Likewise the sounding of two eights when one is touched, must be done within a certain distance: the same may be said of all Infectious and catching Diseases amongst Animals, where the Infection, be it the Infected Air, or a Poysonous Vapour, or any thing else, must needs touch the body, and enter either through the Mouth, or Nostrils, or Ears, or Pores of the body; for though the like Antipathies of Infectious Diseases, as of the Plague, may be in several places far distant and remote from each other at one and the same time, yet they cannot infect particular Creatures, or Animals, without coming near, or without the sense of Touch.[53]

---

[53] Here Cavendish is suggesting that two bodies do not interact unless they come into contact, or unless the bodies that are in between them come into contact. See also letters IV and XXIV, in this chapter.

XVI

Not that I say, Nature in her self is a Magicianess, but it may be called natural Magick or Witchcraft, meerly in respect to our Ignorance; for though Nature is old, yet she is not a Witch, but a grave, wise, methodical Matron, ordering her Infinite family, which are her several parts, with ease and facility, without needless troubles and difficulties; for these are onely made through the ignorance of her several parts or particular Creatures, not understanding their Mistress, Nature, and her actions and government, for which they cannot be blamed; for how should a part understand the Infinite body, when it doth not understand it self;[54] but Nature understands her parts better, then they do her.

XX

Man in this particular goes beyond others, as having not onely a natural, but also a revealed knowledg of the most Holy God; for he knows Gods Will, not onely by the light of Nature, but also by revelation, and so more then other Creatures do, whose knowledg of God is meerly Natural. But this Revealed Knowledg makes most men so presumptuous, that they will not be content with it, but search more and more into the hidden mysteries of the Incomprehensible Deity, and pretend to know God as perfectly, almost, as themselves; describing his Nature and Essence, his Attributes, his Counsels, his Actions, according to the revelation of God, (as they pretend) when as it is according to their own Fancies. So proud and presumptuous are many: But they shew thereby rather their weaknesses and follies, then any truth; and all their strict and narrow pryings into the secrets of God, are rather unprofitable, vain and impious, then that they should benefit either themselves, or their neighbour; for do all we can, God will not be perfectly known by any Creature: The truth is, it is a meer impossibility for a finite Creature, to have a perfect Idea of an Infinite Being, as God is; be his Reason never so acute or sharp, yet he cannot penetrate what is Impenetrable, nor comprehend what is Incomprehensible: Wherefore, in my opinion, the best way is humbly to adore what we cannot conceive, and believe as much as God has been pleased to reveal, without any further search; lest we diving too deep, be swallowed up in the bottomless depth of his Infiniteness: Which I wish every one may observe, for the benefit of his own self, and of others, to spend his time in more profitable Studies, then vainly to seek for what cannot be found.[55]

[54] But compare to *Grounds of Natural Philosophy*, chapter XII of the First Part.
[55] See also *Philosophical and Physical Opinions*, the poem at the end of chapter 210.

XXI

Your *Author* is so much for Spirits, that he doth not stick to affirm *That Bodies scarce make up a moity or half part of the world; but Spirits, even by themselves, have or possess their moity, and indeed the whole world.*[56] If he mean bodiless and incorporeal Spirits, I cannot conceive how Spirits can take up any place, for place belongs onely to body, or a corporeal substance, and millions of immaterial Spirits, nay, were their number infinite, cannot possess so much place as a small Pinspoint, for Incorporeal Spirits possess no place at all: which is the reason, that an Immaterial and a Material Infinite cannot hinder, oppose, or obstruct each other; and such an Infinite, Immaterial Spirit is God alone.

XXIII

These motions and actions of Nature, since they are so infinitely various, when men chance to observe some of their variety, they call them by some proper name, to make a distinguishment, especially those motions which belong to the figure of their own kind; and therefore when they will express the motions of dissolution of their own figure, they call them Death; when they will express the motions of Production of their figure, they call them Conception and Generation; when they will express the motions proper for the Consistence, Continuance and Perfection of their Figure, they call them Health;[57] but when they will express the motions contrary to these, they call them Sickness, Pain, Death, and the like: and hence comes also the difference between regular and irregular motions; for all those Motions that belong to the particular nature and consistence of any figure, they call regular, and those which are contrary to them, they call irregular. And thus you see, *Madam*, that there is no such thing in Nature, as Death, Sickness, Pain, Health, &c. but onely a variety and change of the corporeal motions, and that those words express nothing else but the variety of motions in Nature; for men are apt to make more distinctions then Nature doth: Nature knows of nothing else but of corporeal figurative Motions, when as men make a thousand distinctions of one thing, and confound and entangle themselves so, with Beings, Non-beings, and Neutral-beings, Corporeals and Incorporeals, Substances and Accidents, or manners and modes of Substances, new Creations, and Annihilations, and the like, as neither they themselves, nor any body else, is able to make any sense thereof.

---

[56] This is from Van Helmont, *A ternary of paradoxes, the magnetick cure of wounds, nativity of tartar in wine, image of God in man*, ed. and trans. Walter Charleton (London: Printed by James Flesher for William Lee, 1650), 75.

[57] See also *Philosophical and Physical Opinions*, chapter 59.

XXIX

Nevertheless, all these motions, whether regular or irregular, are natural; for regularity and irregularity hath but a respect to particulars, and to our conceptions, because those motions which move not after the ordinary, common or usual way or manner, we call *Irregular*. But the curiosity and variety in Nature is unconceiveable by any particular Creature.

XXX

Natures actions are not onely curious, but very various; and not onely various, but very obscure; in so much, as the most ingenious Artists cannot trace her ways, or imitate her actions; for Art being but a Creature, can do or know no more then a Creature; and although she is an ingenious Creature, which can and hath found out some things profitable and useful for the life of others, yet she is but a handmaid to Nature, and not her Mistress.[58]

XXXIV

[S]ome diseases have such sudden alterations, by the sudden changes of motions, that a wise Physician will not, nor cannot venture to apply so many several medicines so suddenly as the alteration requires; and shall therefore Physicians be condemned? And not onely condemned for what cannot be helped by reason of the variety of irregular motions,[59] but what cannot be helped in Nature? For some diseases are so deadly, as no art can cure them, when as otherwise Physicians with good and proper medicines, have, and do as yet rescue more people from death, then the Laws do from ruine. Nay, I have known many that have been great enemies to Physick, die in the flower of their age, when as others which used themselves to Physick, have lived a very long time.

---

[58] See also *Philosophical and Physical Opinions*, chapter 141.

[59] Cavendish refers to the irregularities of nature in other passages as well, for example in *Grounds of Natural Philosophy*, chapter XII of the Sixth Part, and chapter I of the Eighth Part; and *Appendix to Grounds of Natural Philosophy*, chapter IV and V of the First Part. If Cavendish holds that there are actual irregularities that occur in nature—and that all events do not occur in a perfectly regular and orderly manner—that would add support to the view that she conceives of freedom in libertarian terms. See also note 11 for *Philosophical and Physical Opinions*, but also *Philosophical Letters*, letters IV and XXXIII of section four.

XLII

[T]hose cures which are performed exteriously, as to heal inward affects by an outward bare co-touching, are all made by natural motions in natural substances, and not by *Non*-beings, substanceless Ideas, or spiritual Rays; for those that will cure diseases by Non-beings, will effect little or nothing; for a disease is corporeal or material, and so must the remedies be, there being no cure made but by a conflict of the remedy with the disease; and certainly, if a *non*-being fight against a being, or a corporeal disease, I doubt it will do no great effect; for the being will be too strong for the non-being: Wherefore my constant opinion is, that all cures whatsoever, are perfected by the power of corporeal motions, working upon the affected parts either interiously or exteriously, either by applying external remedies to external wounds, or by curing internal distempers, either by medicines taken internally, or by bare external co-touchings.

XLIII

I pray, mistake me not, when I say, that the animal motions are not subject to our exterior senses; for I do not mean all exterior animal motions, nor all interior animal motions; for though you do see no interior motion in an animal body, yet you may feel some, as the motion of the Heart, the motion of the Pulse, the motion of the Lungs, and the like; but the most part of the interior animal motions are not subject to our exterior senses; nay, no man, he may be as observing as he will, can possibly know by his exterior senses all the several and various interior motions in his own body, nor all the exterior motions of his exterior parts: and thus it remains still, that neither the subtillest motions and parts of matter, nor the obscure passages in several Creatures, can be known but by several parts; for what one part is ignorant of, another part is knowing, and what one part is knowing, another part is ignorant thereof; so that unless all the Parts of Infinite Matter were joyned into one Creature, there can never be in one particular Creature a perfect knowledg of all things in Nature. Wherefore I shall never aspire to any such knowledg, but be content with that little particular knowledg, Nature has been pleased to give me.

Section 4

[In this last section, Cavendish elaborates on some of the themes from earlier, and she addresses the views of some new figures as well.]

I

[Y]ou are pleased to desire my opinion of a very difficult and intricate argument in Natural Philosophy, to wit, of Generation, or Natural Production. I must beg leave to tell you, first, that some (though foolishly) believe, it is not fit for Women to argue upon so subtil a Mystery.

II

[T]here is but one Matter, which is Infinite and Eternel, and this Matter has self-motion in it, both Matter, and Motion must of necessity transmigrate, or be transferred together without any separation, as being but one thing, to wit, Corporeal Motion. 'Tis true, one part of animate or self-moving Matter, may without Translation move, or rather occasion other parts to move; but one Creature cannot naturally produce another without the transferring of its corporeal motions. . . . But you may say, If the producer transfers its own Matter, or rather its own corporeal motions into the produced, many productions will soon dissolve the producer, and he will become a sacrifice to his off-spring. I answer; That doth not follow: for as one or more Creatures contribute to one or more other Creatures; so other Creatures do contribute to them, although not after one and the same manner or way, but after divers manners or ways; but all manners and ways must be by translation to repair and assist; for no Creature can subsist alone and of it self, but all Creatures traffick and commerce from and to each other, and must of necessity do so, since they are all parts of the same Matter: Neither can Motion subsist without Matter, nor quit Matter, nor act without Matter, no more, then an Artificer can work without materials, and without selfmotion Matter would be dead and useless; Wherefore Matter and Motion must upon necessity not onely be inseparable, but be one body, to wit, corporeal motion; which motion by dividing and composing its several parts, and acting variously, is the cause of all Production, Generation, Metamorphosing, or any other thing that is done in Nature.

IV

And as for Irregularities, properly there is none in Nature, for Nature is Regular; but that, which Man (who is but a small part of Nature, and therefore but partly knowing) names Irregularities, or Imperfections, is onely a change and alteration of motions; for a part can know the variety of motions in Nature no more, then Finite can know Infinite, or the bare exterior shape and figure of a mans body can know the whole body, or the head can know the mind.

VI

[T]he motion by which (for example) the bowl is moved, is the bowls own motion, and not the hands that threw it; for the hand cannot transfer its own motion, which hath a material being, out of it self into the bowl, or any other thing it handles, touches, or moves; or else if it did, the hand would in a short time become weak and useless, by losing so much substance, unless new motions were as fast created, as expended. You'l say, perhaps, that the hand and the bowl may exchange motions, as that the bowls own motion doth enter into the hand, and supply that motion which went out of the hand into the bowl, by a close joyning or touch, for in all things moving and moved, must be a joyning of the mover to the moved, either immediate, or by the means of another body. I answer: That this is more probable, then that the hand should give out, or impart motion to the bowl, and receive none from the bowl; but by reason motion cannot be transferred without matter, as being both inseparably united, and but one thing; I cannot think it probable, that any of the animate or self-moving matter in the hand, quits the hand, and enters into the bowl; nor that the animate matter, which is in the bowl, leaves the bowl, and enters into the hand, because that self-moving substance is not readily prepared for so sudden a Translation or Transmigration.[60] . . . It is very true, that all Creatures have more power and strength by a joyned assistance, then if every part were single, and subsisted of it self. But as some parts do assist each other, so on the other side, some parts do resist each other.

X

[Y]our *Author* [Gideon Harvey] doth speak so presumptuously of Gods Actions, Designs, Decrees, Laws, Attributes, Power, and secret Counsels, and describes the manner, how God created all things, and the mixture of the Elements to an hair, as if he had been Gods Counsellor and Assistant in the work of Creation; which whether it be not more impiety, then to say, Matter is Infinite, I'le let others judg. Neither do I think this expression to be against the holy Scripture; for though I speak as a natural Philosopher, and am unwilling to cite the Scripture, which onely treats of things belonging to Faith and, and not to Reason; yet I think there is not any passage which plainly denies Matter to be Infinite, and Eternal, unless it be drawn by force to that sense: *Solomon* says, *That there is not any thing new:* and in another place it is said, *That God is all fulfilling;* that is, The Will of God is the fulfilling of the actions of Nature: also the Scripture says, *That Gods ways are unsearchable, and past finding out.* Wherefore,

---

[60] See also note 4 for *Philosophical and Physical Opinions.*

it is easier to treat of Nature, then the God of Nature; neither should God be treated of by vain Philosophers, but by holy Divines, which are to deliver and interpret the Word of God without sophistry, and to inform us as much of Gods Works, as he hath been pleased to declare and make known.

XXVII

[Y]ou desire to know, *Whether any truth may be had in Natural Philosophy*: for since all this study is grounded upon probability, and he that thinks he has the most probable reasons for his opinion, may be as far off from truth, as he who is thought to have the least; nay, what seems most probable today, may seem least probable tomorrow, especially if an ingenious opposer, bring rational arguments against it: Therefore you think it is but vain for any one to trouble his brain with searching and enquiring after such things wherein neither truth nor certainty can be had. To which, I answer: That the undoubted truth in Natural Philosophy, is, in my opinion, like the Philosopher's Stone in Chymistry, which has been sought for by many learned and ingenious Persons, and will be sought as long as the Art of Chymistry doth last; but although they cannot find the Philosophers Stone, yet by the help of this Art they have found out many rare things both for use and knowledg.[61] The like in Natural Philosophy, although Natural Philosophers cannot find out the absolute truth of Nature, or Natures ground-works, or the hidden causes of natural effects; neverthelss they have found out many necessary and profitable Arts and Sciences, to benefit the life of man; for without Natural Philosophy we should have lived in dark ignorance, not knowing the motions of the Heavens, the cause of the Eclipses, the influences of the Stars, the use of Numbers, Measures, and Weights, the vertues and effects of Vegetables and Minerals, the Art of Architecture, Navigation, and the like: Indeed all Arts and Sciences do ascribe their original to the study of Natural Philosophy; and those men are both unwise and ungrateful, that will refuse rich gifts because they cannot be masters of all Wealth; and they are fools, that will not take remedies when they are sick, because Medicines can onely recover them from death for a time, but not make them live for ever. But to conclude, Probability is next to truth, and the search of a hidden cause finds out visible effects; and this truth do natural Philosophers find, that there are more fools, then wise men, which fools will never attain to the honour of being Natural Philosophers.

---

[61] See also note 16 for *Philosophical and Physical Opinions*.

XXX

[T]o make it more plain and perspicuous, humane sense and reason may perceive, that wood, stone, or metal, acts as wisely as an animal: As for example; Rhubarb, or the like drugs, will act very wisely in Purging; and Antimony, or the like, will act very wisely in Vomiting; and Opium will act very wisely in Sleeping; also Quicksilver or Mercury will act very wisely, as those that have the French disease can best witness: likewise the Loadstone acts very wisely; as Mariners or Navigators will tell you: Also Wine made of Fruit, and Ale of Malt, and distilled Aqua-vitae will act very subtilly; ask the Drunkards, and they can inform you; Thus Infinite examples may be given, and yet man says, all Vegetables and Minerals are insensible and irrational, as also the Planets and Elements; when as yet the Planets move very orderly and wisely, and the Elements are more active, nay, more subtil and searching then any of the animal Creatures.[62]

XXXIII

[I]t is impossible but that all her particular creatures or parts must be knowing as well as self-moving, there being not one part or particle of Nature that has not its share of animate or self-moving matter, and consequently of knowledge and self-love, each according to its own kind and nature; but by reason all the parts are of one matter, and belong to one body, each is unalterable so far, that although it can change its figure, yet it cannot change or alter from being matter, or a part of Infinite Nature; and this is the cause there cannot be a confusion amongst those parts of Nature, but there must be a constant union and harmony betwixt them; for cross and opposite actions make no confusion, but onely a variety; and such actions which are different, cross and opposite, not moving always after their usual and accustomed way, I name Irregular, for want of a better expression; but properly there is no such thing as Irregularity in Nature, nor no weariness, rest, sleep, sickness, death or destruction, no more then there is place, space, time, modes, accidents, and the like, any thing besides body or matter.

[62] This passage calls to mind the argumentation in Hume, *Dialogues Concerning Natural Religion*, 75, 81. Hume and Cavendish agree on the sophistication of the behavior of non-human creatures, but Cavendish would say that these are guided by intelligence, whereas Hume would not. Part of the disagreement here is because Hume does not identify an entity as intelligent or minded unless it is aware of its behavior.

CHAPTER 4

Observations Upon Experimental Philosophy

To the Reader

But as for Learning, that I am not versed in it, no body, I hope, will blame me for it, since it is sufficiently known, that our Sex is not bread up to it, as being not suffer'd to be instructed in Schools and Universities; I will not say, but many of our Sex may have as much wit, and be capable of Learning as well as Men; but since they want Instructions, it is not possible they should attain to it; for Learning is Artificial, but Wit is Natural.[1]

I. Of Humane Sense and Perception

And thus Nature may be called both *Individual*, as not having single parts subsisting without her, but all united in one body; and *Divideable*, by reason she is partable in her own several corporeal figurative motions, and not otherwise; for there is no *Vacuum* in Nature, neither can her parts start or remove from the Infinite body of Nature, so as to separate themselves from it, for there's no place to flee to, but body and place are all one thing, so that the parts of Nature can onely joyn and disjoyn to and from parts, but not to and from the body of Nature.[2] And since Nature is but one body, it is intirely wise and knowing, ordering her self-moving parts with all facility and ease, without any disturbance, living in pleasure and delight, with infinite varieties and curiosities, such as no single Part or Creature of hers can ever attain to.

---

[1] See also note 1 for *Worlds Olio*.

[2] See also the similar language in Descartes, "Synopsis of the following six Meditations," CSM 2:10, and Spinoza, *Ethics*, Part I, Proposition 14, p. 224

III. *Of* Micrography, *and of* Magnifying *and* Multiplying Glasses

Although I am not able to give a solid judgment of the Art of *Micrography*, and the several dioptrical instruments belonging thereto, by reason I have neither studied nor practised that Art; yet of this I am confident, that this same Art, with all its Instruments, is not able to discover the interior natural motions of any part or creature of Nature; nay, the question is, whether it can represent yet the exterior shapes and motions so exactly, as naturally they are; for Art doth more easily alter then inform: As for example; Art makes Cylinders, Concave and Convex-glasses, and the like, which represent the figure of an Object in no part exactly and truly, but very deformed and misshaped: also a Glass that is flaw'd, crack'd, or broke, or cut into the figure of Lozenges, Triangles, Squares, or the like, will present numerous pictures of one Object. Besides, there are so many alterations made by several lights, their shadows, refractions, reflexions, as also several lines, points, mediums, interposing and intermixing parts, forms and positions, as the truth of an Object will hardly be known; for the perception of sight, and so of the rest of the Senses, goes no further then the exterior Parts of the Object presented; and though the Perception may be true, when the object is truly presented, yet when the presentation is false, the information must be false also. And it is to be observed, that Art, for the most part, makes Hermaphroditical, that is, mixt Figures, partly Artificial, and partly Natural: for Art may make some Metal, as Pewter, which is between Tin and Lead, as also Brass, and numerous other things of mixt natures; In the like manner may Artificial Glasses present Objects, partly Natural, and partly Artificial; nay, put the case they can present the natural figure of an Object, yet that natural figure may be presented in as monstrous a shape, as it may appear mis-shapen rather then natural: For example; a Lowse by the help of a Magnifying-glass, appears like a Lobster, where the Microscope enlarging and magnifying each part of it, makes them bigger and rounder then naturally they are. The truth is, the more the Figure by Art is magnified, the more it appears mis-shapen from the Natural, in so much as each joynt will appear as a diseased, swell'd and tumid Body, ready and ripe for Incision. But, mistake me not; I do not say, that no Glass presents the true picture of an Object: but onely that Magnifying, Multiplying, and the like Optick Glasses, may, and do oftentimes present falsly the Picture of an Exterior Object; I say, the Picture, because it is not the real Body of the Object which the Glass presents, but the Glass onely Figures or Patterns out the picture presented in and by the Glass, and there mistakes may easily be committed in taking Copies from Copies.[3]

---

[3] See also *Philosophical Letters*, letter XXIV of section one. One of the reasons that Cavendish is skeptical of microscopes and other human-made artifacts is that she holds that the (perceptive)

Nay, Artists do confess themselves, that Flies, and the like, will appear of several Figures or shapes, according to the several Reflections, Refractions, Mediums and Positions of several Lights; which if so, how can they tell or judg which is the truest Light, Position, or Medium, that doth present the Object naturally as it is? . . . [I]f the Picture of a young Beautiful Lady should be drawn according to the representation of the Microscope, or according to the various refraction and reflection of light through such like Glasses; it would be so far from being like her, as it would not be like a Humane face, but rather a Monster, then a picture of Nature. Wherefore those that invented Microscopes, and such like dioptrical Glasses, at first, did, in my opinion, the World more injury then benefit; for this Art has intoxicated so many Mens brains, and wholly imployed their thoughts and bodily actions about Phaenomena, or the Exterior Figures of Objects, as all better Arts and Studies are laid aside; nay, those that are not as earnest and active in such imployments as they, are, by many of them, accounted unprofitable Subjects to the Commonwealth of Learning. . . . But, as Boys that play with watry Bubbles, or fling Dust into each others Eyes, or make a Hobby-horse of Snow, are worthy of reproof rather then praise, for wasting their time with useless sports; so those that addict themselves to unprofitable Arts, spend more time then they reap benefit thereby. Nay, could they benefit men either in Husbandry, Architecture, or the like necessary and profitable imployments; yet before the Vulgar sort would learn to understand them, the World would want Bread to eat, and Houses to dwell in, as also Cloths to keep them from the inconveniences of the inconstant weather. But truly, although Spinsters were most experienced in their Art, yet they will never be able to spin Silk, Thred, or Wool, &c. from loose Atoms; neither will Weavers weave a Web of Light from the Sun's Rays; nor an Architect build an House of the bubbles of Water and Air, (unless they be Poetical Spinsters, Weavers and Architects), and if a Painter should draw a Lowse as big as a Crab, and of that shape as the Microscope presents, can any body imagine that a Beggar would believe it to be true? But if he did, what advantage would it be to the Beggar? For it doth neither instruct him how to avoid breeding them, or how to catch them, or to hinder them from biting. . . . Wherefore the best Optick is a perfect natural Eye, and a regular sensitive Perception;[4] and the best

bodies that compose a natural production (like the human eye) have a much longer history of coordination and collaboration, whereas the bodies that compose an artefact are, relatively speaking, just thrown together. She then points to instances of actual distortion (a Lowse, a young beautiful lady) to make the case more concretely. See also *Observations Upon Experimental Philosophy*, sections XXV, XXXIV, and XXXVII, q.11–12.

[4] Cavendish does not anywhere in her corpus take seriously the skeptical worry that our sensory perceptions of the external world might not be veridical; she seems to just take for granted that what we identify as errors of perception are perceptions that depart from our normal waking perceptions, and she appears to regard the latter as our best possible point of departure. If we have to choose

Judg, is Reason, and the best Study is Rational Contemplation joyned with the Observations of Regular Sense, but not deluding Arts; for Art is not onely gross in comparison to Nature, but, for the most part, deformed and defective, and at best produces mixt or hermaphroditical figures, that is, a third figure between Nature and Art: which proves, that natural Reason is above artificial Sense, as I may call it: wherefore those Arts are the best and surest Informers, that alter Nature least, and they the greatest deluders that alter Nature most.[5]

IX. Of the Eyes of Flies

I cannot wonder enough at the strange Discovery made by the help of the Microscope concerning the great number of Eyes observed in Flies; as that, for example, In a gray Drone-flie should be found clusters which contain about 14000 eyes. . . . But a greater wonder it is to me, that Man with the twinkling of one Eye, can observe so many in so small a Creature, if it be not a deceit of the Optick Instrument: for as I have mentioned above, Art produces most commonly Hermaphroditical Figures, and it may be, perhaps, that those little Pearls or Globes, which were taken for Eyes in the mentioned Flie, are onely transparent Knobs, or glossie shining Spherical parts of its Body, making Refractions of the rayes of Light, and reflecting the Pictures of Exterior Objects; there being many Creatures, that have such shining Protuberances and Globular parts, and those full of quick Motion, which yet are not Eyes. Truly, my Reason can hardly be perswaded to believe, that this Artificial Informer (I mean the Microscope) should be so true as it is generally thought; for, in my opinion it more deludes, then informs. . . . Nay, if Flies should have so many numerous Eyes, why can they not see the approach of a Spider until it be just at them; also, how comes it that sometimes (as for example, in cold weather) they seem blind, so as one may take or kill them, and they cannot so much as perceive their enemie's approach? Surely if they had 14000 Eyes, all this number would seem useless to them; since other Creatures which have but two, can make more advantage of those two Eyes, then they of their vast number. But perchance some will say, that Flies having so many Eyes, are more apt to be blind then others that have but few, by reason the number is the cause that each particular is the weaker. To

between artificial instruments, on the one hand, and sense organs that are productions of nature, she will opt for the latter every time. (See also *Observations Upon Experimental Philosophy*, section XIV, and note 19 for *Worlds Olio*.) But when it comes to a proof that our sense organs provide us with veridical representations, Cavendish does not provide one. She admits that dreams can sometimes seem just as realistic as waking perceptions (for example in *Philosophical and Physical Opinions*, chapters 153–154), and leaves it at that.

[5] See also *Worlds Olio*, "The Power of Natural Works."

which I answer, That if two Eyes be stronger then a Thousand, then Nature is to be blamed that she gives such numbers of Eyes to so little a Creature. But Nature is wiser then we or any Creature is able to conceive; and surely she works not to no purpose, or in vain; but there appears as much Wisdom in the Fabrick and Structure of her works, as there is variety in them.

XIV. Of Natural Productions

I cannot wonder with those, who admire that a Creature which inhabits the air, doth yet produce a Creature, that for some time lives in the water as a Fish, and afterward becomes an inhabitant of the air; for this is but a Production of one animal from another: but, what is more, I observe that there are productions of and from Creatures of quite different kinds; as for example, that Vegetables can and do breed Animals, and Animals, Minerals and Vegetables, and so forth: Neither do I so much wonder at this, because I observe that all Creatures of Nature are produced but out of one matter, which is common to all, and that there are continual and perpetual Generations and Productions in Nature, as well as there are perpetual Dissolutions. But yet I cannot believe, that some sorts of Creatures should be produced on a sudden by the way of transmigration or translation of parts, which is the most usual way of Natural Productions; for both Natural and Artificial Productions are performed by Degrees, which requires time, and is not done in an instant.

XV. Of the Seeds of Vegetables

I suppose some conceive Nature to be like a Granary or Store-house of Pinebarley, or the like; which if so, I would fain know in what grounds those Seeds should be sown to produce and increase: for no Seeds can produce of themselves if they be not assisted by some other matter; which proves, that Seeds are not the prime or principal Creatures in Nature, by reason they depend upon some other matter which helps them in their Productions: for if Seeds of Vegetables did lie never so long in a store-house, or any other place, they would never produce, until they were put into some proper and convenient ground: It is also an argument, that no Creature or part of Nature can subsist singly and divided from all the rest, but that all parts must live together;[6] and since no part can subsist and live

---

[6] See also *Philosophical Letters*, letter II of section one and letter II of section four; *Grounds of Natural Philosophy*, chapter XVII of the First Part; and *Observations Upon Experimental Philosophy*, section XXXI.

without the other, no part can also be called prime or principal. . . . But I rather cease to wonder at those strange and Irregular opinions of Mankind, since even they themselves do justifie and prove the variety of Nature;[7] for what we call Irregularities in Nature, are really nothing but a variety of Natures motions; and therefore if all Men's Conceits, Fancies and Opinions were Rational, there would not be so much Variety as there is.

XVIII. Of the blackness of a Charcoal, and of Light

If Man knew Natures Geometry, he might perhaps do something, but his artificial figures will never find out the architecture of Nature, which is beyond his perception or capacity.

XIX. Of the Pores of a Charcoal, and of Emptiness

But yet although Pores are passages for other bodies to issue or enter, nevertheless they are not empty, there being no such thing as an emptiness in Nature; for surely God, the Fulness and Perfection of all things, would not suffer any *Vacuum* in Nature, which is a Pure Nothing; *Vacuum* implies a want and imperfection of something, but all that God made by his All-powerful Command, was good and perfect; Wherefore, although Charcoals and other bodies have Pores, yet they are fill'd with some subtile Matter not subject to our sensitive perception, and are not empty, but onely call'd so, by reason they are not fill'd up with some solid and gross substance perceptible by our senses. But some may say, If there be no emptiness in Nature, but all fulness of body, or bodily parts, then the Spiritual or Divine Soul in Man, which inhabits his body, would not have room to reside in it. I answer, The Spiritual or Divine Soul in Man is not Natural, but Supernatural, and has also a Supernatural way of residing in man's body; for Place belongs onely to bodies, and a Spirit being bodiless, has no need of a bodily place. But then they will say, That I make Spirit and *Vacuum* all one thing, by reason I describe a Spirit to be a Natural Nothing, and the same I say of *Vacuum*; and hence it will follow, that particular Spirits are particular Emptinesses, and an Infinite Spirit an

[7] This is a very interesting aside from Cavendish, given that her *Orations of Divers Sorts* and *Sociable Letters* contain speeches and other offerings on a wide range of topics from a wide range of perspectives. It can be tricky to make sense of how the two texts fit into her larger corpus, given that the passages on their own never indicate which of the views are Cavendish's own. One possibility is that she is using the two texts to call attention to another of the many arenas in nature where variety and diversity are found—human opinion—and appreciating it, as she appreciates the variety and diversity in nature more generally. See also *Observations Upon Experimental Philosophy*, section XXVIII.

Infinite *Vacuum*. My answer is, That although a Spirit is a Natural Nothing, yet it is a Supernatural Something; but a *Vacuum* is a Pure Nothing, both Naturally and Supernaturally; and God forbid I should be so irreligious, as to compare Spirits, and consequently God, who is an Infinite Spirit, to a *Vacuum*; for God is All-fulfilling, and an Infinite Fulness and Perfection, though not a Corporeal or Material, yet a Supernatural, Spiritual, and Incomprehensible Fulness; when as *Vacuum*, although it is a corporeal Word, yet in effect or Reality is nothing, and expresses a want or imperfection, which cannot be said of any Supernatural Creature, much less of God.[8]

XXI. Whether an Idea have a Colour, and of the Idea of a Spirit

I have declared in my former Discourse, that there is no Colour without Body, nor a Body without Colour, for we cannot think of a Body without we think of Colour too. To which some may object, That if Colour be as proper to a Body as Matter, and if the Mind be Corporeal, then the Mind is also Coloured. I answer, The Mind, in my opinion, has as much Colour as other parts of Nature. But then perhaps they will ask me, what Colour the Mind is of? My answer is, That the Mind, which is the rational part of Nature, is no more subject to one Colour, then the Infinite parts of Nature are subject to one corporeal figurative motion; for you can no more confine the corporeal Mind to a particular complexion, then you can confine Infinite matter to one particular Colour, or all Colours to one particular Figure. Again, they may ask, Whether an Idea have a Colour? And if so, whether the Idea of God be coloured? To which I answer, If the Ideas be of corporeal finite Figures, they have Colours according to the nature, or property, or Figure of the Original; but as for the Idea of God, it is impossible to have a corporeal Idea of an infinite incorporeal Being; for though the finite parts of Nature may have a perception or knowledg of the existence of God, yet they cannot possibly pattern or figure him; he being a Supernatural, Immaterial, and Infinite Being: But put the case (although it is very improbable, nay, against sense and reason) there were natural immaterial Ideas, if those Ideas were finite, and not infinite, yet they could not possibly express an infinite,[9] which is without limitation, by a finite figure which hath a Circumference. Some may say, An Immaterial Idea hath no Circumference.

---

[8] See also note 20 for *Worlds Olio*.

[9] Here Cavendish might have in mind Descartes's Third Meditation contention (CSM 2:28–31) that finite minds have a finite (and immaterial) idea of God that is still able to represent God's infinitude. See also *Philosophical Letters*, letter XX of section one, and letter II of section two.

But then I answer, It is not a finite Idea, and it is impossible for an Idea to be Infinite: for I take an Idea to be the picture of some Object, and there can be no picture without a perfect form; neither can I conceive how an Immaterial can have a form, not having a body; wherefore it is more impossible for Nature to make a picture of the Infinite God, then for Man, which is but a part of Nature, to make a picture of Infinite Nature; for Nature being Material, has also Figure and Matter, they being all one, so that none can be without the other, no more then Nature can be divided from her self. Thus it is impossible for Man to make a Figure, or Picture of that which is not a part of Nature; for Pictures are as much parts of Nature, as any other parts; nay, were they Monstrous, as we call them: for Nature being material, is also figurative, and being a Self-moving matter or substance, is dividable, and composable: and as she hath infinite corporeal, figurative motions, and infinite parts; so she hath infinite figures, of which some are Pictures, others Originals: And if any one particular Creature could picture out those infinite figures, he would picture out Nature; but Nature being Infinite, cannot be pictured or patterned by any finite and particular Creature, although she is material; nevertheless she may be patterned in parts: And as for God, He being Individable, and Immaterial, can neither be patterned in Part, nor in Whole, by any part of Nature which is material, nay, not by infinite Nature her self: Wherefore the notions of God can be no otherwise but of His Existence, to wit, that we know there is Something above Nature, who is the Author, and God of Nature; for though Nature hath an infinite natural knowledg of the Infinite God; yet being dividable as well as composable, her parts cannot have such an infinite knowledg or perception; and being composable as much as dividable, no part can be so ignorant of God, as not to know there is a God. Thus Nature hath both an infinite and finite perception; infinite in the whole (as I may say for better expressions sake), and finite in parts. But mistake me not, I do not mean, that either the infinite perception of Nature, or the finite perceptions of natural parts and Creatures, are any otherwise of that supernatural and divine Being then Natural; but yet they are the most purest parts, being of the rational part of Nature, moving in a most elevating and subtile manner, as making no exact figure or form, because God hath neither form nor figure; but that subtile matter, or corporeal perceptive motion patterns out onely an over-ruling power: which power all the parts of Nature are sensible of, and yet know not what it is; like as the perception of Sight seeeth the ebbing and flowing of the Sea, or the motion of the Sun, yet knows not their cause; and the perception of Hearing hears Thunder, yet knows not how it is made; and if there be such ignorance of the corporeal parts of Nature, what of God? For whatsoever is corporeal, hath a being; but what being and Immaterial hath, no Corporeal can perceive: Wherefore no part of Nature (her parts Being corporeal) can perceive an Immaterial; because it is impossible to have a perception of what which is not perceptible, as not being an Object fit or proper for corporeal perception.[10]

XXV. Of the Motions of Heat and Cold

But I observe, Experimental Philosophers do first cry up several of their Artificial Instruments, then make doubts of them, and at last disprove them, so that there is no trust nor truth in them, to be relied on: For, it is not an age, since [the time when] Weather-glasses were held the onely divulgers of Heat and Cold, or change of Weather, and now some do doubt they are not such infallible Informers of those Truths. By which it is evident, that Experimental Philosophy has but a brittle, inconstant and uncertain Ground. And these Artificial Instruments, as Microscopes, Telescopes, and the like, which are now so highly applauded, who knows but they may within a short time have the same fate; and upon a better and more rational enquiry, be found Deluders rather then true Informers. The truth is, there's not any thing that has, and doth still delude most mens understandings more, then that they do not consider enough the variety of Nature's actions, and do not employ their Reason so much in the search of Nature's actions, as they do their Senses; preferring Art and Experiments, before Reason; which makes them stick so close to some particular Opinions, and particular sorts of Motions or Parts; as if there were no more Motions, Parts, or Creatures in Nature, than what they see and find out by their Artificial Experiments.

[T]hat particular Sensitive knowledg in man, which is built meerly upon artificial Experiments, will never make him a good Philosopher, but regular Sense and Reason must do it; that is, a regular, sensitive, and rational inquisition, into the various actions of Nature; For, put the case a Microscope be true, concerning the magnifying of an exterior Object; but yet the Magnitude of the Object cannot give a true information of its interior parts, and their Motions; or else great and large Bodies would be interiorly known, even without Microscopes. The truth is, our exterior Senses can go no further than the exterior figures of Creatures, and their exterior actions: but our Reason may pierce deeper, and consider their inherent natures, and interior actions.[11] And although it do sometimes erre, (for there can be no perfect or universal knowledg in a finite Part concerning the Infinite actions of Nature) yet it may also probably guess at them,

---

[10] See also *Philosophical Letters*, letter II of section one.

[11] Cavendish appears to hold that the (rational) matter that composes our ideas is able to copy information about the external world that our sensory organs cannot. (See also *Observations Upon Experimental Philosophy*, section XXXVII, Q12.) Perhaps she has in mind ideas that we recognize are not copies of sensory perceptions. Cavendish is fallibilistic about such ideas, however, calling them here a matter of probable guesswork that "may chance to hit the Truth."

and may chance to hit the Truth. Thus Sense and Reason shall be the ground of my Philosophy, and no particular Natural Effects, nor Artificial Instruments; and if any one can shew me a better and surer Ground or Principle than this, I shall most willingly and joyfully embrace it.

XXVI. Of the Measures, Degrees, and different sorts of Heat and Cold

[A]s much as a Natural man differs from an Artificial Statue or Picture of a Man, so much differs a Natural Effect from an Artificial, which can neither be so good, nor so lasting as a Natural one. If *Charles's Wain*,[12] the Axes of the Earth, and the motions of the Planets, were like the pole, or axes, or wheels of a Coach, they would soon be out of order. Indeed, Artificial things are pretty toys to imploy idle time: Nay, some are very useful for our conveniency; but yet they are but Nature's Bastards or Changelings, if I may so call them; And though Nature takes so much delight in variety, that she is pleased with them, yet they are not to be compared to her wise and fundamental actions: for, Nature being a wise and provident Lady, governs her parts very wisely, methodically and orderly: also she is very industrious, and hates to be idle, which makes her employ her time as a good Huswife doth, in Brewing, Baking, Churning, Spinning, Sowing, &c. as also in Preserving, for those that love Sweet-meats; and in Distilling, for those that take delight in Cordials; for she has numerous employments; and being in-finitely self-moving, never wants work; but her Artificial works, are her works of delight, pleasure and pastime: Wherefore those that employ their time in Artificial Experiments, consider onely Natures sporting or playing-actions; but those that view her wise Government, in ordering all her parts, and consider her changes, alterations and tempers in particulars, and their causes, spend their time more usefully and profitably: and truly, To what purpose should a man beat his brains, and weary his body with labours about that wherein he shall lose more Time, than gain Knowledg? But if any one would take delight in such things, my opinion is, That our Female-sex would be the fittest for it, for they most com-monly take pleasure in making of Sweet-meats, Possets, several sorts of Pyes, Puddings, and the like; not so much for their own eating, as to employ their idle time;[13] and it may be, they would prove good Experimental Philosophers,

---

[12] This is a cluster of stars that in medieval times was associated with the ruler Charlemagne.

[13] The issue is arising again about whether or not Cavendish is a kind of proto-feminist, or whether she supposes that there are respects in which women are inherently inferior to men. (See also note 1 for *Worlds Olio*.) In this particular passage she is clearly suggesting that seventeenth-century women tend to engage in trivial pursuits, but it is not clear from the passage itself if she is supposing that it is part of the natural order of things that women tend to engage in such pursuits, or if this is a more

and inform the world how to make Artificial Snow, by their Creams, or Possets beaten into froth: and Ice, by their clear, candied or crusted Quiddities, or Conserves of fruits: and Frost, by their candied herbs and flowers: and Hail, by their small Comfits made of water and sugar, with whites of Eggs: And many other the like figures, which resemble Beasts, Birds, Vegetables, Minerals, &c. But the men should study the Causes of those Experiments: and by this Society, the Commonwealth would find a great benefit. For the Woman was given to Man, not onely to delight, but to help and assist him; and I am confident, Women would labour as much with Fire and Furnace, as Men; for they'l make good Cordials and Spirits; but whether they would find out the Philosophers-stone, I doubt; for our sex is more apt to wast[e], than to make Gold: However, I would have them try, especially those that have Means to spend; for, who knows but Women might be more happy in finding it out, than Men; and then would Men have reason to employ their time in more Profitable studies, then in useless Experiments.

XXVII. Of Congealation and Freezing

Nature is neither absolutely necessitated, nor has an absolute free-will: for, she is so much necessitated, that she depends upon the All-powerful God, and cannot work beyond her self, or beyond her own nature; and yet hath so much liberty, that in her particulars she works as she pleaseth, and as God has given her power; but she being wise, acts according to her infinite natural Wisdom, which is the cause of her orderly Government in all particular productions, changes and dissolutions; so that all Creatures in their particular kinds, do move and work as Nature pleases, orders and directs: And therefore, as it is impossible for Nature to go beyond her self; so it is likewise impossible, that any particular body should extend beyond it self, or its natural figure. . . .

[N]ot that living animals have more natural life then those we call dead; for animals, when dissolved from their animal figure, although they have not animal life, yet they have life according to the nature of the figure into which they did change; but, because of their different perceptions; for a dead or dissolved animal, as it is of another kind of figure then a living animal, so it has also another kind of perception.[14] . . .

---

contingent matter having to do with the beliefs and expectations that men and women have about proper gender roles.

[14] See also *Philosophical and Physical Opinions*, chapter 23, and *Philosophical Letters*, letter X of section one.

But to return to Artificial Congelations: There is as much difference between Natural and Artificial Ice and Snow, as there is between Chalk and Cheese, or between a natural Child, and a Baby made of Paste or Wax, and Gummed-silk; or between artificial Glass, and natural Diamonds: The like may be said of Hail, Frost, Wind, &c. for though their exterior figures do resemble, yet their interior natures are quite different; and therefore, although by the help of Art, some may make Ice of Water or Snow, yet we cannot conclude from hence, that all natural Ice is made the same way, by Saline particles, or acid Spirits, and the like; for if Nature should work like Art, she would produce a Man like as a Carver makes a Statue, or a Painter draws a Picture.

XXVIII. Of Thawing or dissolving of Frozen bodies

But some may say, If Nature be but one Body, and the Infinite parts are all united into that same Body; How comes it that there is such an opposition, strife and war, betwixt the parts of Nature? I answer: Nature being Material, is composable and dividable; and as Composition is made by a mutual agreement of parts, so Division is made by an opposition or strife betwixt parts; which opposition or division, doth not obstruct the Union of Nature, but, on the contrary, rather proves, That without an opposition of parts, there could not be a union or com-position of so many several parts and creatures, nor no change or variety in Nature; for if all the parts did unanimously conspire and agree in their motions, and move all but one way, there would be but one act or kind of motion in Nature; whenas an opposition of some parts, and a mutual agreement of others, is not onely the cause of the Miraculous variety in Nature, but it poyses and ballances, as it were, the corporeal, figurative motions, which is the cause that Nature is steady and fixt in Herself, although her Parts be in a perpetual Motion.

XXXI. Of the Parts of Nature, and of Atoms

Although I am of opinion, That Nature is a self-moving, and consequently a self-living and self-knowing infinite Body, dividable into infinite parts; yet I do not mean, That these parts are Atoms; for there can be no Atom, that is, an indivisible Body in Nature; because whatsoever has Body, or is mate-rial, has quantity; and what has quantity is divisible. But some may say, If a part be finite, it cannot be divisible into Infinite. To which I answer, That there is no such thing as one finite single part in Nature: for when I speak of the parts of Nature, I do not understand, that those parts are like grains of Corn or Sand in one heap, all of one figure or magnitude, and separable from each other: but, I conceive Nature to be an infinite Body, bulk or magnitude, which by its own self-motion, is divided into infinite parts, not single or indivisible parts, but parts of one continued Body, onely discernable from each other by their proper figures, caused by the changes of particular motions: for, it is well to be observed, first, That Nature is corporeal, and therefore divisible. . . . [I]t is evident, first, That no certain quantity or figure can be assigned to the parts of Nature, as I said before of the grains of Corn or Sand; for infinite changes of Motions, produce infinite varieties of Figures; and all the degrees of density, rarity, levity, gravity, slowness, quickness; nay, all the effects that are in Nature. Next, That it is impossible to have single parts in Nature, that is, parts which are indivisible in themselves, as Atoms; and may subsist single, or by themselves, precised or separated from all other parts: for, although there are perfect and whole figures in Nature, yet are they nothing else but parts of Nature, which consist of a composition of other parts, and their figures make them discernable from other parts or figures of Nature. For example: An Eye, although it be composed of parts, and has a whole and perfect figure, yet it is but a part of the Head, and could not subsist without it. Also the Head, although it has a whole and perfect figure, yet 'tis a part of the Body, and could not subsist without it. The same may be said of all other particular and perfect figures: As for example, An Animal, though it be a whole and perfect figure, yet it is but a part of Earth, and some other Elements, and parts of Nature, and could not subsist without them; nay, for any thing we know to the contrary, the Elements cannot subsist without other Creatures. All which proves, That there are no single Parts, nor *Vacuum*.[15] . . .

[I]t remains firm, That Self-motion is the onely cause of the various parts and changes of figures; and that when parts move or separate themselves from parts, they move and joyn to other parts, at the same point of time: I do not mean that parts do drive or press upon each other; for those are forced and constraint actions; when as natural Self-motions are free and voluntary. And although there are pressures and re-actions in Nature, yet they are not universal actions. Neither is there any such thing as a stoppage in the actions of Nature, nor do parts move through Empty spaces; but as some parts joyn, so others divide by the same act: for, although some parts can quit such or such parts, yet they cannot quit all parts: For example, a man goes a hundred miles, he leaves or quits those parts from whence he removed first; but as soon as he removes from such parts, he joyns to other parts, were his motion no more then a hairs breadth; so that all his journey is nothing else but a division and composition of parts, wheresoever he goes, by Water, or by Land; for it is impossible for him to quit parts in general,

---

[15] See also *Observations Upon Experimental Philosophy*, section XV.

although it be in his choice to quit such or such particular parts, and to join to what parts he will.[16] ...

But some may say, How is it possible that there can be a motion of bodies, without an empty space; for one body cannot move in another body? I answer: Space is change of division, as Place is change of magnitude; but division and magnitude belong to body; therefore Space and Place cannot be without body, but wheresoever is body, there is place also: neither can a body leave a place behind it. So that the distinction of interior and exterior place, is needless; because no body can have two places, but place and body are but one thing; and whensoever the body changes, its place changes also.

XXXIV. Of Telescopes

Many Ingenious and Industrious Artists take much labour and pains in studying the natures and figures of Celestial objects, and endeavour to discover the causes of their appearances, by Telescopes, and such like Optick Instruments; but if Art be not able to inform us truly of the natures of those Creatures that are near us; How may it delude us in the search and enquiry we make of those things that are so far from us? We see how Multiplying-glasses do present numerous pictures of one object, which he that has not the experience of the deceitfulness of such Glasses, would really think to be so many objects. The like deceits may be in other optick Instruments, for ought man knows. 'Tis true, we may, perhaps, through a Telescope, see a Steeple a matter of 20 or 30 miles off; but the same can a natural Eye do, if it be not defective, nor the medium obstructed, without the help of any such Instrument, especially if one stand upon a high place. But,

[16] In "To the Reader," Cavendish offers a few clarifications to the claims that she has put forward in *Observations Upon Experimental Philosophy*. She writes, *"When I say, that* The parts of Nature do not drive or press upon each other, but that all natural actions are free and easie, and not constrained; *My meaning is not, as if there was no pressing or driving of parts at all in Nature, but onely that they are not the universal or principal actions of Nature's body, as it is the opinion of some Philosophers, who think there is no other motion in nature, but by pressure of parts upon parts: Nevertheless, there is pressure and reaction in Nature, because there are infinite sorts of motions. Also, when I say in the same place, That Natures actions are voluntary; I do not mean, That all Actions are made by rote, and none by imitation; but by Voluntary-Actions I understand Self actions; that is, such actions whose Principle of Motion is within themselves, and doth not proceed from such an exterior Agent, as doth the motion of the inanimate part of Matter; which, having no motion of it self, is moved by the animate parts, yet so, that it receives no motion from them, but moves by the motion of the animate parts, and not by an infused motion into them; for the animate parts in carrying the inanimate along with them, lose nothing of their own motion, nor impart no motion to the inanimate; no more than a man who carries a stick in his hand, imparts motion to the stick, and loses so much as he imparts; but they bear the inanimate parts along with them, by vertue of their own Self-motion, and remain Self-moving parts, as well as the inanimate remain without motion."* See also note 11 for *Philosophical and Physical Opinions*.

put the case a man should be upon the *Alps,* he would hardly see the City of *Paris* from thence, although he looked through a Telescope never so perfect, and had no obstruction to hinder his sight. And truly, the Starrs and Planets are far more distant from us, than *Paris* from the *Alps.* It is well known, that the sense of Sight requires a certain proportion of distance betwixt the Eye and the Object; which being exceeded, it cannot perform its office: for, if the object be either too near, or too far off, the sight cannot discern it; and, as I have made mention in my Philosophical Letters of the nature of those Guns, that according to the proportion of the length of the barrel, shoot either further or shorter; for the Barrel must have its proportioned length, which being exceeded, the Gun will shoot so much shorter as the barrel is made longer: so may Prospective-glasses perhaps direct the sense of seeing within a certain compass of distance; which distance, surely the Stars and Planets do far exceed.[17]

XXXV. Of Knowledg and Perception in General

No part can subsist singly, or by it self, precised from the rest; but they are all parts of one infinite Body; for though such parts may be separated from such parts, and joined to other parts, and by this means may undergo infinite changes, by infinite compositions and divisions; yet no part can be separated from the Body of Nature. . . .

As there can be no annihilation; so there can neither be a new Creation of the least part or particle of Nature, or else Nature would not be infinite.

Nature is purely corporeal or material, and there is nothing that belongs to, or is a part of Nature, which is not corporeal; so that natural and material, or corporeal, are one and the same; and therefore spiritual-beings, non-beings, mixt beings, and whatsoever distinctions the Learned do make, are no ways belonging to Nature. Neither is there any such thing as an Incorporeal motion;[18] for all actions of Nature are corporeal, being natural; and there can no abstraction be made of Motion or Figure, from Matter or Body, but they are inseparably one thing.[19] Wherefore no spiritual Being, can have local motion. . . .

---

[17] Cavendish's distrust of instruments does not extend to those whose results can be confirmed with the naked eye or other non-artificial organs. Part of the concern that she appears to be expressing here is that if we cannot confirm the appearance of a distant object with the naked eye, but can only see it through a telescope, we cannot check to see whether or not the telescope is representing it accurately. She will then err on the side of concluding that the instrument is probably misleading us, given that it is an artifact and not a natural production. See also note 3 in this chapter, and *Worlds Olio,* "The Power of Natural Works."

[18] See also note 43 for *Philosophical Letters.*

[19] See also *Philosophical Letters,* letter XXX of section one.

I conclude, That no particular parts are bound to certain particular actions, no more than Nature her self, which is self-moving Matter; for as Nature is full of variety of motions or actions, so are her Parts; or else she could not be said self-moving, if she were bound to certain actions, and had not liberty to move as she pleases: for, though God, the Author of Nature, has ordered her, so that she cannot work beyond her own nature, that is, beyond Matter; yet has she freedom to move as she will; neither can it be certainly affirmed, that the successive propagation of the several species of Creatures, is decreed and ordained by God, so that Nature must of necessity work to their continuation, and can do no otherwise; but humane sense and reason may observe, that the same Parts keep not always to the same particular Actions, so as to move to the same species or figures; for, those parts that join in the composition of an Animal, alter their actions in its dissolution, and in the framing of other figures; so that the same Parts which were joined in one particular Animal, may, when they dissolve from that composed figure, join severally to the composition of other figures; as for example, of Minerals, Vegetables, Elements, &c. and some may join with some sorts of Creatures, and some with others, and so produce creatures of different sorts, when as before they were all united in one particular Creature: for, particular parts are not bound to work or move to a certain particular action, but they work according to the wisdom and liberty of Nature, which is onely bound by the Omnipotent God's Decree, not to work beyond her self, that is, beyond Matter; and since Matter is dividable, Nature is necessitated to move in Parts; for Matter can be without Parts, no more then Parts can be without a Whole; neither can Nature, being material, make her self void of figure, nor can she rest, being self-moving; but she is bound to divide and compose her several Parts into several particular figures, and dissolve and change those figures again infinite ways: All which proves the variety of Nature, which is so great, that even in one and the same species, none of the particulars resemble one another so much, as not to be discerned from each other.

But to return to Knowledg and Perception; I say, They are general and fundamental actions of Nature; it being not probable that the infinite parts of Nature should move so variously, nay, so orderly and methodically as they do, without knowing what they do, or why, and whether they move; and therefore all particular actions whatsoever in Nature, as Respiration, Digestion, Sympathy, Antipathy, Division, Composition, Pressure, Re-action, &c. are all particular perceptive and knowing actions: for, if a Part be divided from other Parts, both are sensible of their division: The like may be said of the composition of Parts. . . .

Next, as Colour, according to their opinion, is not inherent any otherwise in the object, but by an effect thereof upon us, caused by such a motion in the object; so, neither (say they) is Sound in the thing we hear, but in our selves:[20] for, as a man may see, so he may hear double, or treble, by multiplication of Ecchoes, which are Sounds as well as the Original; and not being in one and the same place, cannot be inherent in the Body; for the Clapper has no sound in it, but Motion, and maketh motion in the inward parts of the Bell: neither has the Bell Motion, but Sound, and imparts motion to the Air, the Air again imparts motion to the ear and nerves, until it comes to the brain, which has Motion, not Sound: from the brain it rebounds back into the nerves outward, and then it becomes an apparition without, which we call Sound. But, good Lord! What a confusion would all this produce, if it were thus! What need is there of imparting Motion, when Nature can do it a much easier way? I wonder how rational men can believe that Motion can be imparted without Matter: Next, that all this can be done in an instant: Again, that it is the Organ of the Sentient that makes Colour, Sound, and the like, and that they are not really inherent in the object it self. For were there no men to perceive such or such a colour, figure or sound; can we rationally think that Object would have no colour, figure nor sound at all? I will not say, That there is no Pressure or Reaction, but they do not make Sense or Reason: several parts may produce several effects by their several compositions; but yet this does not prove that there can be no perception but by pressure upon the Organ, and consequently the Brain; and that the thing perceived, is not really existent in the Object, but a bare apparition to the Sentient: the Clapper gives no Motion to the Bell, but both the Clapper, and the Bell, have each their own Motion, by which they act in striking each other; and the conjunction of such or such parts, makes a real sound, were there no Ear to hear it.

Again, Concerning the Sense of Touch, the heat, say they, we feel from the Fire, is in us; for it is quite different from that in the Fire: our heat is pleasure, or pain, according as it is, great or moderate; but in the Coal there is no such thing. I answer: They are so far in the right, that the Heat we feel, is made by the perceptive motions of, and in our own parts, and not by the Fire's parts acting upon us: but yet, if the Fire were not really such a thing as it is, that is, a hot and burning Body, our sense would not so readily figure it out, as it does: which proves, it is a real copy of a real object, and not a meer fantasm, or bare imparted motion from the object to the sentient, made by pressure and reaction.

[20] Here (and also in section XXI) Cavendish is referring to a common view in the early modern period that so-called secondary qualities like color and sound are not literally in objects, but instead bodies impact our senses and produce in our minds an experience of such qualities. See for example Descartes, *The World*, chapters one and two, CSM 1:81–84; and Locke, *An Essay concerning Human Understanding*, II.viii.1–16, pp. 132–143.

XXXVI. Of the different Perceptions of Sense
and Reason

Having declared in the former discourse, that there is a double Perception in all Parts of Nature, to wit, Rational and Sensitive; some might ask, How these two degrees of Motions work; whether differently or unitedly in every part to one and the same perception.

I answer: That regularly the animal perception of exterior objects, is made by its own sensitive, rational, corporeal and figurative motions; the sensitive patterning out the figure or action of an outward object in the sensitive organ; and the Rational making a figure of the same object in their own substance; so that both the rational and sensitive motions, work to one and the same perception, and that at the same point of time, and, as it were, by one act; but yet it is to be observed, that many times they do not move together to one and the same perception; for the sensitive and rational motions do many times move differently even in one and the same part: As for the rational, they being not incumbred with any other parts of Matter, but moving in their own degree, are not at all bound to work always with the sensitive, as is evident in the production of Fancies, Thoughts, Imaginations, Conceptions, &c. which are figures made onely by the Rational Motions in their own matter or substance, without the help of the sensitive; and the sensitive, although they do not commonly work without the rational, yet many times they do; and sometimes both the rational and sensitive work without patterns, that is, voluntarily and by rote; and sometimes the sensitive take patterns from the rational, as in the invention of Arts, or the like; so that there is no necessity that they should always work together to the same perception. Concerning the perception of exterior objects, I will give an instance, where both the rational and sensitive motions do work differently, and not to the same perception: Suppose a man be in a deep contemplative study, and some-body touch or pinch him, it happens oft that he takes no notice at all of it, nor doth feel it; when as yet his touched or pinched parts are sensible, or have a sensitive perception thereof; also a man doth often see or hear something without minding or taking notice thereof,[21] especially when his thoughts

---

[21] This claim might call to mind the (very different) view that Descartes expresses in the Second Meditation: "Lastly, it is also the same 'I' who has sensory perceptions, or is aware of bodily things as it were through the senses. For example, I am now seeing light, hearing a noise, feeling heat. But I am asleep, so all this is false. Yet I certainly *seem* to see, to hear, and to be warmed. This cannot be false; what is called 'having a sensory perception' is strictly just this, and in this restricted sense of the term it is simply thinking" (CSM 2:19). For Descartes, we should never say of a creature that it sees or hears something if it is not having a conscious visual or auditory experience, etc. In that case the creature would be *as-if* seeing.

are busily imployed about some other things; which proves, that his Mind, or rational motions, work quite to another perception then his sensitive do. . . .

Some Learned conceive, That all knowledg is in the Mind, and none in the senses: For the senses, say they, present onely exterior objects to the Mind; which sits as a Judg in the Kernel or fourth Ventricle of the Brain, or in the Orifice of the Stomack, and judges of them; which, in my apprehension, is a very odd opinion: For first, they allow, that all knowledg and perception comes by the senses, and the sensitive spirits; who, like faithful servants, run to and fro, as from the sensitive organs, to the brain and back, to carry news to the mind; and yet they do not grant, that they have any knowledg at all: which shews, they are very dull servants, and I wonder how they can inform the mind of what they do not know themselves. . . . [I]t is absurd, in my opinion, to say, That the senses bring all knowledg of exterior objects to the mind, and yet have none themselves; and that the Mind chiefly resides but in one part of the Body; so that when the Heel is touched, the sensitive spirits, who watch in that place, do run up to the Head, and bring News to the Mind.[22]

XXXVII. Several Questions and Answers concerning Knowledg and Perception

Q. 3. *Whether the Inanimate Matter could have Parts, without Self-motion?*

I answer, Yes: For wheresoever is Body or Matter, there are also Parts; because Parts belong to Body, and there can be no Body without Parts; but yet, were there no Self-motion, there could be no various changes of Parts or Figures. The truth is, Nature considered as she is, and as much as our sense and reason can perceive by her various effects, must of necessity be composed, or consist of a commixture of animate, both rational and sensitive, and inanimate matter; for, were there no inanimate matter, there would be no ground, or grosser substance to work on, and so no solid figures: and, were there no animate sensitive matter, there would be no Labourer, or Workman, as I may call it, to form the inanimate part of matter into various figures; nor would there be such infinite changes, compositions, divisions, productions, dissolutions, &c. as we see there are. Again, Were there no animate rational Matter, there would be no Designer or Surveigher, to order and direct all things methodically; nor no Fancies, Imaginations, Conceptions, Memory, &c. so that this *Triumvirate* of the

---

[22] Here Cavendish might have in mind the discussion in Descartes' Sixth Meditation, CSM 2:59–61.

degrees of Matter, is so necessary a constitutive principle of all natural effects, that Nature could not be without it[23]: I mean, Nature considered, not what she might have been, but as she is, and as much as we are able to perceive by her actions; for, Natural Philosophy is no more but a rational inquisition into the causes of natural effects: and therefore, as we observe the effects and actions of Nature, so we may probably guess at their Causes and Principles.

Q. 10. *Whether there could be Self-knowledg without Perception.*

[S]ome may ask, Whether, in such a case, that is, in the perception of an Object which is distant from the Sentient, the intermediate parts are as well perceived, as the Object it self, to which the perception directly tends? I answer, That, if the intermediate parts be subject to that kind of perception, they may as well be perceived, as the Object that is distant; nay, sometimes better: but most commonly, the intermediate parts are but slightly or superficially perceived: For example, in the fore-mentioned sense of Seeing, if the Organ of Sight be directed to some certain Object that is distant, and there be some parts between the Organ and the Object, perceptible by the same sense, but such as do not hinder or obstruct the perception of the said Object: not onely the Object, but also those intermediate parts will be perceived by the optick sense.[24] Also, if I cast my eye upon an object that is before me, in a direct line, the eye will not onely perceive the Object to which it is chiefly directed, but also those parts that are joined to it, either beneath, or above, or on each side of that Object, at the same point of time, and by the same act; the sole difference is, That the said Object is chiefly,

---

[23] Cavendish posits the existence of three kinds of matter, although she supposes that these are thoroughly intermingled in every individual body. Rational matter is active and intelligent and swift; it constitutes a large percentage of our imagistic ideas, which (from experience) we know are able to go in and out of different configurations very quickly. Rational matter also constitutes a percentage of the bulkier bodies that we encounter in the external world, guiding those bodies in their pursuit of aims and goals and order. Sensitive matter is active as well; it is not as directive as rational matter, but instead takes and executes orders from it. Cavendish then posits inanimate matter to account for the slow and gradual unfolding of the order that is exhibited in external bodies. She appears to hold that if rational matter was the only matter that existed, we would encounter organized configurations that go in and out of existence quickly and on a regular basis (but we don't). She also appears to hold that if there existed only rational matter and (slower but still active and intelligent) sensitive matter, then bodies like mountains and planets would not persist as long as they do, because creative rational matter would often (and successfully) attempt to upend their figure and form on a whim. But mountains and many other bodies exist for long stretches of time. See, in this chapter, *Further Observations Upon Experimental Philosophy*, section VI; and *Grounds of Natural Philosophy*, chapters III, V and X of the First Part, and chapter VI of the Second Part.

[24] In this passage Cavendish is suggesting that perception of faraway objects is a matter of perceiving not only those objects, but also the intermediate objects in the plenum (though not as distinctly). See also *Philosophical Letters*, letters IV and XXIV of section one.

and of purpose patterned out by the sensitive and rational figurative motions of the eye; when as the other intermediate or adjoining parts, are but superficially and slightly looked over.

Q. 11. *Whether Perception be made by Patterning?*

I answer: My Sense and Reason does observe, That the Animal, at least, Human Perception, performed by the sensitive and rational motions in the Organs appropriated for it, is made by patterning or framing of figures, according to the patterns of exterior objects; but whether all other kinds and sorts of perceptions in the infinite parts of Nature, be made the same manner or way, neither my self, nor no particular Creature is able to determine, by reason there are as many various sorts of perceptions, as there are of other actions of Nature; and according as the corporeal figurative motions do alter and change, so do particular perceptions; for, Perception is a corporeal, figurative action, and is generally in all parts and actions of Nature: and, as no part can be without self-motion and self-knowledg, so none can be without perception. And therefore, I dare truly say, That all perceptions are made by figuring, though I cannot certainly affirm, that all are made by imitation or patterning. . . .

Others again say, That the species of the Objects, pass from the Objects to the Optick Organ, and make figures in the air; but then the multitude of those figures in the Air, would make such a confusion, as would hinder the species passing through: besides, the species being corporeal, and proceeding from the Object, would lessen its quantity or bulk. Wherefore my opinion is, That the most rare and subtilest parts in the Animal sensitive organs, do pattern out the figures of exterior Objects, and that the perception of the exterior Animal Senses, to wit, Sight, Hearing, Tasting, Touching, Smelling, is certainly made by no other way, than by figuring and imitation.[25]

Q. 12. *How the bare patterning out of the Exterior Figure of an Object, can give us an information of its Interior nature.*

My answer is, That although our sensitive Perception can go no further then the exterior shape, figure and actions of an object; yet, the rational being a more subtil, active and piercing Perception, by reason it is more free then the sensitive, does not rest in the knowledg of the exterior Figure of an Object, but, by its exterior actions, as by several effects, penetrates into its interior nature, and doth probably guess and conclude what its interior figurative motions may be. . . . [T]he interior, figurative Motions of these Creatures, being not subject

---

[25] See also note 21 for *Philosophical and Physical Opinions*.

to the perception of our exterior senses, cannot exactly be known: Nevertheless, although our exterior senses have no perception thereof, yet their own parts which are concern'd in it, as also their adjoining or neighbouring parts may: For example, a man knows he has a digestion in his body, which being an interior action, he cannot know, by his exterior senses, how it is made; but those parts of the body where the digestion is performed, may know it; nay, they must of necessity do so, because they are concerned in it, as being their proper imployment. The same may be said of all other particular parts and actions in an Animal Body, which are like several Workmen employed in the building of a House; for, although they do all work and labour to one and the same end, that is, the Building of the House; and every one may have some inspection or perception of what his Neighbour doth; yet each having his peculiar task and employment, has also its proper and peculiar knowledg how to perform his own work.

Further Observations Upon Experimental Philosophy, Reflecting withal upon some Principal Subjects in Contemplative Philosophy

II. WHETHER ARTIFICIAL EFFECTS MAY BE CALLED NATURAL, AND IN WHAT SENSE

In my former Discourses I have declared, that Art produces Hermaphroditical Effects, that is, such as are partly Natural, and partly Artificial; but the question is, whether those Hermaphroditical Effects may not be called Natural Effects as well as others; or, whether they be Effects quite different and distinct from Natural? My answer is, When I call Artificial effects Hermaphroditical, or such as are not Natural; I do not speak of Nature in general, as if they were something else besides Nature; for Art it self is natural, and an effect of Nature, and cannot produce any thing that is beyond, or not within Nature: wherefore artificial effects can no more be excluded from Nature, then any ordinary effect or Creature of Nature. But when I say they are not natural, I understand the particular nature of every Creature, according to its own kind or species; for as there is Infinite Nature, which may be called General Nature, or Nature in general, which includes and comprehends all the effects and Creatures that lie within her, and belong to her, as being parts of her own Self-moving body; so there are also particular natures in every Creature, which are the innate, proper and inherent interior and substantial forms and figures of every Creature, according to their own kind or species, by which each Creature or part of Nature is discerned or distinguished from the other.

VI. WHETHER THERE BE ANY PRIME OR PRINCIPAL FIGURE IN NATURE; AND OF THE TRUE PRINCIPLES OF NATURE

[I]t is well to be observed, That although I make a distinction betwixt animate and inanimate, rational and sensitive Matter, yet I do not say that they are three distinct and several Matters; for as they do make but one Body of Nature, so they are also but one Matter. . . . [T]hat every part has not onely sensitive, but also rational Matter, is evident, not onely by the bare motion in every part of Nature, which cannot be without sense, for wheresoever is motion, there's sense; but also by the regular, harmonious and well-ordered actions of Nature, which clearly demonstrates, that there must needs be Reason as well as Sense, in every part and particle of Nature; for there can be no order, method or harmony, especially such as appears in the actions of Nature, without there be reason to cause that order and harmony. And thus Motion argues Sense, and the well-ordered Motion argues Reason in Nature, and in every part and particle thereof, without which Nature could not subsist, but would be as a dull indigested and unformed heap and Chaos. Besides, it argues that there is also knowledg in Nature, and all her parts; for wheresoever is sense and reason, there is also sensitive and rational knowledg, it being most improbable that such an exactly ordered and harmonious consort of all the infinitely various actions of Nature should be without any knowledg, moving and acting, producing, transforming, composing, dissolving, &c. and not knowing how, whether, or why to move.

VII. WHETHER NATURE BE SELF-MOVING

I observe, that most of the great and famous, especially our Modern Authors, endeavour to deduce the knowledg of causes from their effects, and not effects from their causes, and think to find out Nature by Art, not Art by Nature. . . . Art is but Nature's foolish Changeling-Child; and the reason is, that some parts of Nature, as some Men, not knowing all other parts, believe there is no reason, and but little sense in any part of Nature, but themselves; nay, that it is irreligious to say that there is, not considering, that God is able to give Sense and Reason to Infinite Nature, as well as to a finite part. But those are rather irreligious, that believe God's Power is confined, or that it is not Infinite.

IX. OF THE DOCTRINE OF THE SCEPTICKS CONCERNING THE KNOWLEDG OF NATURE

Nature being not onely divisible, but also compoundable in her parts, it cannot be absolutely affirmed that there is either a total ignorance, or a universal knowledg in Nature, so as one finite part should know perfectly all other parts of Nature: but as there is an ignorance amongst particulars, caused by the division of Nature's parts, so there is also a knowledg amongst them, caused by the composition and union of her parts. Neither can any ignorance be attributed to Infinite Nature, by reason she being a body comprehending so many parts of her own in a firm bond, and indissoluble union, so as no part can separate it self from her, must of necessity have also an Infinite wisdom and knowledg to govern her Infinite parts. And therefore it is best, in my judgment, for Scepticks and Dogmatists to agree in their different opinions; and whereas now they express their wit by division, to shew their wisdom by composition; for thus they will make an harmonious consort and union in the truth of Nature, where otherwise their disagreement will cause perpetual quarrels and disputes both in Divinity and Philosophy, to the prejudice and ruin of Church and Schools; which disagreement proceeds meerly from self-love: For every Man being a part of Nature, which is self-loving as well as self-moving, would fain be, at least appear wiser than his fellow-creatures.

X. OF NATURAL SENSE AND REASON

Those that believe natural sense and reason to be immaterial, are, in my opinion, in a great error, because Nature is purely corporeal, as I have declared before: And those which affirm, That our Understanding, Will and Reason, are in some manner like to God's, shall never gain my assent; for if there be so great a difference between God's Understanding, Will and Decree, and between Nature's, as no comparison at all can be made betwixt them; much more is there between a part of Nature, *viz.* Man, and the Omnipotent and Incomprehensible God; for there is an infinite difference between Divine Attributes, and Natural Properties; wherefore to similize our Reason, Will, Understanding, Faculties, Passions, and Figures, *&c.* to God, is too high a presumption, and in some manner a blasphemy. Nevertheless, although our natural reason and faculties are not like to Divine Attributes, yet our natural rational perceptions are not always delusions; and therefore it is certain, that Nature's knowing parts, both sensitive and rational, do believe a God, that is, some Being above Nature: But many Writers endeavour rather to make divisions in Religion, than promote the honour and worship of God by a mutual and united agreement, which I confess is an irregularity and imperfection in some parts of Nature; and argues, that Nature is not so perfect, but she has some faults and infirmities, otherwise she would be a God, which she is not.

XI. OF A GENERAL KNOWLEDG AND WORSHIP OF GOD, GIVEN HIM BY ALL NATURAL CREATURES

It is not the sight of the Beauteous Frame of this World (as some do conceive) that makes men believe and admire God; but the knowledg of the Existence of God is natural, and there's no part of Nature but believes a God. . . . Nature being the Eternal Servant and Worshipper of God, God hath been also eternally worshipped and adored: for, surely God's Adoration and Worship has no beginning in time; neither could God be worshipped and adored by himself, so as that one part of him should adore and worship another; for God is an individual and simple Being, not composed of parts; and therefore, as it is impossible for me to believe that there is no general Worship and Adoration of God; so it is impossible also to believe that God has not been adored and worshipped from all Eternity, and that Nature is not Eternal; for although God is the Cause of Nature, and Nature the Effect of God, yet she may be Eternal however, there being nothing impossible to be effected by God; but He, as an Eternal Cause, is able to produce an Eternal Effect; for, although it is against the Rules of Logick, yet it is not above the Power of God.

XII. OF A PARTICULAR WORSHIP OF GOD, GIVEN HIM BY THOSE THAT ARE HIS CHOSEN AND ELECT PEOPLE

Natural Philosophy is the chief of all sorts of Knowledges; for she is a Guide, not onely to other Sciences, and all sorts of Arts, but even to Divine Knowledg it self; for she teaches, that there is a Being above Nature, which is God the Author and Master of Nature, whom all Creatures know and adore. But to adore God after a particular manner, according to his special Will and Command, requires his particular Grace, and divine Instructions, in a supernatural manner or way, which none but the chosen Creatures of God do know, at least believe; nor none but the Sacred Church ought to explain and interpret: And the proof, that all men are not of the number of those elect and chosen people of God, is, That there can be but one True Religion, and that yet there are so many several and different opinions in that Religion; wherefore the Truth can onely be found in some, which are those that serve God truly, according to his special will and command, both in believing and acting that which he has been pleased to reveal and command in his holy Word: And I pray God, of his infinite mercy, to give me grace, that I may be one of them, which I doubt not but I shall, as long as I follow the Instruction of our blessed Church, in which I have been educated. 'Tis true, many persons are much troubled concerning Free-will and Predestination, complaining, that the Christian Church is so divided about this

Article, as they will never agree in one united belief concerning that point; which is the cause of the trouble of so many Consciences, nay, in some even to despair. But I do verily believe, that if man do but love God from his soul, and with all his power, and pray for his saving-graces, and offend not any Creature when offences can or may be avoided, and follow the onely Instructions of the Sacred Church, not endeavouring to interpret the Word of God after his own fancy and vain imagination, but praying zealously, believing undoubtedly, and living virtuously and piously, he can hardly fall into despair, unless he be disposed and inclined towards it through the irregularities of Nature, so as he cannot avoid it. But I most humbly thank the Omnipotent God, that my Conscience is in peace and tranquility, beseeching him of his mercy to give to all men the like.

XIII. OF THE KNOWLEDG OF MAN

Some Philosophical Writers discourse much concerning the knowledg of Man, and the ignorance of all other Creatures; but I have sufficiently expressed my opinion hereof, not onely in this, but in my other Philosophical Works, to wit, that I believe other Creatures have as much knowledg as Man, and Man as much in his kind, as any other particular Creature in its kind; but their knowledges being different, by reason of their different natures and figures, it causes an ignorance of each other's knowledg; nay, the knowledg of other Creatures, many times gives information to Man: As for example; The *Egyptians* are informed how high the River *Nilus* will rise by the Crocodile's building her Nest higher or lower; which shews, that those Creatures fore-see or fore-know more than Man can do: Also, many Birds fore-know the rising of a Tempest, and shelter themselves before it comes; the like examples might be given of several other sorts of Animals, whose knowledg proceeds either from some sensitive perceptions, or from rational observations, or from both; and if there be such a difference in the rational and sensitive knowledg of one kind of Creatures, to wit, Animals; much more in all other kinds, as Vegetables, Minerals, Elements, and so in all Nature's Works.[26]

XX. OF CHYMISTRY, AND CHYMICAL PRINCIPLES

As for God, he being immoveable, and beyond all natural motion, cannot actually move Matter; neither is it Religious, to say, God is the Soul of Nature; for God is no part of Nature, as the Soul is of the Body; and immaterial spirits, being supernatural, cannot have natural attributes or actions, such as is corporeal, natural motion. Wherefore it remains, that Matter must be naturally self-moving, and consequently all parts of Nature, all being Material. . . . 'Tis true, Matter

---

[26] See also *Philosophical Letters*, letter X of section one.

might subsist without Motion, but not Motion without Matter: for, there is no such thing as an Immaterial Motion, but Motion must necessarily be of some-thing: Also, if there be a figure, it must of necessity be a figure of something; the same may be said of magnitude and weight, there being no such thing as a mean between Something and Nothing, that is, between body, and no body in Nature.[27] ...

[N]o Creature that has its reason regular, can almost believe, that such wise and orderly actions should be done either by chance, or by straying Atoms, which cannot so constantly change and exchange parts, and mix and join so properly, and to such constant effects as are apparent in Nature. . . . [I]t is most frequently observed thus amongst all sorts of Animals; and if amongst Animals, I know no reason but all other kinds and sorts of Creatures may do the like; nay, both sense and reason inform us, they do; as appears by the several and proper actions of all sorts of drugs, as also of Minerals and Elements, and the like; so that none ought to wonder how it is possible That medicines that must pass through digestions in the body, should, neglecting all other parts, shew themselves friendly onely to the brain or kidnies, or the like parts; for, if there be sense and reason in Nature, all things must act wisely and orderly, and not confusedly.[28]

Observations Upon the Opinions of Some Ancient Philosophers

[T]he Opinions of the Ancient, though they are not exempt from Errors no more than our Moderns; yet are they to be commended, that their Conceptions are their own, and the issue of their own Wit and Reason; when as most of the Opinions of our Modern Philosophers, are patched up with theirs; some whereof do altogether follow either *Aristotle, Plato, Epicurus, Pythagoras,* &c. others make a mixture of several of their Opinions; and others again take some of their Opinions, and dress them up new with some Additions of their own; and what is worst, after all this, instead of Thanks, they reward them with Scorn, and rail at them; when as, perhaps, without their pains and industry, our Age would hardly have arrived to that knowledg it has done. To which ungrateful and un-conscionable act, I can no ways give my consent, but admire and honour both the Ancient, and all those that are real Inventors of Noble and Profitable Arts and Sciences, before all those that are but Botchers and Brokers; and that I do in this following Part, examine and mark some of their Opinions as erroneous, is not out of a humor to revile or prejudice their Wit, Industry, Ingenuity and Learning,

[27] See also note 43 for *Philosophical Letters.*
[28] See also *Philosophical and Physical Opinions,* "A Condemning Treatise of Atoms."

in the least; but onely to shew, by the difference of their Opinions and mine, that mine are not borrowed from theirs, as also to make mine the more Intelligible and clear; and, if possible, to find out the truth in Natural Philosophy; for which, were they alive, I question not but I should easily obtain their pardon.

II. SOME FEW OBSERVATIONS UPON PLATO'S DOCTRINE

10. As for his [Plato's] Ethicks, where he speaks of Beauty, Strength, Proportion, &c. I'le onely say this, That of all these there are different sorts; for, there's the strength of the Mind, and the strength of the Body; and these are so various in their kinds and particulars, that they cannot be exactly defined: Also Beauty, considering onely that which is of the Body, there are so many several sorts, consisting in features, shapes, and proportions of Bodies, as it is impossible to describe properly what Beauty is, and wherein it really consists: for, what appears beautiful to some, may seem ill-favoured to others; and what seems extraordinary fair or handsome to one, may have but an indifferent character of another; so that, in my opinion, there's no such thing as an Universal Beauty, which may gain a general applause of all, and be judged alike by every one that views it; nay, not by all Immortal Souls, neither in body nor mind; for what one likes, another may dislike; what one loves, another may hate; what one counts Good, another may proclaim Bad; what one names Just, another may call Unjust.[29] And as for Temperance, which he joins to Justice, what may be Temperance to one, may be Intemperance to another: for, no particular knows the just measures of Nature; nay, even one and the same thing which one man loves today, he may chance to hate, or at least dislike, tomorrow; for Nature is too various to be constant in her particulars, by reason of the perpetual alterations and changes they are subject to; which do all proceed from self-moving Matter, and not from incorporeal Ideas.

III. UPON THE DOCTRINE OF PYTHAGORAS

4. *Pythagoras's* Doctrine is, That the World, in its nature, is Corruptible, but the Soul of the World is Incorruptible; and that without the Heavens, there is an Infinite *Vacuum*, into which, and out of which, the World repairs. As for the corruptibility of the World, I cannot understand how the Soul can be incorruptible, and the World itself corruptible: for, if the World should be destroyed, what will become of the Soul? I will not say, That the All-powerfull God may not destroy it when he pleases; but the Infiniteness and perpetual Self-motion of Nature, will not permit that Nature should be corruptible in it self: for, God's Power

---

[29] See also note 5 for *Philosophical and Physical Opinions.*

goes beyond the power of Nature. But it seems, *Pythagoras* understands by the World, no more then his senses can reach; so that beyond the Celestial Orbs, he supposes to be an infinite *Vacuum*; which is as much as to say, an infinite Nothing: and my Reason cannot apprehend how the World can breath and respire into Nothing, and out of Nothing.[30] . . .

I cannot conceive how it is possible that the Soul is a self-moving Number, and yet but a Monad, or Unite; for a Unite, they say, is no Number, but a Principle of Number: Not, how the Soul, being incorporeal, can walk in the Air, like a Body;[31] for, Incorporeal beings cannot have Corporeal Actions, no more then corporeal Beings can have the Actions of Incorporeals. Wherefore I will leave those points to the examination of more Learned Persons than my self. And as for the *Pythagorean* Transmigration of Souls, I have declared my Opinion thereof heretofore.

IV. OF EPICURUS HIS PRINCIPLES OF PHILOSOPHY

1. . . . As for his infinite Worlds, I am not different from his opinion, if by Worlds he mean the parts of infinite Nature; but my Reason will not allow, that those infinite Worlds do subsist by themselves, distinguished from each other by *Vacuum*; for it is meer non-sense to say, The Universe consists of Body and *Vacuum*; that is, of something, and nothing: for nothing cannot be a constitutive principle of any thing, neither can it be measured, or have corporeal dimensions; for what is no Body, can have no bodily affections or properties.[32] God, by his Omnipotency, may reduce the World into nothing; but this cannot be comprehended by natural reason.

2. . . . But put the case there were such Atoms, out of which all things are made; yet no man that has his Sense and Reason regular, can believe, they did move by chance, or at least without Sense and Reason, in the framing of the World, and all Natural Bodies; if he do but consider the wonderful order and harmony that is in Nature, and all her Parts.[33] . . . Nature, being an infinite self-moving body, has

[30] Here Cavendish is suggesting that since there is no empty space into which the material universe might expand, the "infinite" universe is composed of a fixed and constant amount of matter. See also *Observations Upon Experimental Philosophy*, section XXXV, and *Grounds of Natural Philosophy*, chapter XII of the First Part and chapter VI of the Third Part. Note that in some passages Spinoza also identifies the infinitude of the universe with its totality, for example in *Short Treatise on God, Man and His Well-Being*, I.ii, 40. Part of Cavendish's motivation for the view would be her commitment to the doctrine that, in the natural word, something cannot come from nothing, and hence no matter is produced that is new.

[31] See also note 44 for *Philosophical Letters*. Locke came very close to offering the argument that since our minds travel with us as we move from place to place, and since it is only material things that move, our minds must be material. See *An Essay Concerning Human Understanding*, II.xxiii.20, 307.

[32] See also note 20 for *Worlds Olio*.

[33] See also *Philosophical and Physical Opinions*, "A Condemning Treatise of Atoms."

also infinite knowledg; and therefore she knows of no Chance: nor is this visible World, or any part of her, made by chance, or a casual concourse of senseless and irrational Atoms; but by the All-powerful Decree and Command of God, out of that preexistent Matter that was from all Eternity, which is, infinite Nature; for though the Scripture expresses the framing of this World, yet it doth not say, that Nature her self was then created; but onely that this World was put into such a frame and state, as it is now; and, Who knows but there may have been many other Worlds before, and of another figure than this is: nay, if Nature be infinite, there must also be infinite Worlds; for I take, with *Epicurus*, this World but for a part of the Universe; and as there is self-motion in Nature, so there are also perpetual changes of particulars, although God himself be immovable; for God acts by his All-powerful Decree or Command, and not after a natural way.

3. . . . I shall never be able to conceive, how, senseless and irrational Atomes can produce sense and reason, or a sensible and rational body, such as the soul is; although he affirms it to be possible: 'Tis true, different effects may proceed from one cause or principle; but there is no principle, which is senseless, can produce sensitive effects; nor no rational effects can flow from an irrational cause; neither can order, method and harmony, proceed from chance or confusion.[34]

5. . . . But, in my opinion, God must either be Corporeal, or Incorporeal; if Corporeal, he must be Nature it self; for there's nothing corporeal, but what is Natural; if Incorporeal, he must be Supernatural; for there is nothing between Body, and no Body; Corporeal and Incorporeal; Natural, and Supernatural: and therefore to say, God is of a Corporeal Nature, and yet not a Body, but like a Body, is contrary to all Sense and Reason. 'Tis true, God hath Actions, but they are not Corporeal, but Supernatural, and not Comprehensible by a humane or

---

[34] See also section 17 of Leibniz's *Monadology*. In the famous passage, Leibniz writes, "We must confess that the perception, and what depends on it, is inexplicable in terms of mechanical reasons, that is, through shapes and motions. If we imagine that there is a machine whose structure makes it think, sense, and have perceptions, we could conceive it enlarged, keeping the same proportions, so that we could enter into it, as one enters into a mill. Assuming that, when inspecting its interior, we will find only parts that push one another, and we will never find anything to explain a perception." See also Descartes, *Principles of Philosophy* I.53, CSM 1:210–211; and Malebranche, *Dialogues on Metaphysics and on Religion*, 6. Locke does not rule out the possibility that matter thinks, but he does agree with Descartes, Leibniz, and Malebranche that unthinking matter cannot combine to result in thinking; he holds that the only way that matter could think is if God super-added thinking to matter, by means of a miracle. (See *An Essay Concerning Human Understanding*, III.iv.6, 540.) Cavendish agrees with all three figures that unthinking matter cannot combine to result in thought, but she holds that mentality is already a basic feature of matter. She does not hold that thought *arises* from the organized interactions of non-thinking bodies; she supposes that any such organized interactions would have to involve intelligence to begin with (for example, *Philosophical Letters*, letter XII of section one).

finite Capacity: Neither is God naturally moving; for he has no local or natural Motion, nor doth he trouble himself with making any thing, but by his All-powerful Decree and Command he produces all things; and Nature, which is his Eternal servant, obeys his Commands: Wherefore the Actions of Nature cannot be a disturbance to his Incomprehensible felicity, no not to Nature, which being self-moving, can do no otherwise, but take delight in acting, for her Actions are free and easie, and not forced or constrained.[35]

6. . . . [F]or Nature, although she be Infinite and Eternal, yet she depends upon the Incomprehensible God, the Author of Nature, and his All-powerful Commands, Worshipping and Adoring Him in her Infinite Particulars; for, God being Infinite, must also have an Infinite Worship; and if Nature had no Dependance on God, she would not be a servant, but God her self.

V. ON ARISTOTLE'S PHILOSOPHICAL PRINCIPLES

1. . . . I would fain know what he means by the action of the first Mover, Whether he be actually moving the world, or not? If he be actually moving, he must of necessity have natural Motion in Himself; but natural Self-motion is Corporeal; and a Corporeal Propriety cannot be attributed to an Incorporeal Substance; But if he be not actually moving, he must move Nature by his powerful Decree and Command; and thus the first Mover is none else but God, who may be called so, because he has endued Nature with Self-motion, and given it a principle of Motion within it self, to move according as he has decreed and ordered it from all Eternity; for God, being Immovable and Incorporeal, cannot actually move the Universe, like the chief Wheel in a Watch.

Of Scepticism, and some other Sects of the Ancients

Heraclitus is of opinion, That Contraries are in the same things; and *Scepticks* affirm, That Contraries appear in the same thing; but I believe they may be partly both in the right, and partly both in the wrong. If their opinion be, That there are, or appear Contraries in Nature, or in the essence of Matter, they are both in the wrong; but, if they believe that Matter has different and contrary actions, they are both in the right: for there are not onely real, but also apparent, or seeming Contraries in Nature, which are her irregularities.[36]

---

[35] See also *Philosophical and Physical Opinions*, chapter 59.
[36] See also *Philosophical Letters*, letters XXIII and XXIX of section three.

CHAPTER 5

Grounds of Natural Philosophy

To all the Universities in Europe

Most Learned Societies,

All Books, without exception, being undoubtedly under your Jurisdiction, it is very strange that some Authors of good note, are not asham'd to repine at it; and the more forward they are in judging others, the less liberty they will allow to be judg'd themselves. But, if there was not a necessity, yet I would make it my choice, To submit, willingly, to your Censures, these Grounds of Natural Philosophy, in hopes that you will not condemn them, because they want Art, if they be found fraught with Sense and Reason. You are the Starrs of the First Magnitude, whose Influence governs the World of Learning; and it is my confidence, That you will be propitious to the Birth of this beloved Child of my Brain, whom I take the boldness to recommend to your Patronage; and as, if you vouchsafe to look on it favourably, I shall be extreamly obliged to your Goodness, for its everlasting Life: So, if you resolve to Frown upon it, I beg the favour, That it be not buried in the hard and Rocky Grave of your Displeasure; but be suffer'd, by your gentle silence, to lye still in the soft and easie Bed of Oblivion, which is incomparably the less Punishment of the Two. It is so commonly the error of indulgent Parents, to spoil their Children out of Fondness, that I may be forgiven for spoiling This, in never putting it to suck at the Breast of some Learned Nurse, whom I might have got from among your Students, to have assisted me; but would, obstinately, suckle it my self, and bring it up alone, without the help of any Scholar: Which having caused in the First Edition, (which was published under the name of Philosophical and Physical Opinions) many Imperfections; I have endeavoured in this Second, by many Alterations and Additions, (which have forc'd me to give it another Name) to correct them; whereby, I fear, my Faults are rather changed and encreased, than amended.

The First Part

CHAPTER I. OF MATTER

Matter is that we name *Body*; which Matter cannot be less, or more, than Body: Yet some Learned Persons are of opinion, That there are Substances that are not Material Bodies. But how they can prove any sort of Substance to be no Body, I cannot tell: neither can any of Nature's Parts express it, because a Corporeal Part cannot have an Incorporeal Perception.[1] But as for Matter, there may be degrees, as, *more pure,* or *less pure*; but there cannot be any Substances in Nature, that are between Body, and no Body: Also, Matter cannot be figureless, neither can Matter be without Parts. Likewise, there cannot be Matter without Place, nor Place without Matter; so that Matter, Figure, or Place, is but one thing: for, it is as impossible for One Body to have Two Places, as for One Place to have Two Bodies; neither can there be Place, without Body.[2]

CHAPTER II. OF MOTION

Though Matter might be without Motion, yet Motion cannot be without Matter; for it is impossible (in my opinion) that there should be an Immaterial Motion in Nature:[3] and if Motion is corporeal, then Matter, Figure, Place, and Motion, is but one thing, viz. a corporeal figurative Motion. As for a First Motion, I cannot conceive how it can be, or what that First Motion should be: for, an Immaterial cannot have a Material Motion; or, so strong a Motion, as to set all the Material Parts in Nature, or this World, a-moving;[4] but (in my opinion) every particular

---

[1] Cavendish holds that we cannot have ideas of immaterials or think or detect or speak of them (for example, *Philosophical and Physical Opinions*, chapter 160), but she does not thereby want to deny their existence. See also *Observations Upon Experimental Philosophy*, section XIX; and *Philosophical Letters*, letter XVIII of section two.

[2] See also note 20 for *Worlds Olio*.

[3] See also note 43 for *Philosophical Letters*. Descartes had faced objections from commentators like Princess Elisabeth of Bohemia and Pierre Gassendi that minds and ideas have characteristics that are had only by bodies, and hence that minds and ideas would appear to be material themselves. (See Princess Elisabeth, "To Descartes, 16 May 1643," in *The Princess and the Philosopher*, 9–10; and Gassendi, *Fifth Objections*, CSM 2:238–239.) To address the objection, Descartes in some cases appeals to the limitations of human understanding (for example, in "To Princess Elizabeth, 29 June 1643," CSMK 226–228), and in others he suggests that immaterial things are more exalted and more noble than bodies and hence contain the reality of physical objects eminently and in a purer form (for example, in the Sixth Meditation, CSM 2:55).

[4] See also *Observations Upon the Opinions of Some Ancient Philosophers*, section V.1.

part moves by its own Motion: If so, then all the Actions in Nature are self-corporeal, figurative Motions. But this is to be noted, That as there is but one Matter, or there is but one Motion; and as there are several Parts of Matter, so there are several Changes of Motion: for, as Matter, of what degree soever it is, or can be, is but Matter; so Motion, although it make Infinite Changes, can be but Motion.

CHAPTER III. OF THE DEGREES OF MATTER

Though Matter can be neither more nor less than Matter; yet there may be degrees of Matter, as *more pure*, or *less pure*; and yet the purest Parts are as much material, in relation to the nature of Matter, as the grossest: Neither can there be more than two sorts of Matter, namely, that sort which is Self-moving, and that which is not Self-moving. Also, there can be but two sorts of the Self-moving Parts; as, that sort that moves intirely without Burdens, and that sort that moves with the Burdens of those Parts that are not Self-moving: So that there can be but these three sorts; Those parts that are not moving, those that move free, and those that move with those parts that are not moving of themselves: Which degrees are (in my opinion) the Rational Parts, the Sensitive Parts, and the Inanimate Parts; which three sorts of Parts are so join'd, that they are but as one Body; for, it is impossible that those three sorts of Parts should subsist single, by reason Nature is but one united material Body.

CHAPTER V. THE DIFFERENCE OF THE TWO SELF-MOVING PARTS OF MATTER

The Self-moving Parts of Nature seem to be of two sorts, or degrees; one being purer, and so more agil and free than the other; which (in my opinion) are the Rational Parts of Nature. The other sort is not so pure; and are the Architectonical Parts, which are the Labouring Parts, bearing the grosser Materials about them, which are the Inanimate Parts; and this sort (in my opinion) are the Sensitive Parts of Nature; which form, build, or compose themselves with the Inanimate Parts, into all kinds and sorts of Creatures, as Animals, Vegetables, Minerals, Elements, or what Creatures soever there are in Nature: Whereas the Rational are so pure, that they cannot be so strong Labourers, as to move with Burdens of Inanimate Parts, but move freely without Burdens: for, though the Rational and Sensitive, with the Inanimate, move together as one Body; yet the Rational and Sensitive, do not move as one Part, as the sensitive doth with the Inanimate.[5]

---

[5] See also note 23 for *Observations Upon Experimental Philosophy*.

But, pray mistake me not, when I say, the Inanimate Parts are grosser; as if I meant, they were like some densed Creature; for, those are but Effects, and not Causes: but, I mean gross, dull, heavy Parts, as, that they are not Self-moving; nor do I mean by Purity, Rarity; but Agility: for, Rare or Dense Parts, are Effects, and not Causes: And therefore, if any should ask, Whether the Rational and Sensitive Parts were Rare, or Dense; I answer, They may be Rare or Dense, according as they contract, or dilate their Parts; for there is no such thing as a Single Part in Nature: for Matter, or Body, cannot be so divided, but that it will remain Matter, which is divisible.

CHAPTER VIII. OF NATURE'S KNOWLEDG AND PERCEPTION

If Nature were not Self-knowing, Self-living, and also Perceptive, she would run into Confusion: for, there could be neither Order, nor Method, in Ignorant motion; neither would there be distinct kinds or sorts of Creatures, nor such exact and methodical Varieties as there are: for, it is impossible to make orderly and methodical Distinctions, or distinct Orders, by Chances: Wherefore, Nature being so exact (as she is) must needs be Self-knowing and Perceptive: And though all her Parts, even the Inanimate Parts, are Self-knowing, and Self-living; yet, onely her Self-moving Parts have an active Life, and a perceptive Knowledg.[6]

CHAPTER X. OF DOUBLE PERCEPTION

There is a *Double Perception* in Nature, the Rational Perception, and the Sensitive: The Rational Perception is more subtil and penetrating than the Sensitive; also, it is more generally perceptive than the Sensitive; also, it is a more agil Perception than the Sensitive: All which is occasioned not onely through the *purity* of the Rational parts, but through the *liberty* of the Rational parts; whereas the Sensitive being incumbred with the Inanimate parts, is obstructed and retarded. Yet all Perceptions, both Sensitive and Rational, are in parts; but, by reason the Rational is freer, (being not a painful Labourer) can more easily make an united Perception, than the Sensitive; which is the reason the Rational parts can make a Whole Perception of a Whole Object: Whereas the Sensitive makes but Perceptions in part, of one and the same Object.

[6] See also note 2 for *Philosophical and Physical Opinions*, and note 19 for *Worlds Olio*.

CHAPTER XII. WHETHER NATURE CAN KNOW HER SELF, OR HAVE AN ABSOLUTE POWER OF HER SELF, OR HAVE AN EXACT FIGURE

I Was of an opinion, That Nature, because Infinite, could not know her Self; because Infinite hath no limit. Also, That Nature could not have an Absolute Power over her own Parts, because she had Infinite Parts; and, that the Infiniteness did hinder the Absoluteness: But since I have consider'd, That the Infinite Parts must of necessity be Self-knowing[7]; and that those Infinite Self-knowing Parts are united in one Infinite Body, by which Nature must have both an United Knowledg, and an United Power. Also, I questioned, Whether Nature could have an Exact Figure, (but, mistake me not; for I do not mean the Figure of Matter, but a composed Figure of Parts) because Nature was composed of Infinite Variety of Figurative Parts: But considering, that those Infinite Varieties of Infinite Figurative Parts, were united into one Body; I did conclude, That she must needs have an Exact Figure,[8] though she be Infinite: As for example, This World is composed of numerous and several Figurative parts, and yet the World hath an exact Form and Frame, the same which it would have if it were Infinite. But, as for Self-knowledg, and Power, certainly God hath given them to Nature, though her Power be limited: for, she cannot move beyond her Nature; nor hath she power to make her self any otherwise than what she is, since she cannot create, or annihilate any part, or particle: nor can she make any of her Parts, Immaterial; or any Immaterial, Corporeal: Nor can she give to one part, the Nature (*viz.* the Knowledg, Life, Motion, or Perception) of another part; which is the reason one Creature cannot have the properties, or faculties of another; they may have the like, but not the same.[9]

CHAPTER XVI. OF EFFECTS, AND CAUSE

To treat of Infinite Effects, produced from an Infinite Cause, is an endless Work, and impossible to be performed, or effected; only this may be said, That the Effects, though Infinite, are so united to the material Cause, as that not any single effect can be, nor no Effect can be annihilated; by reason all Effects are in the

---

[7] Note that for Cavendish self-knowledge is not necessarily conscious knowledge that a mind has of its states. One of the reasons she holds that bodies have self-knowledge, or knowledge of their own states—whether this knowledge is conscious or not—is that she supposes that bodies must be in possession of information about themselves if they are to communicate such information to the bodies that surround them. See, for example, *Grounds of Natural Philosophy*, chapters VI and IX of the Second Part.

[8] See also *Observations Upon the Opinions of Some Ancient Philosophers*, section III.4.

[9] See also *Observations Upon Experimental Philosophy*, section XIII.

power of the Cause. But this is to be noted, That some Effects producing other Effects, are, in some sort or manner, a Cause.

CHAPTER XVII. OF INFLUENCE

An *Influence* is this; When as the Corporeal Figurative Motions, in different kinds, and sorts of Creatures, or in one and the same sorts, or kinds, move sympathetically: And though there be antipathetical Motions, as well as sympathetical;[10] yet, all the Infinite parts of Matter, are agreeable in their nature, as being all Material, and Self-moving; and by reason there is no *Vacuum,* there must of necessity be an Influence amongst all the Parts of Nature.[11]

CHAPTER XVIII. OF FORTUNE AND CHANCE

Fortune, is only various Corporeal Motions of several Creatures, design'd to one Creature, or more Creatures; either to *that* Creature, or *those* Creatures Advantage, or Disadvantage: If Advantage, Man names it *Good Fortune*; if Disadvantage, Man names it *Ill Fortune.* As for *Chance,* it is the visible Effects of some hidden Cause; and *Fortune,* a sufficient Cause to produce such Effects: for, the conjunction of sufficient Causes, doth produce such or such Effects; which Effects could not be produced, if any of those Causes were wanting: So that, *Chances* are but the Effects of *Fortune.*[12]

CHAPTER XIX. OF TIME AND ETERNITY

Time is not a Thing by it self; nor is *Time* Immaterial: for, *Time* is only the variations of Corporeal Motions; but *Eternity* depends not on Motion, but of a Being without Beginning, or Ending.

The Second Part

CHAPTER I. OF CREATURES

All *Creatures* are Composed-Figures, by the consent of Associating Parts; by which Association, they joyn into such, or such a figured Creature: And though

---

[10] See also *Philosophical and Physical Opinions*, chapters 19 and 22. Bodies sometimes work in synchrony with each other, of course, but in many cases they oppose and struggle against each other.

[11] See also *Observations Upon Experimental Philosophy*, section XV.

[12] See also Chapter XVI of the First Part, in this chapter, and the similar view in Descartes, *Passions of the Soul*, II.145, CSM 1:380; Spinoza, *Ethics*, Part I, axiom 3, p. 218; and Malebranche, *The Search After Truth*, VI.ii.3, 446–452. See also note 11 for *Philosophical and Physical Opinions*.

every Corporeal Motion, or Self-moving Part, hath its own motion; yet, by their Association, they all agree in proper actions, as actions proper to their Compositions: and, if every particular Part, hath not a perception of all the Parts of their Association; yet, every Part knows its own Work.

CHAPTER III. OF PERCEPTION OF PARTS, AND UNITED PERCEPTION

[A]ll the Parts of one and the same Creature, perceive their Adjoining Parts, as they perceive Foreign Parts; only, by their close conjunction and near relation, they unite in one and the same actions. I do not say, they always agree: for, when they move irregularly, they disagree: And some of those United Parts, will move after one manner, and some after another; but, when they move regularly, then they move to one and the same Design, or one and the same United Action. So, although a Creature is composed of several sorts of Corporeal Motions; yet, these several sorts, being properly united in one Creature, move all agreeably to the Property and Nature of the whole Creature;[13] that is, the particular Parts move according to the property of the whole Creature; because the particular Parts, by conjunction, make the Whole: So that, the several Parts make one Whole; by which, a Whole Creature hath both a general Knowledg, and a Knowledg of Parts; whereas, the Perceptions of Foreign Objects, are but in the Parts: and this is the reason why one Creature perceives not the Whole of another Creature, but only some Parts. Yet this is to be noted, That not any Part hath another Part's Nature, or Motion, nor therefore, their Knowledg, or Perception; but, by agreement, and unity of Parts, there is composed Perceptions.

CHAPTER VI. WHETHER THE MIND OF ONE CREATURE, CAN PERCEIVE THE MIND OF ANOTHER CREATURE

Some may ask the reason, *Why one Creature, as Man, cannot perceive the Thoughts of another Man, as well as he perceives his exterior Sensitive Parts?* I answer, That the Rational Parts of one Man, perceive as much of the Rational Parts of another Man, as the Sensitive Parts of that Man doth of the Sensitive Parts of the other Man; that is, as much as is presented to his Perception: for, all Creatures, and every part and particle, have those three sorts of Matter; and therefore, every part of a Creature is perceiving, and perceived. But, by reason all Creatures are composed of Parts, (*viz.* both of the Rational and Sensitive) all Perceptions are in parts, as well the Rational, as the Sensitive Perception: yet, neither the Rational, nor the Sensitive, can perceive all the Interior Parts or Corporeal Motions,

---

[13] See also note 20 for *Worlds Olio*.

unless they were presented to their perception: Neither can one Part know the Knowledg and Perception of another Part: but, what Parts of one Creature are subject to the perception of another Creature, those are perceived.

CHAPTER IX. OF INFORMATION BETWEEN SEVERAL CREATURES

No question but there is *Information* between all Creatures:[14] but, several sorts of Creatures, having several sorts of Informations, it is impossible for any particular sort to know, or have perceptions of the Infinite, or Numberless Informations, between the Infinite and Numberless Parts, or Creatures of Nature: Nay, there are so many several Informations amongst one sort (as of Mankind) that it is impossible for one Man to perceive them all; no, nor can one Man generally perceive the particular Informations that are between the particular Parts of his Sensitive Body; or between the particular Informations of his Rational Body; or between the particular Rational and Sensitive Parts: much less can Man perceive, or know the several Informations of other Creatures.

The Third Part

CHAPTER I. OF PRODUCTIONS IN GENERAL

The Self-moving Parts, or Corporeal Motions, are the Producers of all Composed Figures, such as we name *Creatures*: for, though all Matter hath Figure, by being Matter; for it were non-sense to say, *Figureless Matter*; since the most pure Parts of Matter, have Figure, as well as the grossest; the rarest, as well as the densed: But, such Composed Figures which we name *Creatures*, are produced by particular Associations of Self-moving Parts, into particular kinds, and sorts; and particular Creatures in every kind, or sort. The particular kinds, that are subject to Human Perceptions, are those we name Animals, Vegetables, Minerals, and Elements; of which kinds, there are numerous sorts; and of every sort, infinite particulars: And though there be Infinite Varieties in Nature, made by the Corporeal Motions, or Self-moving Parts, which might cause a Confusion: Yet, considering Nature is intire in her self, as being only Material, and as being but one United Body; also, poysing all her Actions by Opposites; 'tis impossible to be any ways in Extreams, or to have a Confusion.

---

[14] See also note 7 in this chapter, and note 19 for *Worlds Olio.*

CHAPTER VI. OF PRODUCTIONS IN GENERAL

All Creatures are Produced, and Producers; and all these Productions partake more or less of the Producers; and are necessitated so to do, because there cannot be any thing New in Nature:[15] for, whatsoever is produced, is of the same Matter; nay, every particular Creature hath its particular Parts: for, not any one Creature can be produced of any other Parts than what produced it; neither can the same Producer produce one and the same double . . . for, though the same Producers may produce the like, yet not the same: for, every thing produced, hath its own Corporeal Figurative Motions.

The Fifth Part

CHAPTER V. OF THE SEVERAL PERCEPTIONS AMONGST THE SEVERAL PARTS OF MAN

There being infinite several Corporeal Figurative Motions, or Actions of Nature, there must of necessity be infinite several Self-knowledges and Perceptions: but I shall only, in this Part of my Book, treat of the Perception proper to Mankind: And first, of the several and different Perceptions, proper for the several and different Parts: for, though every Part and Particle of a Man's Body, is perceptive; yet, every particular Part of a Man, is not generally perceived; for, the Interior Parts do not generally perceive the Exterior; nor the Exterior, generally or perfectly, the Interior; and yet, both Interior and Exterior Corporeal Motions, agree as one Society; for, every Part, or Corporeal Motion, knows its own Office; like as Officers in a Common-wealth, although they may not be acquainted with each other, yet they know their Employments: So every particular Man in a Common-wealth, knows his own Employment, although he knows not every Man in the Common-wealth. The same do the Parts of a Man's Body, and Mind.

CHAPTER IX. OF THE EXTERIOR SENSITIVE ORGANS OF HUMAN CREATURES

As for the manner, or ways, of all the several sorts, and particular perceptions, made by the different composed parts of Human Creatures; it is impossible, for a Human Creature, to know any otherwise, but in part: for, being composed of parts, into Parties, he can have but a parted knowledg, and a parted perception of himself: for, every different composed part of his Body, have different sorts of

---

[15] See also *Observations Upon Experimental Philosophy*, section XXXV; and *Grounds of Natural Philosophy*, chapter VI of the Third Part.

Self-knowledg, as also, different sorts of Perceptions; but yet, the manner and way of some Human Perceptions, may probably be imagined, especially those of the exterior parts, Man names the *Sensitive Organs*; which Parts (in my opinion) have their perceptive actions, after the manner of patterning, or picturing the exterior Form, or Frame, of Foreign Objects: As for example, The present Object is a Candle; the Human Organ of Sight pictures the Flame, Light, Week, or Snuff, the Tallow, the Colour, and the dimension of the Candle; the Ear patterns out the sparkling noise; the Nose patterns out the scent of the Candle; and the Tongue may pattern out the tast of the Candle: but, so soon as the Object is removed, the figure of the Candle is altered into the present Object, or as much of one present Object, as is subject to Human Perception. Thus the several parts or properties, may be patterned out by the several Organs. Also, every altered action, of one and the same Organ, are altered Perceptions; so as there may be numbers of several pictures or Patterns made by the Sensitive Actions of one Organ; I will not say, by one act; yet there may be much variety in one action. But this is to be noted, That the Object is not the *cause* of Perception, but is only the *occasion*: for, the Sensitive Organs can make such like figurative actions, were there no Object present; which proves, that the Object is not the Cause of the Perception.[16] Also, when as the Sensitive parts of the Sensitive Organs, are Irregular, they will make false perceptions of present Objects; wherefore the Object is not the Cause. But one thing I desire, not to be mistaken in; for I do not say, that all the parts belonging to any of the particular Organs, move only in one sort or kind of perception; but I say, Some of the parts of the Organ, move to such, or such perception: for, all the actions of the Ears, are not only hearing; and all the actions of the Eye, seeing; and all the actions of the Nose, smelling; and all the actions of the Mouth, tasting; but, they have other sorts of actions: yet, all the sorts of every Organ, are according to the property of their figurative Composition.

CHAPTER X. OF THE RATIONAL PARTS OF THE HUMAN ORGANS

As for the Rational parts of the Human Organs, they move according to the Sensitive parts, which is, to move according to the Figures of Foreign Objects; and their actions are (if Regular) at the same point of time, with the Sensitive: but, though their Actions are alike, yet there is a difference in their Degree; for, the figure of an Object in the Mind, is far more pure than the figure in the Sense. But, to prove that the Rational (if Regular) moves with the Sense, is, That all the

---

[16] See also note 21 for *Philosophical and Physical Opinions*.

several Sensitive perceptions of the Sensitive Organs, (as all the several Sights, Sounds, Scents, Tasts, and Touches) are thoughts of the same.[17]

CHAPTER XV. OF THE AGREEING, OR DISAGREEING, OF THE SENSITIVE AND RATIONAL PARTS OF HUMAN CREATURES

There is, for the most part, a general agreement between the Rational and Sensitive Parts of Human Creatures; not only in their particular, but general actions; only the Rational are the Designing-parts; and the Sensitive, the Labouring parts: As for proof, The Mind designs to go to such, or such Foreign Parts, or Places; upon which design the Sensitive Parts will labour to execute the Mind's intention, so as the whole Sensitive Body labours to go to the designed place, without the Mind's further Concern: for, the Mind takes no notice of every action of the Sensitive parts; neither of those of the Eyes, Ears; or of the Leggs, or feet; nor of their perceptions: for, many times, the Mind is busied in some Conception, Imagination, Fancy, or the like; and yet the Sensitive Parts execute the Mind's Design exactly.[18]

The Sixth Part

CHAPTER I. OF THE MOTIONS OF SOME PARTS OF THE MIND; AND OF FORREIN OBJECTS

Notions, Imaginations, Conceptions, and the like, are such Actions of the Mind, as concern not Forrein Objects: and some Notions, Imaginations, or Conceptions of one man, may be like to another man, or many men. Also, the Mind of one man may move in the like Figurative Actions, as the Sensitive Actions of other sorts of Creatures; and that, Man names *Understanding*: and if those Conceptions be afterwards produced, Man names them *Prudence,* or *Foresight*; but if those Parts move in such Inventions as are capable to be put into Arts, Man names that, *Ingenuity*: but, if not capable to be put into the practice of Arts, Man names it, *Sciences*: if those Motions be so subtile, that the Sensitive cannot imitate them, Man names them, *Fancies*:[19] but, when those Rational Parts move

[17] See also Hume's doctrine that all ideas are copies of prior impressions, in *An Enquiry Concerning Human Understanding*, section two, 96–100. Unlike Hume, however, Cavendish does seem to allow that there are some instances in which ideas copy information that the senses do not. See, for example, *Observations Upon Experimental Philosophy*, section XXV.

[18] See also *Worlds Olio*, "Epistle," and the corresponding note 4. Cavendish appears to hold that instances of embodied intelligence abound.

[19] See also *Worlds Olio*, "Allegory 20."

promiscuously, as partly after their own inventions, and partly after the manner of Forrein or outward Objects; Man names them, Conjectures, or Probabilities.

CHAPTER IV. OF THE REPETITIONS OF THE SENSITIVE AND RATIONAL ACTIONS

[T]he Rational can make as perfect Copies in the absence, as in the presence of the Object; which is the cause that the Mind is as much delighted, or grieved, in the absence of an Object, as with the presence: As for example, A Man is as much grieved when he knows his Friend is wounded, or dead, as if he had seen his Wounds, or had seen him dead: for, the Picture of the dead Friend, is in the mind of the living Friend; and if the dead Friend was before his Eyes, he could but have his Picture in his mind; which is the same for an absent Friend alive; only, as I said, there is wanting the Sensitive Perception of the absent Object: And certainly, the Parts of the Mind have greater advantage than the Sensitive Parts; for, the Mind can enjoy that which is not subject to the Sense; as those things Man names, *Castles in the Air*, or *Poetical Fancies*; which is the reason Man can enjoy Worlds of its own making, without the assistance of the Sensitive Parts; and can govern and command those Worlds; as also, dissolve and compose several Worlds, as he pleases: but certainly, as the pleasures of the Rational Parts are beyond those of the Sensitive, so are their Troubles.[20]

CHAPTER V. OF THE PASSIONATE LOVE, AND SYMPATHETICAL ENDEAVOURS, AMONGST THE ASSOCIATE PARTS OF A HUMAN CREATURE

In every Regular Human Society, there is a Passionate Love amongst the Associated Parts, like fellow-Students of one Colledg, or fellow-Servants in one House, or Brethren in one Family, or Subjects in one Nation, or Communicants in one Church: So the Self-moving Parts of a Human Creature, being associated, love one another, and therefore do endeavour to keep their Society from dissolving. But perceiving, by the example of the lives of the same sort of Creatures, that the property of their Nature is such, that they must dissolve in a short time, this causes these Human sorts of Creatures, (being very ingenuous) to endeavour an after-life: but, perceiving again, that their after-life cannot be

---

[20] Here Cavendish is expressing a view that we see elsewhere in her corpus—that vivid bouts of imagination, in which we picture scenes in our thought, can be just as satisfying, and in some cases even more satisfying, than our experience of the external world. See for example *Worlds Olio*, "Allegory 20"; *Philosophical and Physical Opinions*, chapter 152; and in "Fiction," *Blazing World*, "To all Noble and Worthy Ladies" and "The Epilogue to the Reader."

the same as the present life is, they endeavour (since they cannot keep their own Society from dissolving) that their Society may remain in remembrance amongst the particular and general Societies of the same sort of Creatures, which we name *Mankind*: And this Design causes all the Sensitive and Rational Parts, in one Society, to be industrious, to leave some Mark for a lasting Remembrance, amongst their fellow-Creatures: which general remembrance, Man calls *Fame*; for which *Fame*, the Rational Parts are industrious to design the manner and way, and the Sensitive Parts are industrious to put those Designs in execution; as, their Inventions, into Arts or Sciences; or to cause their Heroick or Prudent, Generous or Pious Actions; their Learning, or witty Fancies, or subtile Conceptions, or their industrious Observations, or their ingenious Inventions, to be set in Print; or their Exterior Effigies to be cast, cut, or engraven in Brass, or Stone, or to be painted; or they endeavour to build Houses, or cut Rivers, to bear their Names; and millions of other Marks, for remembrance, they are industrious to leave to the perception of after-Ages: And many men are so desirous of this after-life, that they would willingly quit their present life, by reason of its shortness, to gain this after-life, because of the probability of a long continuance; and not only to live so in many several Ages, but in many several Nations. And amongst the number of those that prefer a long after-life, before a short present life, I am one. But, some men dispute against these Desires, saying, That *it doth a man no good to be remembred when he is dead.* I answer: It is very pleasing, whilst as man lives, to have in his Mind, or in his Sense, the Effigies of the Person, and of the good Actions of his Friend, although he cannot have his present company.[21] Also, it is very pleasant to any body to believe, that the Effigies either of his own Person, or Actions, or both, are in the Mind of his Friend, when he is absent from him; and, in this case, Absence and Death are much alike. But, in short, God lives no other ways amongst his Creatures, but in their Rational Thoughts, and Sensitive Worship.

CHAPTER XII. OF HUMAN PERCEPTION, OR DEFECTS OF A HUMAN CREATURE

Nature poysing her Actions by Opposites, there must needs be Irregularities, as well as Regularities; which is the cause that seldom any Creature is so exact,

[21] Note that given her animistic view of matter (for example, in *Grounds of Natural Philosophy*, Chapter XV of the Fifth Part), an idea of a creature that survives in our thought is not just a static image or picture, but is an active being that in the course of an episode of imagination will sometimes take on a life of its own; it is a sort of miniature of the version of itself that existed in real life. This miniature is still dissimilar from a living human being, but Cavendish is supposing that it is the most that can survive of a material individual when it perishes. She also supposes that we have an investment in how things transpire for that version of ourselves after we are gone.

but there is some Exception. But, when the Sensitive and Rational Corporeal Motions are regular, and move sympathetically, then the Body is healthful and strong, the Mind in peace and quiet, understands well, and is judicious: and, in short, there are perfect Perceptions, proper Digestions, easie Respirations, regular Passions, temperate Appetites. But when the Rational Corporeal Motions are curious in their change of Actions, there are subtile Conceptions, and elevated Fancies: and when the Sensitive Corporeal Motions move with curiosity, (as I may say) then there are perfect Senses, exact Proportions, equal Temperaments; and that, Man calls *Beauty*.

The Seventh Part

CHAPTER IV. OF THE ACTIONS OF DREAMS

When the Figures of those Friends and Acquaintants that have been dead a long time, are made in our Sleep, we never, or seldom question the truth of their being alive, though we often question them how they came to be alive: And the reason that we make no doubt of their being alive, is, That those Corporeal Motions of Sleep, make the same pattern of that Object in Sleep, as when that Object was present, and patterned awake; so as the Picture in Sleep seems to be the Original awake: and until such times that the Corporeal Motions alter their Sleeping-Actions to Waking-Actions, the truth is not known. Though Sleeping and Dreaming, is somewhat after the manner of Forgetfulness and Remembrance; yet, perfect Dreams are as perceptive as Waking-patterns of present Objects; which proves, That both the Sensitive and Rational Motions, have Sleeping Actions; but both the Sensitive and Rational Corporeal Actions in Sleep, moving partly by rote, and partly voluntarily, or by invention, make Walking-Woods, or Wooden Men; or make Warrs and Battels, where some Figures of Men are kill'd, or wounded, others have victory: They also make Thieves, Murderers, falling Houses, great Fires, Floods, Tempests, high Mountains, great Precipices; and sometimes pleasant Dreams of Lovers, Marriage, Dancing, Banquetting, and the like: And the Passions in Dreams are as real, as in waking actions.

CHAPTER XII. OF FOREKNOWLEDG

I have had some Disputes amongst the Parts of my Mind, *Whether Nature hath Foreknowledg?* The Opinion of the Minor Parts was, That Nature had Foreknowledg, by reason all that was Material, was part of her self; and those Self-parts having Self-motion, she might foreknow what she would act, and so what they should know. The Opinion of the Major Parts was, That by reason every Part had Self-motion, and natural Free-will, Nature could not foreknow how they would move, although she might know how they have moved, or how they do move.[22]

The Eighth Part

CHAPTER I. OF THE IRREGULARITY OF NATURE'S PARTS

Some may make this Question, that, *If Nature were Self-moving, and had Free-will, it is probable that she would never move her Parts so irregularly, as to put her self to pain.* I answer, first, That Nature's Parts move themselves, and are not moved by any Agent. Secondly, Though Nature's Parts are Self-moving, and Self-knowing, yet they have not an infinite or uncontrolable Power; for, several Parts, and Parties, oppose, and oft-times obstruct each other;[23] so that many times they are forced to move, and they may not when they would. Thirdly, Some Parts may occasion other Parts to be irregular, and keep themselves in a regular posture. Lastly, Nature's Fundamental actions are so poysed, that Irregular actions are as natural as Regular.

The Thirteenth Part

CHAPTER XII. OF ARTIFICIAL THINGS

Artificial Things, are Natural Corporeal Figurative Motions: for, all Artificial Things are produced by several produced Creatures. But, the differences of those Productions we name *Natural* and *Artificial*, are, That the Natural are produced from the Producer's own Parts; whereas the Artificial are produced by composing, or joyning, or mixing several Forrein Parts; and not any of the particular Parts of their composed Society: for, Artificial things are not produced as Animals, Vegetables, Minerals, or the like: but only, they are certain several Mixtures of some of the divided, or dead Parts, as I may say, of Minerals, Vegetables, Elements, and the like.[24] But this is to be noted, That all, or at least, most, are but Copied, and not Originals.

But some may ask, *Whether Artificial Productions have Sense, Reason, and Perception?* I answer: That if all the Rational and Sensitive Parts of Nature, are

---

[22] Compare to chapter VI of the First Part of *Appendix to Grounds of Natural Philosophy*, where Cavendish speaks to the question of God's foreknowledge, as opposed to the foreknowledge of Nature. See also note 11 for *Philosophical and Philosophical Opinions*.

[23] See also note 7 for *Philosophical and Physical Opinions*.

[24] See also note 19 for *Worlds Olio*.

Perceptive, and that no part is without Perception; then all Artificial Productions are Perceptive.

CHAPTER XIII. OF SEVERAL KINDS AND SORTS OF SPECIES

According to my Opinion, though the *Species* of this World, and all the several Kinds and Sorts of *Species* in this World, do always continue; yet, the particular Parts of one and the same Kind or sort of *Species*, do not continue: for, the particular Parts are perpetually altering their Figurative Actions. But, by reason some Parts compose or unite, as well as some Parts dissolve or disunite; all kinds and sorts of *Species*, will, and must last so long as Nature lasts. But mistake me not, I mean such kinds and sorts of *Species* as we name *Natural*, that is, the Fundamental *Species*; but not such *Species*, as we name *Artificial*.

CHAPTER XIV. OF DIFFERENT WORLDS

Tis probable if Nature be Infinite, there are several kinds and sorts of those Species, Societies, or Creatures, we name *Worlds*; which may be so different from the Frame, Form, Species, and Properties of this World, and the Creatures of this World, as not to be any ways like this World, or the Creatures in this World. But mistake me not, I do not mean, not like this World, as it is Material and Self-moving; but, not of the same Species, or Properties: as for example, That they have not such kind of Creatures, or their Properties, as Light, Darkness, Heat, Cold, Dry, Wet, Soft, Hard, Leight, Heavy, and the like.

But some may say, *That is impossible: for, there can be no World, but must be either Light or Dark, Hot or Cold, Dry or Wet, Soft or Hard, Heavy or Leight; and the like.* I answer, That though those Effects may be generally beneficial to most of the Creatures in this World; yet, not to all the Parts of the World: as for example, Though Light is beneficial to the Eyes of Animals; yet, to no other Part of an Animal Creature. And, though Darkness is obstructive to the Eyes of Animals; yet, to no other Parts of an Animal Creature. Also, Air is no proper Object for any of the Human Parts, but Respiration. So Cold and Heat, are no proper Objects for any Part of a Human Creature, but only the Pores, which are the Organs of Touch. The like may be said for Hard and Soft, Dry and Wet: and since they are not Fundamental actions of Nature, but Particular, I cannot believe, but that there may be such Worlds, or Creatures, as may have no use of Light, Darkness, and the like: for, if some Parts of this World need them not, nor are any ways beneficial to them, (as I formerly proved) surely a whole World may be, and subsist without them. . . . [A]nd certainly, there may be, in Nature, other Worlds as full of varieties, and as glorious and beautiful as this World; and are, and may be more glorious or beautiful, as also, more full of variety than this World, and yet be quite different in all kinds and sorts, from this World: for, this is to be noted, That the different kinds and sorts of Species, or Creatures, do not make Particulars more or less perfect, but according to their kind. And one thing I desire, That my *Readers* would not mistake my meaning, when I say, *The Parts dissolve*: for, I do not mean, that Matter dissolves; but, that their particular Societies dissolve.

Appendix to Grounds of Natural Philosophy

THE FIRST PART

Chapter II. Of an Immaterial

I cannot conceive how an Immaterial can be in Nature: for, first, An Immaterial cannot, in my opinion, be naturally created; nor can I conceive how an Immaterial can produce particular Immaterial Souls, Spirits, or the like. Wherefore, an Immaterial, in my opinion, must be some uncreated Being; which can be no other than GOD alone. Wherefore, Created Spirits, and Spiritual Souls, are some other thing than an Immaterial: for surely, if there were any other Immaterial Beings, besides the Omnipotent God, those would be so near the Divine Essence of God, as to be petty gods; and numerous petty gods, would, almost, make the Power of an Infinite God. But, God is Omnipotent, and only God.[25]

Chapter III. Whether an Immaterial be Perceivable

Whatsoever is Corporeal, is Perceivable; that is, may be perceived in some manner or other, by reason it hath a Corporeal Being: but, what Being an Immaterial hath, no Corporeal can perceive. Wherefore, no Part in Nature can perceive an Immaterial, because it is impossible to have a perception of that, which is not to be perceived, as not being an Object fit and proper for Corporeal Perception. In truth, an Immaterial is no Object, because no Body.

But some may say, that, *A Corporeal may have a Conception, although not a Perception, of an Immaterial*. I answer, That, surely, there is an innate Notion of God, in all the Parts of Nature; but not a perfect knowledg: for if there was, there would not be so many several Opinions, and Religions, amongst one Kind, or

---

[25] Note that in most of the other passages in which Cavendish speaks of finite immaterial souls, she says that we have no idea of them and cannot conceive of them, but she does not deny that they exist (for example in *Philosophical Letters*, letter XXXIII of section 2). Here she goes further and posits that the only immaterial entity of any kind is God.

rather, sort of Creatures, as Mankind, as there are; insomuch, that there are but few of one and the same Opinion, or Religion: but yet, that Innate Notion of God, being in all the Parts of Nature, God is infinitely and eternally worshipped and adored, although after several manners and ways; yet, all manners and ways, are joyned in one Worship, because the Parts of Nature are joyned into one Body.

Chapter IV. Of the Differences between God, and Nature

GOD is an Eternal Creator; Nature, his Eternal Creature. GOD, an Eternal Master: Nature, God's Eternal Servant. GOD is an Infinite and Eternal Immaterial Being:[26] Nature, an Infinite Corporeal Being. GOD is Immovable, and Immutable: Nature, Moving, and Mutable. GOD is Eternal, Indivisible, and of an Incompoundable Being: Nature, Eternally Divisible and Compoundable. GOD, Eternally Perfect: Nature, Eternally Imperfect. GOD, Eternally Inalterable: Nature Eternally Alterable. GOD, without Error: Nature, full of Irregularities.[27] GOD knows exactly, or perfectly, Nature: Nature doth not perfectly know. GOD is Infinitely and Eternally worshipped: Nature is the Eternal and Infinite Worshipper.

Chapter V. All the Parts of Nature worship God

All Creatures (as I have said) have an Innate Notion of GOD; and as they have a Notion of God, so they have a Notion to worship GOD: but, by reason Nature is composed of Parts; so is the Infinite Worship to God: and, as several Parts are dividing and uniting after several kinds, sorts, manners and ways; so is their Worship to GOD: but, the several manners and ways of Worship, make not the Worship to GOD less: for certainly, all Creatures Worship and Adore GOD; as we may perceive by the Holy Scripture, where it says, *Let the Heavens, Earth, and all that therein is, praise God.* But 'tis probable, that some of the Parts being Creatures of Nature, may have a fuller Notion of GOD than others; which may cause some Creatures to be more Pious and Devout, than others: but, the Irregularity of Nature, is the cause of Sin.

Chapter VI. Whether God's Decrees are limited

In my opinion, though God is Inalterable, yet no ways bounded or limited: for, though GOD's Decrees are fixt, yet, they are not bound: but, as GOD hath an Infinite Knowledg, He hath also an Infinite Fore-knowledg; and so, fore-knows Nature's Actions, and what He will please to decree Nature to do: so that, GOD knows what Nature can act, and what she will act; as also, what He will decree: and this is the cause, that some of the Creature's or Parts of Nature,

---

[26] See also notes 1 and 4 for *Philosophical Letters.*
[27] See also note 59 for *Philosophical Letters.*

especially Man, do believe *Predestination.* But surely, GOD hath an Omnipotent Divine Power, which is no ways limited: for GOD, being above the nature of Nature, cannot have the Actions of Nature, because GOD cannot make Himself no GOD; neither can He make Himself more than what he is, He being the All-powerful, Omnipotent, Infinite, and Everlasting Being.

Chapter VII. Of God's Decrees concerning the particular Parts of Nature
Though Nature's Parts have Free-will, of Self-motion; yet, they have not Free-will to oppose *GOD's Decrees*: for, if some Parts cannot oppose other Parts, being over-power'd, it is probable, that the Parts of Nature cannot oppose the All-powerful Decrees of *GOD.*[28] But, if it please the All-powerful *GOD* to permit the Parts of Nature to act as they please, according to their own natural Will; and, upon condition, if they act so, they shall have such Rewards as Nature may be capable to receive; or such Punishments as Nature is capable of; then the Omnipotent *God* doth not predestinate those Rewards, or Punishments, any otherwise than the Parts of Nature do cause by their own Actions. Thus all Corporeal Actions, belong to Corporeal Parts; but, the Rewards and Punishments, to *GOD* alone: but, what those Punishments and Blessings are, no particular Creature is capable to know: for, though a particular Creature knows there is a *GOD*; yet, not what *GOD* is: so, although particular Creatures know there are Rewards and Punishments; yet, not what those Rewards and Punishments are. But mistake me not; for I mean the general Rewards and Punishments to all Creatures: but 'tis probable, that *GOD* might decree Nature, and her Parts, to make other sorts of Worlds, besides this World; of which Worlds, this may be as ignorant, as a particular Human Creature is of *GOD.* And therefore, it is not probable (since we cannot possibly know all the Parts of Nature, of which we are parts) that we should know the Decrees of *GOD*, or the manners and ways of Worship, amongst all kinds and sorts of Creatures.

Chapter XI. Sins and Punishments, are Material
As all *Sins* are *Material*, so are *Punishments*: for, Material Creatures, cannot have Immaterial Sins; nor can Material Creatures be capable of Immaterial Punishments; which may be proved out of the Sacred Scripture: for, all the Punishments that are declared to be in Hell, are Material Tortures: nay, Hell it self is described to be Material; and not only Hell, but Heaven, is described to be Material.[29] But, whether Angels, and Devils, are Material, that is not declared: for, though they are named Spirits, yet we know not whether those Spirits be Immaterial. But, considering that Hell and Heaven is described to be

---

[28] See also note 11 for *Philosophical and Physical Opinions.*
[29] See also note 43 for *Philosophical Letters.*

Material, it is probable, Spirits are also Material: nay, our blessed Saviour Christ, who is in Heaven, with God the Father, hath a Material Body; and in that Body will come attended by all the Hosts of Heaven, to judg the quick and the dead; which quick and dead, are the Material Parts of Nature: which could not be actually judged and punished, but by a Material Body, as Christ hath. But, pray mistake me not; I say, They could not be actually judged and punished; that is, not according to Nature, as Material Actions: for, I do not mean here, Divine and Immaterial Decrees. But Christ, being partly Divine, and partly Natural; may be both a Divine and Natural Judg.

Chapter XII. Of Human Conscience

[A]s for Conscience, and holy Notions, they being Natural, cannot be altered by force, without a Free-will: so that the several Societies, or Communicants, commit an Error, if not a Sin, to endeavour to compel their Brethren to any particular Opinion: and, to prove it is an Error, or Sin, the more earnest the *Compellers* are, the more do the *Compelled* resist; which hath been the cause of many Martyrs. But surely, all Christians should follow the Example of Christ, who was like a meek Lamb, not a raging Lyon: neither did Christ command his Apostles to Persecute; but, to suffer Persecution patiently. Wherefore, *Liberty of Conscience* may be allowed, conditionally, it be no ways a prejudice to the Peaceable Government of the State or Kingdom.[30]

THE THIRD PART

Chapter VIII. Whether it is not Irregular, for one Creature to feed on another

The Minor Part's Opinion, was, That the Milk of Animals, and the Fruits of Vegetables, and the Herbs of the Earth, had as much Life as their Producers.

The Major Part's Opinion, was, That though they had as much Life as their Producers; yet, it was natural for such off-springs to change and alter their Lives, by being united to other sorts of Creatures: as for example, An Animal eats Fruit and Herbs; and those Fruits and Herbs convert themselves into the nature of those Animals that feed of them. The same is of Milk, Eggs, and the like; out of which, a condition of Life is endeavoured for: and, for proof, such sorts of Creatures account an Animal Life the best; and therefore, all such superfluous Parts of Creatures, endeavour to unite into an Animal Society; as we

---

[30] Cavendish does not offer a full-fledged political philosophy, but she does speak in favor of the relative stability of monarchical forms of government (for example in *The She-Anchoret*, in "Fiction," the responses both to "The Third sort that visited her, . . . *Moral Philosophers*" and "The Eighth Sort of Visiters . . . States-men"). She also addresses other factors that she thinks would help to keep the peace—here, the latitude that comes with allowing subjects to believe and worship as they will.

may perceive, that Fruits and Herbs, are apt to turn into Worms, and Flies; and some Parts of Milk, as Cheese, will turn into Maggots; so that when Animals feed of such Meats, they occasion those Parts they feed on, to a more easie Transformation; and not only such Creatures, but Humans also, desire a better Change: for, what Human would not be a glorious Sun, or Starr?[31]

After which Discourse, all the Parts of my Mind agreed unanimously, That Animals, and so Human Creatures, might feed on such sorts of Food, as afore-said; but not on such Food as is an united Society: for, the Root and Foundation of any kind and sort of Creature, ought not to be destroyed.[32]

[31] See also *Poems and Fancies*, "A Dialogue Between an Oake, and a Man cutting him downe."
[32] Cavendish was not a vegetarian, but she does frequently speak against the ill-treatment of non-human animals for sport. See for example *Poems and Fancies*, "A Dialogue betwixt Man, and Nature."

CHAPTER 6

Poems and Fancies

A World made by Atomes

Small *Atomes* of themselves a *World* may make,
As being subtle, and of every shape:
And as they dance about, fit places finde,
Such *Formes* as best agree, make every kinde.
For when we build a house of Bricke, and Stone,
We lay them even, every one by one:
And when we finde a gap that's big, or small,
We seeke out Stones, to fit that place withall.
For when not fit, too big, or little be,
They fall away, and cannot stay we see.
So *Atomes*, as they dance, finde places fit,
They there remaine, lye close, and fast will sticke.
Those that unfit, the rest that rove about,
Do never leave, untill they thrust them out.
Thus by their severall *Motions*, and their *Formes*,
As severall work-men serve each others turnes.
And thus, by chance, may a New *World* create:
Or else predestinated to worke my *Fate*.[1]

---

[1] Note that this is a very early view in the work of Cavendish. *Poems and Fancies* appeared in 1653, and by 1655, she embraced the view that bodies are inherently divisible, and she held to that view throughout the rest of her corpus. See, for example, *Philosophical Letters*, letter XXI of section two, and "A Treatise Condemining of Atoms," in *Philosophical and Physical Opinions*.

The weight of Atomes

If *Atomes* are as small, as small can bee,
They must in *quantity* of *Matter* all agree:
And if consisting *Matter* of the same (be right,)
Then every *Atome* must weigh just alike.
Thus *Quantity, Quality* and *Weight,* all
Together meets in every *Atome* small.

The bignesse of Atomes

When I say *Atomes* small, as small can bee;
I mean *Quantity, quality*, and *Weight* agree
Not in the *Figure*, for some may shew
Much bigger, and some lesser: so
Take *Water* fluid, and *Ice* thats firme,
Though the *Weight* be just, the *Bulke* is not the same.
So *Atomes* are some soft, others more knit,
According as each *Atome's Figured*;
Round and *Long Atomes* hollow are, more slacke
Then *Flat,* or *Sharpe*, for they are more compact:
And being hollow they are spread more thin,
Then other *Atomes* which are close within:
And *Atomes* which are thin more tender far,
For those that are more close, they harder are.

The joyning of severall Figur'd Atomes make other Figures

Severall *Figur'd Atomes* well agreeing,
When joyn'd, do give another *Figure* being.
For as those *Figures* joyned, severall waies,
The *Fabrick* of each severall *Creature* raise.

All things are govern'd by Atomes

Thus *Life* and *Death*, and *young* and *old*,
Are, as the severall *Atomes* hold.

So *Wit*, and *Understanding* in the *Braine*,
Are as the severall *Atomes* reigne:
And *Dispositions* good, or ill,
Are as the severall *Atomes* still.
And every *Passion* which doth rise,
Is as the severall *Atomes* lies.
Thus *Sicknesse, Health*, and *Peace*, and *War*;
Are alwaies as the severall *Atomes* are.

Of Vacuum

And though that *Vapour* fills those places small,
We cannot thinke, but first were empty all:
For were they all first full, they could not make
Roome for succession, their places for to take.
But as those *Atomes* passe, and repasse through,
Yet still in empty places must they go.[2]

Of many Worlds in this World

Just like unto a Nest of Boxes round,
Degrees of sizes within each Boxe are found.
So in this *World*, may many *Worlds* more be,[3]
Thinner, and lesse, and lesse still by degree;
Although they are not subject to our *Sense*,
A *World* may be no bigger then *two-pence*.
Nature is curious, and such *worke* may make,
That our dull *Sense* can never finde, but escape.
For *Creatures*, small as *Atomes*, may be there,
If every *Atome* a *Creatures Figure* beare.
If four *Atomes* a *World* can make, then see,
What severall *Worlds* might in an *Eare-ring* bee.
For *Millions* of these *Atomes* may bee in
The *Head* of one *small*, little, *single Pin*.
And if thus *small*, then *Ladies* well may weare
A *World* of *Worlds* as *Pendents* in each *Eare*.

---

[2] See the contrasting position that Cavendish defends in her later works, for example in *Observations Upon Experimental Philosophy*, section XIX. See also note 20 for *Worlds Olio*.

[3] See also *Worlds Olio*, "Of going round the World."

To Morall Philosophers

Morall Philosophy is a *severe Schoole*, for there is no *Arithmetitian* so exact in his Accounts, or doth *Divide* and *Substract* his *Numbers* more subtlely, then they the *Passions*; & as *Arithmetick* can multiply *Numbers* above all use, so *Passions* may be divided beyond all *Practice*. But *Moralists* live the happiest lives of Man-kind, because most contented, for they do not onely subdue the *Passions*, but can make the best use of them, to the Tranquility of the mind: As *Feare* to make them *Circumspect, Hate* to *Evill, Desire* to *Good, Love* to *Vertue, Hope* makes *Industry Jealous* of *Indiscretions, Angry* at *Follies*, and so the like of all the rest. For they do not only subdue the feircest of them, making them Slaves to execute several works, in several places. But those *Passions* that are *mild*, & of *gentle Nature*, they make perfect *Friend-ship* with: for the *Passions* are like Privie *Counsellors*, where some Counsell for *Peace*, others for *Warre*, and some being brib'd with the *World*, and *Appetite*, perswade to mutiny, which uses a *Rebellion*. But *Moralists* are like powerfull *Monarchs*, which can make their *Passions* obedient at their pleasure, condemning them at the Bar of *Justice*, cutting of their heads with the sword of *Reason*; or, like skilfull *Musitians*, making the *Passions Musicall Instruments*, which they can tune so exactly, and play so well, and sweetly, as every severall *Note* shall strike the *Eares* of the Soule with delight: and when they play Concords, the Mind dances in *Measure*, the *Sarabrand of Tranquillity*. Whereas when they are out of Tune, they do not only sound *harsh* and *unpleasant*, but when the *Notes disagreeing*, the *Mind* takes *wrong Steps*, and keeps *false time*, and the *Soule* is disquieted with the noise. But there is no *Humour*, or *Passion* so troublesome as *Desire*, because it yeilds no *sound satisfaction*; for all it is mixt most commonly with *pleasing hopes*; but *hope* is a greater pleasure then *Injoyment*, just as *Eating* is a greater pleasure to the *Hungry*, then when the *Stomacke* is fully satisfied.[4] Yet *Desire*, and *Curiosity* make a *Man* to be above other *Creatures*: for by desiring Knowledge, *Man* is as much above a *Beast*, as *want of perfect Knowledge* makes him lesse then *God*; and *Man*, as he hath a *transcending Soule* to out-live the *World* to all Eternity; so he hath a *transcending desire* to live in the Worlds *Memory*, . . . that he might not dye like a *Beast*, and be forgotten;[5] but that his *Works* may beget

[4] See also *Worlds Olio*, "Of a Solitary Life" and "Of the Vastness of Desires."
[5] See also *Grounds of Natural Philosophy*, chapter V of the Sixth Part.

another *Soule*, though of shorter life, which is *Fame*; and *Fame* is like a *Soule*, an *Incorporeall Thing*.

A Dialogue betwixt Man, and Nature

Man
Tis strange,
How we do change.
First to live, and then to dye,
Is a great misery.
To give us sense, great paines to feele,
To make our lives to be *Deaths wheele*;
To give us *Sense*, and *Reason* too,
Yet know not what we're made to do.
Whether to *Atomes* turne, or *Heaven* up flye,
Or into new *Formes* change, and never dye.
Or else to *Matter Prime* to fall againe,
From thence to take new *Formes*, and so remaine.
Nature gives no such *Knowledge* to *Man-kind*,
But *strong Desires* to torment the *Mind*:
And *Senses*, which like *Hounds* do run about,
Yet never can the *perfect Truth* find out.
O *Nature! Nature!* cruell to *Man-kind*,
Gives *Knowledge* none, but *Misery* to find.

Nature.
Why doth *Man-kind* complaine, and make such Moane?
May not *I* work my *will* with what's my owne?
But *Men* among themselves contract, and make
A *Bargaine* for my *Tree*; that *Tree* will take:
Most cruelly do chop in peeces small,
And formes it as he please, then builds withall.
Although that *Tree* by me was made to stand,
Just as it growes, not to be cut by *Man*.

Man.
O *Nature, Trees* are dull, and have no *Sense*,
And therefore feel not paine, nor take offence.
But *Beasts* have *life* and *Sense*, and *Passion* strong,

Yet *cruell man* doth kill, and doth them wrong.
To take that *life,* I *gave,* before the time
I did ordaine, the *injury is mine.*
What *Ill* man doth, *Nature* did make him do,
For he by *Nature* is prompt thereunto.
For it was in great *Natures power,* and *Will,*
To make him as *she* pleas'd, either *good,* or *ill.*
Though *Beast* hath *Sense,* feels paine, yet whilst they live,
They *Reason* want, for to dispute, or grieve.
Beast hath no paine, but what in *Sense* doth lye,
Nor troubled *Thoughts,* to think how they shall dye.
Reason doth stretch *Mans mind* upon the Rack,
With *Hopes,* with *Joyes,* pull'd up, with *Feare* pull'd back.
Desire whips him forward, makes him run,
Despaire doth wound, and pulls him back agen.
For *Nature,* thou mad'st *Man* betwixt *Extreames,*
Wants *perfect Knowledge,* yet thereof he dreames.
For had he bin like to a *Stock,* or *Stone,*
Or like a *Beast,* to live with *Sense* alone.
Then might he eate, or drink, or lye *stone*-still,
Nere troubled be, either for *Heaven,* or *Hell.*
Man knowledge hath enough for to inquire,
Ambition great enough for to aspire:
And *Knowledge* hath, that yet he knowes not all,
And that himselfe he knoweth least of all:
Which makes him wonder, and thinks there is mixt
Two severall *Qualities* in *Nature* fixt.
The one like *Love,* the other like to *Hate,*
By striving both hinders *Predestinate.*
And then sometimes, *Man* thinks, as *one* they be,
Which makes *Contrariety* so well agree;
That though the *World* were made by *Love and hate,*
Yet all is rul'd, and governed by *Fate.*
These are *Mans feares;* mans *hopes* run smooth, and high,
Which thinks his *Mind* is some great *Deity.*
For though the body is of *low* degree,
In *Sense* like *Beasts,* their *Soules* like *Gods* shall be.

Saies *Nature,* why doth *Man* complaine, and crye,
If he beleives his *Soule* shall never dye?

A Dialogue between an Oake, and a Man cutting him downe

Oake.

Why cut you off my *Bowes*, both large, and long,
That keepe you from the *heat*, and *scortching Sun*;
And did refresh your *fainting Limbs* from sweat?
From *thundring Raines I* keepe you free, from *Wet;*
When on my *Barke* your weary head would lay,
Where *quiet sleepe* did take all *Cares* away.
The whilst my *Leaves* a gentle noise did make,
And blew *coole Winds*, that you *fresh Aire* night take.
Besides, *I* did invite the *Birds* to sing,
That their sweet voice might you some pleasure bring.
Where every one did strive to do their best,
Oft chang'd their *Notes*, and strain'd their tender *Breast.*
In *Winter time*, my *Shoulders* broad did hold
Off *blustring Stormes*, that wounded with *sharpe Cold.*
And on my *Head* the *Flakes* of *snow* did fall,
Whilst you under my *Bowes* sate free from all.
And will you thus requite my *Love, Good Will,*
To take away my *Life*, and *Body* kill?
For all my *Care*, and *Service I* have past,
Must *I* be cut, and laid on *Fire* at last?
And thus true *Love* you cruelly have *slaine,*
Invent alwaies to torture me with *paine.*
First you do peele my *Barke*, and flay my *Skinne,*
Hew downe my *Boughes*, so chops off every *Limb.*
With *Wedges* you do peirce my *Sides* to wound,
And with your *Hatchet* knock me to the ground.
I mine'd shall be in *Chips*, and *peeces* small,
And thus doth *Man* reward *good Deeds* withall.

Man.

Why grumblest thou, *old Oake*, when thou hast stood
This hundred yeares, as *King* of all the *Wood.*
Would you for ever live, and not resigne
Your *Place* to one that is of your owne Line?
Your *Acornes young*, when they grow big, and tall,
Long for your *Crowne*, and wish to see your fall;

Thinke every minute lost, whilst you do live,
And grumble at each *Office* you do give.
Ambitien flieth high, and is above
All sorts of *Friend-ship* strong, or *Naturall Love.*
Besides, all *Subjects* they in *Change* delight,
When *Kings* grow *Old*, their *Government* they slight:
Although in *ease*, and *peace*, and *wealth* do live,
Yet all those *happy times* for *Change* will give.
Growes *discontent*, and *Factions* still do make;
What *Good* so ere *he* doth, as *Evill* take.
Were *he* as *wise*, as ever *Nature* made,
As *pious, good*, as ever *Heaven sav'd*:
Yet when *they* dye, such *Joy* is in their *Face*,
As if the *Devill* had gone from that place.
With *Shouts* of *Joy* they run anew to *Crowne*,
Although *next day* they strive to pull *him* downe.

Why, said the *Oake*, because that *they* are mad,
Shall *I* rejoyce, for my owne *Death* be glad?
Because my *Subjects* all ingratefull are,
Shall *I* therefore my *health*, and *life* impaire.
Good Kings governe justly, as they ought,
Examines not their Humours, but their Fault.
For when their *Crimes* appeare, t'is *time to strike*,
Not to examine Thoughts how they do like.
If *Kings* are never *lov'd*, till they do dye,
Nor *wisht* to *live*, till in the *Grave* they lye:
Yet he that loves *himselfe* the lesse, because
He cannot get every mans *high applause*:
Shall by my *Judgment* be condemn'd to weare,
The *Asses Eares*, and *burdens* for to beare.
But let me live the *Life* that *Nature* gave,
And not to please my *Subjects*, dig my *Grave.*

Man.
But here, *Poore Oake*, thou liv'st in *Ignorance*,
And never seek'st thy *Knowledge* to advance.
I'le cut the downe, 'cause *Knowledge* thou maist gaine,[6]

---

[6] Cavendish holds that knowledge and perception are ubiquitous in nature. See also *Appendix to Grounds of Natural Philosophy*, chapter VIII of the Third Part.

Shalt be a *Ship*, to traffick on the *Maine*:
There shalt thou *swim*, and cut the *Seas* in two,
And trample downe each *Wave*, as thou dost go.
Though they rise high, and big are sweld with *pride*,
Thou on their *Shoulders broad*, and *Back*, shalt ride:
Their *lofty Heads* shalt *bowe*, and make them *stoop*,
And on their *Necks* shalt set thy *steddy Foot*:
And on their *Breast* thy *Stately Ship* shalt beare,
Till thy *Sharpe Keele* the *watry Wombe* doth teare.
Thus shalt thou round the *World*, new *Land* to find,
That from the rest is of *another kind*.

O, said the *Oake*, *I* am contented well,
Without that *Knowledge*, in my *Wood* to dwell.
For *I* had rather live, and simple be,
Then dangers run, some new strange *Sight* to see.
Perchance my *Ship* against a *Rock* may hit;
Then were *I* strait in sundry peeces split.
Besides, no rest, nor quiet *I* should have,
The *Winds* would tosse me on each *troubled Wave*.
The *Billowes rough* will beat on every side,
My *Breast* will *ake* to swim against the *Tide*.
And *greedy Merchants* may me over-fraight,
So should *I* drowned be with my owne weight.
Besides with *Sailes*, and *Ropes* my *Body* tye,
Just like a *Prisoner*, have no *Liberty*.
. . . *I* care not for that *Wealth*, wherein the *paines*,
And *trouble*, is farre greater then the *Gaines*.
I am contented with what *Nature* gave,
I not Repine, but one *poore wish* would have,
Which is, that you my *aged Life* would save.

Man.
To build a *Stately House* *I'le* cut thee downe,
Wherein shall *Princes* live of great renowne.
There shalt *thou* live with the best Companie,
All their delight, and pastime *thou* shalt see.
Where *Playes*, and *Masques*, and *Beauties* bright will shine,
Thy *Wood* all oyl'd with Smoake of *Meat*, and *Wine*.
There thou shalt heare both *Men*, and *Women* sing,
Farre pleasanter then *Nightingals* in Spring.

Like to a *Ball*, their *Ecchoes* shall rebound
Against the *Wall*, yet can no *Voice* be found.

Oake.
Alas, what *Musick* shall *I* care to heare,
When on my *Shoulders I* such burthens beare?
Both *Brick*, and *Tiles*, upon my *Head* are laid,
Of this *Preferment I* am sore afraid.
And many times with *Nailes*, and *Hammers* strong,
They peirce my *Sides*, to hang their *Pictures* on.
My *Face* is sinucht with Smoake of *Candle Lights*,
In danger to be burnt in *Winter Nights*.
No, let me here a poore *Old Oake* still grow;
I care not for these vaine *Delights* to know.
For *fruitlesse Promises I* do not care,
More *Honour* tis, my owne *green Leaves* to beare.
More *Honour* tis, to be in *Natures* dresse,
Then any *Shape*, that *Men* by *Art* expresse.
I am not like to *Man*, would Praises have,
And for *Opinion* make my selfe a *Slave*.

Man.
Why do you wish to live, and not to dye,
Since you no *Pleasure* have, but *Misery?*
For here you stand against the *scorching Sun*:
By's *Fiery Beames,* your *fresh green Leaves* become
Wither'd; with *Winter's* cold you quake, and shake:
Thus in no *time*, or *season*, rest can take.

Yet *I* am happier, said the *Oake*, then *Man*;
With my condition *I* contented am.
He nothing loves, but what he cannot get,
And soon doth surfet of one dish of meat:
Dislikes all Company, displeas'd alone,
Makes *Griefe* himselfe, if *Fortune* gives him none.
And as his *Mind* is restlesse, never pleas'd;
So is his *Body* sick, and oft diseas'd.
His *Gouts*, and *Paines*, do make him sigh, and cry,
Yet in the midst of *Paines* would live, not dye.[7]

[7] But see also *Appendix to Grounds of Natural Philosophy*, chapter VIII of the Third Part; and *Philosophical Letters*, letter XXIII of section three.

Man.

Alas, *poore Oake*, thou understandst, nor can
Imagine halfe the misery of *Man*.
All other *Creatures* onely in *Sense* joyne,[8]
But *Man* hath something more, which is *divine*.
He hath a *Mind*, doth to the *Heavens* aspire,
A *Curiosity* for to inquire:
A *Wit* that nimble is, which runs about
In every *Corner*, to seeke *Nature* out.
For *She* doth hide her selfe, as fear'd to shew
Man all *her workes*, lest *he* too powerfull grow.
Like to a *King*, his *Favourite* makes so great,
That at the last, *he* feares his *Power* hee'll get.
And what creates *desire* in *Mans Breast*,
A *Nature* is *divine*, which seekes the best:
And never can be satisfied, untill
He, like a *God*, doth in *Perfection* dwell.
If you, as *Man*, desire like *Gods* to bee,
I'le spare your *Life*, and not cut downe your *Tree*.

A Dialogue betwixt Peace, and War

Peace.

War makes the *Vulgar Multitude* to drink
In at the *Eare* the foule, and muddy *Sinck*
Of *Factious Tales*, by which they *dizzy* grow,
That the cleare sight of *Truth* they do not know.
And reeling stand, know not what way to take,
But when they chuse, 'tis wrong, so a *War* make.

War.

Thou *Flattering Peace*, and most unjust, which drawes
The *Vulgar* by thy *Rhet'rick* to *hard Lawes*:
Which makes them *silly Ones*, content to be,
To take up *Voluntary Slavery*.
And mak'st great *Inequalities* beside,
Some like to *Asses* beare, others on *Horsback* ride.

---

[8] See also *Worlds Olio*, "The difference Betwixt Man and Beast."

Peace.
O *War*, thou cruell *Enemy* to *Life*,
Unquieted Neighbour, breeding alwaies *Strife*.
Tyrant thou art, to *Rest* will give no time,
And *Blessed Peace* thou punishest as a *Crime*.
Factions thou mak'st in every *Publick-weale*,
From *Bonds* of *Friendship* tak'st off *Wax*, and *Seale*.
On *Naturall Affections* thou dost make
A *Massacre*, that hardly one can 'scape.
The *Root* of all *Religion* thou pull'st up,
And every *Branch* of *Ceremony* cut.
Civill Society is turn'd to *Manners base*,
No *Lawes*, or *Customes* can by thee get place.
Each *Mind* within it selfe cannot agree,
But all do strive for *Superiority*:
In the whole *World* dost such *disturbance* make,
To save themselves *none* knowes what waies to take.

War.
O *Peace*, thou *idle Drone*, which lov'st to dwell,
If it but keep the safe, in a *poore Cell*.
Thy *Life* thou sleep'st away, *Thoughts* lazy lye.
Sloath buries *Fame*, makes all great *Actions* dye.

Peace.
I am the *Bed* of *Rest*, and *Couch* of *Ease*,
My *Conversation* doth all *Creatures* please.
I the *Parent* of *Learning* am, and *Arts*,
Nurse to *Religion*, and *Comfort* to all *Hearts*.
I am the *Guardian*, which keepes *Vertue* safe,
Under my *Roofe security shee* hath.
I am adorn'd with *Pastimes*, and with *Sports*,
Each severall *Creature* still to me resorts.

War.
I a great *Schoole* am, where all may grow wise:
For *Prudent Wisdome* in *Experience* lyes.
And am a *Theater* to all *Noble Minds*,
A *Mint* of true *Honour*, that *Valour* still coines.
I am a high *Throne* for *Valour* to sit,
And a great *Court* where all *Fame* may get.

I am a *large Feild*, where doth *Ambition* run,
Courage still seekes me, though *Cowards* me shun.

A Morall Discourse betwixt Man, and Beast

Beast.
Man is a *Creature* like himselfe alone,
In him all *qualities* do joyne as one.
When *Man* is injurd, and his *Honour* stung,
He seemes a *Lion*, furious, feirce, and strong.
With greedy *Covetousnesse*, like to *Wolves*, and *Beares*,
Devoures *Right*, and *Truth* in peeces teares.
. . . Most like to ravenous *Beasts* in *blood* delight,
And onely to do *mischiefe*, love to fight.[9]
. . . Proper for *Flyes* to buzze, *Birds* sing, and chatter,
Onely for *Men* to *promise*, *sweare*, and *flatter*:
So *Men* these *Properties* can imitate,
But not their *Faculties* that *Nature* made.
Men have no *Wings* to flye up to the *Skie*,
Nor can they like to *Fish* in *waters* lye.
What *Man* like *Roes* can run so swift, and long?
Nor are they like to *Horse*, or *Lions* strong.
Nor have they *Scent*, like *Dogs*, a *Hare* to find,
Or *Sight* like *Swine* to see the subtle *wind*.
Thus severall *Creatures*, by severall *Sense*,
Have better far (then *Man*) *Intelligence*.[10]

Man.
These severall *Creatures*, severall *Arts* do well,
But *Man* in generall, doth them far excell.
For *Arts* in *Men* as well did *Nature* give,
As other *qualities* in *Beast* to live.
And from *Mens Braines* such fine *Inventions* flow,
As in his *Head* all other *heads* do grow.
What *Creature* builds like *Man* such *Stately Towers*,

[9] Note that the voice of "Beast" does represent human beings in a positive light in some parts of the speech, but the comments of that voice are for the most part negative.
[10] See also *Further Observations Upon Experimental Philosophy*, section XIII.

And make such things, as *Time* cannot devoure?
What *Creature* makes such *Engines* as *Man* can?
To traffick, and to use at *Sea*, and *Land*.
To *kill*, to *spoile*, or else alive to *take*,
Destroying all that other *Creatures* make.
This makes *Man* seem of all the *World* a *King*,
Because *hee* power hath of every *thing*.
He'l teach *Birds* words, in measure *Beast* to go,
Makes *Passions* in the *Mind*, to ebb, and *flow*.
And though he cannot flye as *Birds*, with *wings*,
Yet he can take the height, and breadth of things.
He knowes the course and number of the *Stars*,
But *Birds*, and *Beasts* are no *Astrologers*.
And though he cannot like to *Fishes* swim,
Yet *Nets He* makes, to catch those *Fishes* in.
And with his *Ships* hee'l circle the *World* round.
What *Beast*, or *Bird* that can do so, is found?
Hee'l fell downe *Woods*, with *Axes* sharp will strike;
Whole *Hoards* of *Beasts* can never do the like.
What *Beast* can plead, to save anothers *Life*,
Or by his *Eloquence* can end a *Strife*?
Or *Counsels* give, great *Dangers* for to shun,
Or tell the *Cause*, of how *Eclipses* come?
Hee'l turne the *Current* of the *Water* cleare,
And make them like new *Seas* for to appeare.
Where *Fishes* onely in old *waters* glide.
Can cut new *Rivers* out on any side.
Hee Mountaines makes so high, the *Cloudes* will touch,
Mountaines of *Moles*, or *Ants*, scarce do so much.
What *Creature* like to *Man* can *Reasons* shew,
Which makes him know, that he thereby doth know?
And who, but *Man*, makes use of every thing,
As *Goodnesse* out of *Poyson Hee* can bring?
Thus *Man* is filled a with strong *Desire*,
And by his *Rhet'rick* sets the *Soule* on *Fire*.
Beasts no *Ambition* have to get a *Fame*,
Nor build they *Tombes*, thereon to write their *Name*.
They never war, *high Honour* for to get,
But to secure themselves, or *Meat* to eat.
But *Men* are like to *Gods*, they live for ever shall;
And *Beasts* are like themselves, to *Dust* shall fall.

Of the Ant

Mark but the little *Ant,* how she doth run,
In what a busie *motion she* goeth on:
As if she ordered all the *Worlds Affaires;*
When tis but onely one small *Straw shee* beares.
But when they find a *Flye,* which on the ground lyes dead,
Lord, how they stir; so full is every *Head.*[11]
Some with their *Feet,* and *Mouths,* draw it along,
Others their *Tailes,* and *Shoulders* thrust it on.
And if a *Stranger Ant* comes on that way,
Shee helpes them strait, nere asketh if *shee* may.
Nor staies to ask *Rewardes,* but is well pleas'd:
Thus paies her selfe with her owne *Paines,* their *Ease.*
They live as the *Lacedemonians* did,
All is in *Common, nothing* is forbid.
No *Private Feast,* but altogether meet,
Wholesome, though *Plaine,* in *Publick* do they eat.
They have no *Envie,* all *Ambition's* downe,
There is no *Superiority,* or *Clowne.*
No *Stately Palaces* for *Pride* to dwell,
Their *House* is *Common,* called the *Ants Hill.*
All help to *build,* and keep it in *repaire,*
No 'speciall *work-men,* all *Labourers* they are.
No *Markets* keep, no *Meat* they have to sell,
For what each one doth eat, all *welcome* is, and well.
No *Jealousie,* each takes his *Neighbors Wife,*
Without *Offence,* which never breedeth *Strife.*
Nor fight they *Duels,* nor do give the *Lye,*
Their greatest *Honour* is to live, not dye.
For they, to keep in *life,* through *Dangers* run,
To get *Provisions* in 'gainst *Winter* comes.
But many loose their *Life,* as *Chance* doth fall,
None is perpetuall, *Death* devoures all.

---

[11] See also *Philosophical Letters,* letter X of section one.

Of Fishes

Who knowes, but *Fishes* which swim in the *Sea*,
Can give a Reason, why so *Salt* it be?
And how it *Ebbs* and *Flowes,* perchance they can
Give *Reasons,* for which never yet could *Man.*

Similizing the Head of Man to the World

As twinckling *Stars* shew in dark *Clouds,* that's cleare,
So *Fancies* quick do in the *Braine* appeare.
Imaginations, like the *Orbes* move so,
Some very quick, others do move more slow.
And solid *Thoughts,* as the twelve *Signes,* are plac'd
About the *Zodiack,* which is *Wisedome* vast.
Where they as constantly in *Wisedome* run,
As in the *Line Ecliptick* doth the *Sun.*

To the *Ecliptick Line* the *Head* compare,
The illustrious *Wit,* to the *Suns* bright *Spheare.*
The *Braine,* unto the *Solid Earth,*
From whence all *Wisdome* hath its *Birth.*
Just as the *Earth,* the *Heads* round *Ball,*
Is crown'd with *Orbes Coelestiall.*
So *Head,* and *World* as one agree;
Nature did make the *Head* a *World* to bee.[12]

Poets have most Pleasure in this Life

Nature most *Pleasure* doth to *Poets* give;
If *Pleasures* in *Variety* do live.
There every *Sense* by *Fancy* new is fed,
Which *Fancy* in a *Torrent Braine* is bred.
Contrary is to all that's borne on *Earth,*
For *Fancy* is delighted most at's *Birth.*
What ever else is borne, with *Paine* comes forth,

---

[12] See also *Philosophical and Physical Opinions,* chapter 160, and *Grounds of Natural Philosophy,* chapter IV of the Sixth Part.

But *Fancy* needs not time to make it grow,
Hath neither Beauty, Strength, nor perfect Growth.
Those *Braine* like *Gods*, from whence all things do flow.

To all Writing Ladies

It is to be observed, that there is a secret working by Nature, as to cast an influence upon the mindes of men: like as in Contagions, when as the Aire is
corrupted, it produces severall Diseases; so severall distempers of the minde,
by the inflammations of the spirits. And as in healthfull Ages, bodies are
purified, so wits are refined; yet it seemes to me as if there were severall invisible spirits, that have severall, but visible powers, to worke in severall Ages
upon the mindes of men. For in many Ages men will be affected, and dis-
affected alike: as in some Ages so strongly, and superstitiously devout, that
they make many gods: and in another Age so Atheisticall, as they beleeve
in no God at all, and live to those Principles. Some Ages againe have such
strong faiths, that they will not only dye in their severall Opinions, but they
will Massacre, and cut one anothers throats, because their opinions are different. In some Ages all men seek absolute power, and every man would be
Emperour of the World; which makes Civil Wars: for their ambition makes
them restlesse, and their restlesnesse makes them seek change. Then in another Age all live peaceable, and so obedient, that the very Governours rule
with obedient power. In some Ages againe, all run after Imitation, like a company of Apes, as to imitate such a Poet, to be of such a Philosophers opinion.
Some Ages mixt, as Moralists, Poets, Philosophers, and the like: and in some
Ages agen, all affect singularity; and they are thought the wisest, that can have
the most extravagant opinions. In some Ages Learning flourisheth in Arts, and
Sciences; other Ages so dull, as they loose what former Ages had taught. And
in some Ages it seemes as if there were a Common-wealth of those governing
spirits, where most rule at one time. Some Ages, as in Aristocracy, when some
part did rule; and other Ages a pure Monarchy, when but one rules; and in
some Ages, it seemes as if all those spirits were at defiance, who should have
most power, which makes them in confusion, and War; so confused are some
Ages, and it seemes as if there were spirits of the Faeminine Gender, as also
the Masculine. There will be many Heroick Women in some Ages, in others
very Propheticall; in some Ages very pious, and devout: For our Sex is won-
derfully addicted to the spirits. But this Age hath produced many effeminate
Writers, as well as Preachers, and many effeminate Rulers, as well as Actors.
And if it be an Age when the effeminate spirits rule, as most visible they doe
in every Kingdome, let us take the advantage, and make the best of our time,

for feare their reigne should not last long;[13] whether it be in the Amazonian Government, or in the Politick Common-wealth, or in flourishing Monarchy, or in Schooles of Divinity, or in Lectures of Philosophy, or in witty Poetry, or any thing that may bring honour to our Sex: for they are poore, dejected spirits, that are not ambitious of Fame. And though we be inferiour to Men, let us shew our selves a degree above Beasts; and not eate, and drink, and sleep away our time as they doe; and live only to the sense, not to the reason; and so turne into forgotten dust. But let us strive to build us Tombs while we live, of Noble, Honourable, and good Actions, at least harmlesse;

> *That though our Bodies dye,*
> *Our Names may live to after memory.*

I Wonder any should laugh, or think it ridiculous to heare of *Fairies*, and yet verily beleeve there are spirits: which spirits can have no description, because no dimension: And of *Witches*, which are said to change themselves into severall formes, and then to returne into their first forme againe ordinarily, which is altogether against nature: yet laugh at the report of *Fairies*, as impossible; which are onely small bodies,[14] not subject to our sense, although it be to our reason. For Nature can as well make small bodies, as great, and thin bodies as well as thicke. We may as well thinke there is no Aire, because we doe not see it; or to thinke there is no Aire in an empty Barrel, or the like, because when we put our hands and armes into the same, we doe not feele it. And why should not they get through doores or walls, as well as Aire doth, if their bodies were as thin? And if we can grant there may be a substance, although not subject to our sense, then wee must grant, that substance must have some forme; And why not of man, as of any thing else? And why not rational soules live in a small body, as well as in a grosse, and in a thin, as in a thicke?

[13] See also *Philosophical and Physical Opinions*, "To the Two Universities," and note 1 for *Worlds Olio*.

[14] See also in this chapter, "Of small Creatures, such as we call Fairies" and "The Fairies in the Braine, may be the causes of many thoughts." In both, Cavendish suggests that perhaps it is mysterious fairies that help to put our thoughts into order when thoughts come to us at just the right time or when we follow a coherent train of thought as it unfolds. Of course, the appeal to fairies is not meant to be a serious explanation of the coherence of our thoughts; Cavendish is just highlighting that our thoughts do tend to come to us in an organized manner and that there must be some cause for this, even if we do not fully understand what that is. See also the very similar explanation (in terms of magic) that Hume provides to account for the way in which thoughts tend to come to us right when we need them. This is in *A Treatise of Human Nature*, I.i.7, 24.

Of small Creatures, such as we call Fairies

Who knowes, but in the *Braine* may dwel
Little small *Fairies;* who can tell?
And by their severall actions they may make
Those *formes* and *figures,* we for *fancy* take.
And when we sleep, those *Visions, dreames* we call,
By *their* industry may be raised all;
And all the *objects,* which through *senses* get,
Within the *Braine* they may in order set.
And some pack up, as *Merchants* do each thing,
Which out sometimes may to the *Memory* bring.
Thus, besides our owne *imaginations,*
Fairies in our *braine* beget *inventions.*

The Fairies in the Braine, may be the causes of many thoughts

When we have *pious thoughts,* and thinke of *heaven,*
Yet goe about, not ask to be forgiven,
Perchance their preaching, or a Chapter saying,
Or on their knees devoutly they are praying.
When we are sad, and know no reason why,[15]
Perchance it is, because *some* there doe dye.
And some *place* in the *Head* is hung with *blacke,*
Which makes us dull, yet know not what we lack.
Our *fancies,* which in *verse,* or *prose* we put,
Are *Pictures* which *they draw,* or Figures *cut,*
And when those *fancies* are both *fine,* and *thin,*
Then they *ingraven* are in *seale,* or *ring.*
When we have *crosse opinions* in the *minde,*

[15] Here Cavendish is gesturing at the possible existence of mental causes of which we are not aware. She appears to hold that unconscious mentality is not uncommon in the case of human beings (*Worlds Olio,* "Epistle," and the corresponding note 4), and that it not uncommon in the rest of nature as well—for example, in ants, bees, immune systems, ecosystems, and other creatures that Cavendish supposes to exhibit intelligence (*Philosophical Letters,* letter X of section one). In "Of small Creatures, such as we call Fairies," she is referring to causes that put our thoughts into a coherent order. If any conscious thought that comes to us is properly identifiable as intelligent, presumably the background processes that select the thought for our awareness should also be identified as intelligent, if not more so.

They in the *Schooles disputing* we shall finde.
When we of *childish toyes* doe thinke upon,
A *Fayre* may be whereto those *people* throng,
And in those *stalles* may all such *knacks* be sold;
As *Bels*, and *Rattles*, or *bracelets* of *Gold*.
Or *Pins, Pipes, Whistles* are to be bought there,
And thus within the *Head* may be a *Fayre*.
When that our *braine* with *amorous thoughts* doth run,
Are marrying there a *Bride* with her *Bride-groom*.
And when our *thoughts* are *merry, humours gay,*
Then they are dancing on their *Wedding day*.[16]

[16] See also chapter V of the Sixth Part of *Grounds of Natural Philosophy*, and the corresponding note 21.

CHAPTER 7

Fiction

Blazing World

To all Noble and Worthy Ladies.

This present *Description of a New World*; was made as an *Appendix* to my *Observations upon Experimental Philosophy*; and, having some Sympathy and Coherence with each other, were joyned together as Two several Worlds, at their Two Poles. But, by reason most Ladies take no delight in *Philosophical Arguments*, I separated some from the mentioned *Observations*, and caused them to go out by themselves, that I might express my Respects, in presenting to Them such *Fancies* as my Contemplations did afford. The First Part is *Romancical*; the Second, *Philosophical*; and the Third is meerly Fancy; or, (as I may call it) *Fantastical*. And if (*Noble Ladies*) you should chance to take pleasure in reading these *Fancies*, I shall account my self a *Happy Creatoress*: If not, I must be content to live a Melancholly Life in my own World; which I cannot call a *Poor World*, if *Poverty* be only want of Gold, and Jewels: for, there is more *Gold* in it, than all the *Chymists* ever made; or, (as I verily believe) will ever be able to make. As for the *Rocks of Diamonds*, I wish, with all my Soul, they might be shared amongst my Noble *Female Friends*; upon which condition, I would willingly quit my Part: And of the *Gold*, I should desire only so much as might suffice to repair my Noble Lord and Husband's Losses: for, I am not Covetous, but as Ambitious as ever any of my Sex was, is, or can be; which is the cause, That though I cannot be *Henry* the Fifth, or *Charles* the Second; yet, I will endeavour to be, *Margaret* the First: and, though I have neither Power, Time, nor Occasion, to be a great Conqueror, like *Alexander*, or *Cesar*; yet, rather than not be Mistress of a World, since Fortune and the Fates would give me none, I have made One of my own. And thus, believing, or, at least, hoping, that no Creature can, or will, Envy me for this World of mine, I remain,

Noble Ladies, Your Humble Servant,
M. NEWCASTLE.

THE DESCRIPTION OF A NEW WORLD, CALLED THE BLAZING-WORLD

A Merchant travelling into a foreign Country, fell extreamly in Love with a young Lady; but being a stranger in that Nation, and beneath her, both in Birth and Wealth, he could have but little hopes of obtaining his desire; however his Love growing more and more vehement upon him, even to the slighting of all difficulties, he resolved at last to Steal her away; which he had the better opportunity to do, because her Father's house was not far from the Sea, and she often gathering shells upon the shore, accompanied not with above two or three of her servants, it encouraged him the more to execute his design. Thus coming one time with a little leight Vessel, not unlike a Packet-boat, mann'd with some few Sea-men, and well victualled, for fear of some accidents, which might perhaps retard their journey, to the place where she used to repair; he forced her away: But when he fancied himself the happiest man of the World, he proved to be the most unfortunate; for Heaven frowning at his Theft, raised such a Tempest, as they knew not what to do, or whither to steer their course; so that the Vessel, both by its own leightness, and the violent motion of the Wind, was carried as swift as an Arrow out of a Bow, towards the North-pole, and in a short time reached the Icy Sea, where the wind forced it amongst huge pieces of Ice; but being little, and leight, it did by the assistance and favour of the gods to this virtuous Lady, so turn and wind through those precipices, as if it had been guided by some experienced Pilot, and skilful Mariner: But alas! Those few men which were in it, not knowing whither they went, nor what was to be done in so strange an Adventure, and not being provided for so cold a Voyage, were all frozen to death; the young Lady onely, by the light of her Beauty, the heat of her Youth, and Protection of the Gods, remaining alive: Neither was it a wonder that the men did freeze to death; for they were not onely driven to the very end or point of the Pole of that World, but even to another Pole of another World, which joined close to it; so that the cold having a double strength at the conjunction of those two Poles, was insupportable: At last, the Boat still passing on, was forced into another World; for it is impossible to round this Worlds Globe from Pole to Pole, so as we do from East to West; because the Poles of the other World, joining to the Poles of this, do not allow any further passage to surround the World that way; but if any one arrives to either of these Poles, he is either forced to return, or to enter into another World. . . .

But to return to the wandering Boat, and the distresed Lady; she seeing all the Men dead, found small comfort in life; their Bodies which were preserved all that while from putrefaction and stench, by the extremity of cold, began now to thaw, and corrupt; whereupon she having not strength enough to fling them over-board, was forced to remove out of her small Cabine, upon the deck, to avoid that nauseous smell; and finding the Boat swim between two plains of Ice, as a stream that runs betwixt two shores, at last perceived land, but covered all with Snow: from which came, walking upon the Ice, strange Creatures, in shape like Bears, only they went upright as men; those Creatures coming near the Boat, catched hold of it with their Paws, that served them instead of hands; some two or three of them entred first; and when they came out, the rest went in one after another; at last having viewed and observed all that was in the Boat, they spake to each other in a language which the Lady did not understand; and having carried her out of the Boat, sunk it, together with the dead men.

The Lady now finding her self in so strange a place, and amongst such wonderful kind of Creatures, was extreamly strucken with fear, and could entertain no other Thoughts, but that every moment her life was to be a sacrifice to their cruelty; but those Bear-like Creatures, how terrible soever they appear'd to her sight, yet were they so far from exercising any cruelty upon her, that rather they shewed her all civility and kindness imaginable; for she being not able to go upon the Ice, by reason of its slipperiness, they took her up in their rough arms, and carried her into their City, where instead of Houses, they had Caves under ground; and as soon as they enter'd the City, both Males and Females, young and old, flockt together to see this Lady, holding up their Paws in admiration; at last having brought her into a certain large and spacious Cave, which they intended for her reception, they left her to the custody of the Females, who entertained her with all kindness and respect, and gave her such victuals as they used to eat; but seeing her Constitution neither agreed with the temper of that Climate, nor their Diet, they were resolved to carry her into another Island of a warmer temper; in which were men like Foxes, onely walking in an upright shape, who received their neighbours the Bear-men with great civility and Courtship, very much admiring this beauteous Lady; and having discoursed some while together, agreed at last to make her a Present to the Emperor of their World; to which end, after she had made some short stay in the same place, they brought her cross that Island to a large River, whose stream run smooth and clear, like Chrystal; in which were numerous Boats, much like our Fox-traps; in one whereof she was carried, some of the Bear- and Fox-men waiting on her; and as soon as they had crossed the River, they came into an Island where there were Men which had heads, beaks, and feathers, like wild-Geese, onely they went in an upright shape, like the Bear-men and Fox-men: their rumps they carried between their legs, their wings were of the same length with their Bodies, and their tails of an indifferent size, trailing after them like a Ladie's Garment; and after the Bear- and Fox-men had declared their intention and design to their Neighbours, the Geese-or Bird-men, some of them joined to the rest, and attended the Lady through that Island, till they came to another great and large River, where there was a preparation made of many Boats, much like Birds nests, onely of a bigger size; and having crost that River, they arrived into another Island, which was of a pleasant and mild temper, full of Woods and the Inhabitants thereof were *Satyrs*, who received both the Bear- Fox- and Bird-men, with all respect and civility; and after some conferences (for they all understood each others language) some chief of the *Satyrs* joining to them, accompanied the Lady out of that Island to another River, wherein were many handsome and commodious Barges; and having crost that River, they entered into a large and spacious Kingdom, the men whereof were of a Grass-Green Complexion, who entertained them very kindly, and provided all conveniences for their further voyage. . . .

At last, having passed by several rich Islands and Kingdoms, they went towards *Paradise*, which was the seat of the Emperor; and coming in sight of it, rejoiced very much; the Lady at first could perceive nothing but high Rocks, which seemed to touch the Skies; and although they appear'd not of an equal height, yet they seemed to be all one piece, without partitions: but at last drawing nearer, she perceived a cleft, which was a part of those Rocks, out of which she spied coming forth a great number of Boats, which afar off shewed like a company of Ants, marching one after another; the Boats appeared like the holes or partitions in a Honey-comb, and when joined together, stood as close; the men were of several Complexions, but none like any of our World; and when both the Boats and Ships met, they saluted and spake to each other very courteously; for there was but one language in all that World: nor no more but one Emperor, to whom they all submitted with the greatest duty and obedience, which made them live in a continued Peace and Happiness; not acquainted with Foreign Wars, or Home-bred Insurrections. . . .

No sooner was the Lady brought before the Emperor, but he conceived her to be some Goddess, and offered to worship her; which she refused, telling him, (for by that time she had pretty well learned their Language) that although she came out of another world, yet was she but a mortal. At which the Emperor rejoycing, made her his Wife, and gave her an absolute power to rule and govern all that World as she pleased. But her subjects, who could hardly be perswaded to believe her mortal, tender'd her all the Veneration and Worship due to a Deity. . . . None was allowed to use or wear Gold but those of the Imperial Race, which were the onely Nobles of the State; nor durst any one wear Jewels but the Emperor, the Empress, and their Eldest Son; notwithstanding that they had an infinite quantity both of Gold and precious Stones in that World; for they had larger extents of Gold, then our *Arabian* Sands; their precious Stones were Rocks, and their Diamonds of several Colours; they used no Coyn, but all their Traffick was by exchange of several Commodities.

Their Priests and Governors were Princes of the Imperial Blood, and made Eunuches for that purpose; and as for the ordinary sort of men in that part of the World where the Emperor resided, they were of several Complexions; not white, black, tawny, olive- or ash-coloured; but some appear'd of an Azure, some of a deep Purple, some of a Grass-green, some of a Scarlet, some of an Orange-colour, &c. Which Colours and Complexions, whether they were made by the bare reflection of light, without the assistance of small particles; or by the help of well-ranged and order'd Atoms; or by a continual agitation of little Globules; or by some pressing and re-acting motion, I am not able to determine.[1] The rest of the Inhabitants of that World, were men of several different sorts, shapes, figures, dispositions, and humors, as I have already made mention, heretofore; some were Bear-men, some Worm-men, some Fish-or Mear-men, otherwise called Syrens; some Bird-men, some Fly-men, some Ant-men, some Geese-men, some Spider-men, some Lice-men, some Fox-men, some Ape-men, some Jack-daw-men, some Magpie-men, some Parrot-men, some Satyrs, some Gyants, and many more, which I cannot all remember; and of these several sorts of men, each followed such a profession as was most proper for the nature of their Species, which the Empress encouraged them in, especially those that had applied themselves to the study of several Arts and Sciences; for they were as ingenious and witty in the invention of profitable and useful Arts, as we are in our world, nay, more; and to that end she erected Schools, and founded several Societies. The Bear-men were to be her Experimental Philosophers, the Bird-men her Astronomers, the Fly- Worm- and Fish-men her Natural Philosophers, the Ape-men her Chymists, the Satyrs her Galenick Physicians, the Fox-men her Politicians, the Spider-and Lice-men her Mathematicians, the Jackdaw-Magpie- and Parrot-men her Orators and Logicians, the Gyants her Architects, &c. But before all things, she having got a Soveraign power from the Emperor over all the World, desired to be informed both of the manner of their Religion and Government; and to that end, she called the Priests and States-men, to give her an account of either. Of the States-men she enquired, first, Why they had so few Laws? To which they answered, That many Laws made many Divisions, which most commonly did breed Factions, and at last brake out into open Wars. Next, she asked, Why they preferred the Monarchical form of Government before any other? They answered, That as it was natural for one Body to have but one Head, so it was also natural for a Politick body to have but one Governor; and that a Common-wealth, which had many Governors was like a Monster with many Heads. Besides, said they, a Monarchy is a divine form of Government, and agrees most with our Religion: For as there is but one God, whom we all

[1] Here Cavendish appears to be having a little bit of fun with the view that sensory perception is by means of impressions and stamping, and also the view that sensory qualities like color, taste, and sound exist only in our subjective experience. She rejects both views. See for example *Philosophical Letters*, letter IV of section one, and *Observations Upon Experimental Philosophy*, sections XXI and XXXV.

unanimously worship and adore with one Faith; so we are resolved to have but one Emperor, to whom we all submit with one obedience.[2]

Then the Empress seeing that the several sorts of her Subjects had each their Churches apart, asked the Priests, whether they were of several Religions? They answered her Majesty, That there was no more but one Religion in all that World, nor no diversity of opinions in that same Religion; for though there were several sorts of men, yet had they all but one opinion concerning the Worship and Adoration of God. The Empress asked them, Whether they were Jews, Turks, or Christians? We do not know, said they, what Religions those are; but we do all unanimously acknowledg, worship and adore the Onely, Omnipotent, and Eternal God, with all reverence, submission, and duty. Again, the Empress enquired, Whether they had several Forms of Worship? They answered, No: For our Devotion and Worship consists onely in Prayers, which we frame according to our several Necessities, in Petitions, Humiliations, Thanksgiving, &c.[3] Truly, replied the Empress, I thought you had been either Jews, or Turks, because I never perceived any Women in your Congregations: But what is the reason, you bar them from your religious Assemblies? It is not fit, said they, that Men and Women should be promiscuously together in time of Religious Worship; for their company hinders Devotion, and makes many, instead of praying to God, direct their Devotion to their Mistresses. But, asked the Empress, Have they no Congregation of their own, to perform the duties of Divine Worship, as well as Men? No, answered they: but they stay at home, and say their Prayers by themselves in their Closets. . . .

[The Bear-men] shewed the Empress a Flea, and a Lowse; which Creatures through the Microscope appear'd so terrible to her sight, that they had almost put her into a swoon; the description of all their parts would be very tedious to relate, and therefore I'le forbear it at this present. . . . But after the Empress had seen the shapes of these monstrous Creatures, she desir'd to know, Whether their Microscopes could hinder their biting, or at least shew some means how to avoid them? To which they answered, That such Arts were mechanical and below that noble study of Microscopical observations. Then the Empress asked them, Whether they had not such sorts of Glasses that could enlarge and magnifie the shapes of great Bodies as well as they had done of little ones? Whereupon they took one of their best and largest Microscopes, and endeavoured to view a Whale thorow it; but alas! The shape of the Whale was so big, that its Circumference went beyond the magnifying quality of the Glass; whether the error proceeded from the Glass, or from a wrong position of the Whale against the reflection

[2] See also *The She-Anchoret*, in this chapter, the response to "The Eighth sort of Visiters," and *Appendix to Grounds of Natural Philosophy*, chapter XII of the First Part.

[3] See also *Philosophical Letters*, letter XX of section three.

of light, I cannot certainly tell.[4] The Empress seeing the insufficiency of those Magnifying-Glasses, that they were not able to enlarge all sorts of Objects, asked the Bear-men, whether they could not make Glasses of a contrary nature to those they had shewed her, to wit, such as instead of enlarging or magnifying the shape or figure of an Object, could contract it beneath its natural proportion: Which, in obedience to her Majesties Commands, they did; and viewing through one of the best of them, a huge and mighty Whale appear'd no bigger then a Sprat; nay, through some no bigger then a Vinegar-Eele; and through their ordinary ones, an Elephant seemed no bigger then a Flea; a Camel no bigger then a Lowse; and an Ostrich no bigger then a Mite. To relate all their Optick observations through the several sorts of their Glasses, would be a tedious work, and tire even the most patient Reader, wherefore I'le pass them by; onely this was very remarkable and worthy to be taken notice of, that notwithstanding their great skil, industry and ingenuity in Experimental Philosophy, they could yet by no means contrive such Glasses, by the help of which they could spy out a *Vacuum*, with all its dimensions, nor Immaterial substances, Non-beings, and Mixt-beings, or such as are between something and nothing; which they were very much troubled at, hoping that yet, in time, by long study and practice, they might perhaps attain to it.[5] . . .

The Empress having hitherto spent her time in the Examination of the Bird-, Fish-, Worm- and Apemen, &c. and received several Intelligences from their several imployments; at last had a mind to divert her self after her serious Discourses, and therefore she sent for the Spider-men, which were her Mathematicians, the Lice-men which were here Geometricians, and the Magpie- Parrot- and Jackdaw-men, which were her Orators and Logicians. The Spider-men came first, and presented her Majesty with a table full of Mathematical points, lines, and figures of all sorts, of squares, circles, triangles, and the like; which the Empress, notwithstanding that she had a very ready wit, and quick apprehension, could not understand; but the more she endeavoured to learn, the more was she confounded: Whether they did ever square the Circle, I cannot exactly tell, nor whether they could make imaginary points and lines; but this I dare say, That their points and lines were so slender, small and thin, that they seem'd next to Imaginary. The Mathematicians were in great esteem with the Empress,

[4] Cavendish holds that scientific instruments and other human artefacts are not as sophisticated as natural productions (like the human eye) and are often misleading and deceptive. See *Observations Upon Experimental Philosophy*, section III.

[5] Cavendish argues throughout her corpus that a vacuum is impossible and also that immaterial things cannot be detected (or conceived) by human beings or any other creatures. See, for example, *Philosophical Letters*, letter XVIII of section two; *Grounds of Natural Philosophy*, chapter I of The First Part; and *Appendix to Grounds of Natural Philosophy*, chapter III of the First Part. See also note 20 for *Worlds Olio*.

as being not onely the chief Tutors and Instructors in many Arts, but some of them excellent Magicians and Informers of Spirits, which was the reason their Characters were so abstruse and intricate, that the Emperess knew not what to make of them. There is so much to learn in your Art, said she, that I can neither spare time from other affairs to busie my self in your profession; nor, if I could, do I think I should ever be able to understand your Imaginary points, lines and figures, because they are Non-beings.[6] . . .

Last of all, when she saw that both Church and State was now in a well-ordered and setled condition, her thoughts reflected upon the World she came from; and though she had a great desire to know the condition of the same, yet could she advise no manner of way how to gain any knowledg thereof; at last, after many serious considerations, she conceived that it was impossible to be done by any other means, then by the help of Immaterial Spirits; where-fore she made a Convocation of the most learned, witty and ingenious of all the forementioned sorts of Men, and desired to know of them, whether there were any Immaterial Spirits in their World. First, she enquired of the Worm-men, whether they had perceived some within the Earth? They answered her Majesty, That they never knew of any such Creatures; for whatsoever did dwell within the Earth, said they, was imbodied and material. Then she asked the Fly-men, whether they had observed any in the Air? For you having numerous Eyes, said she, will be more able to perceive them, than any other Creatures.[7] To which they answered her Majesty, That although Spirits, being immaterial, could not be perceived by the Worm-men in the Earth, yet they perceived that such Creatures did lodg in the Vehicles of the Air. Then the Empress asked, Whether they could speak to them, and whether they did understand each other? The Fly-men answered, That those Spirits were always cloth'd in some sort or other of Material Garments; which Garments were their Bodies, made, for the most part, of Air; and when occasion served, they could put on any other sort of substances; but yet they could not put these substances into any form or shape, as they pleased. The Empress asked the Fly-men, whether it was possible that she could be acquainted, and have some conferences with them? They answered, They did verily believe she might. Hereupon the Empress commanded the Fly-men to ask some of the Spirits, Whether they would be pleased to give her a Visit? This they did; and after the Spirits had presented

---

[6] Here Cavendish seems to have in mind her view that ideas are imagistic pictures and that if we remove all of the imagistic content of an idea—and attempt to converge on a fully abstract and non-sensory idea of the sort that Cartesian philosophers celebrated—we no longer have before our mind an idea of anything at all. See note 19 for *Philosophical and Physical Opinions*.

[7] Cavendish might be having a bit of fun here also, for elsewhere she is skeptical about whether or not flies have as many eyes as a magnifying glass would suggest they do. See for example *Observations Upon Experimental Philosophy*, section IX.

themselves to the Empress, (in what shapes or forms, I cannot exactly tell)[8] after some few Complements that passed between them, the Empress told the Spirits that she questioned not, but they did know how she was a stranger in that World, and by what miraculous means she was arrived there; and since she had a great desire to know the condition of the World she came from, her request to the Spirits was, To give her some Information thereof, especially of those parts of the World where she was born, bred, and educated; as also of her particular friends and acquaintance: all which, the Spirits did according to her desire. At last, after a great many conferences and particular intelligences, which the Spirits gave the Empress, to her great satisfaction and content; she enquired after the most famous Students, Writers, and Experimental Philosophers in that World, which they gave her a full relation of. . . .

She asked them further, Whether Spirits were of a globous or round Figure? They answered, That Figure belonged to body, but they being immaterial, had no Figure. She asked again, Whether Spirits were not like Water or Fire? They answered, that Water and Fire was material, were it the purest and most refined that ever could be; nay, were it above the Heavens: But we are no more like Water or Fire, said they, then we are like Earth; but our Vehicles are of several forms, figures and degrees of substances. Then she desired to know, Whether their Vehicles were made of Air? Yes, answered the Spirits, some of our Vehicles are of thin Air. Then I suppose, replied the Empress, That those airy Vehicles, are your corporeal Summer-suits. She asked further, Whether the Spirits had not ascending and descending-motions, as well as other Creatures? They answered, That properly there was no ascension or descension in Infinite Nature, but onely in relation to particular parts; and as for us Spirits, said they, We can neither ascend nor descend without corporeal Vehicles; nor can our Vehicles ascend or descend, but according to their several shapes and figures, for there can be no motion without body. The Empress asked them further, Whether there was not a World of Spirits, as well as there is of Material Creatures? No, answered they; for the word *World* implies a quantity or multitude of corporeal Creatures, but we being Immaterial, can make no World of Spirits. Then she desired to be informed when Spirits were made? We do not know, answered they, how and when we were made, nor are we much inquisitive after it; nay, if we did, it would be no benefit, neither for us, nor for you Mortals to know it. The Empress replied, That *Cabbalists* and Divine Philosophers said, Mens rational Souls were Immaterial, and stood as much in need of corporeal Vehicles, as Spirits did. If this be so, answered the

[8] Cavendish is insistent in her nonfictional writing that immaterials can have no shape or figure and that if an entity has a feature (like figure) that is only had by bodies, then it is a body itself. See, for example, *Further Observations Upon Experimental Philosophy*, section XX, and note 43 for *Philosophical Letters*.

Spirits, then you are Hermaphrodites of Nature; but your *Cabbalists* are mistaken, for they take the purest and subtilest parts of Matter, for Immaterial Spirits. Then the Empress asked, When the Souls of Mortals went out of their Bodies, whether they went to Heaven or Hell; or whether they remained in airy Vehicles? God's Justice and Mercy, answered they, is perfect, and not imperfect; but if you Mortals will have Vehicles for your Souls, and a place that is between Heaven and Hell, it must be Purgatory, which is a place of Purification, for which action Fire is more proper then Air; and so the Vehicles of those Souls that are in Purgatory, cannot be airy, but fiery; and after this rate there can be but four places for human Souls to be in, *viz.* Heaven, Hell, Purgatory, and this World; but as for Vehicles, they are but fancies, not real truths. Then the Empress asked them, Where Heaven and Hell was? Your Saviour Christ, answered the Spirits, has informed you, that there is Heaven and Hell, but he did not tell you what, nor where they are; wherefore it is too great a presumption for you Mortals to inquire after it. If you do but strive to get into Heaven, it is enough, though you do not know where or what it is; for it is beyond your knowledg and understanding. I am satisfied, replied the Empress; and asked further, Whether there were any Figures or Characters in the Soul? They answered, Where there was no Body, there could be no Figure. Then she asked them, Whether Spirits could be naked? And whether they were of a dark, or a light colour? As for our Nakedness, it is a very odd question, answered the Spirits; and we do not know what you mean by a Naked Spirit; for you judg of us as of corporeal Creatures; and as for Colour, said they, it is according to our Vehicles; for Colour belongs to Body, and as there is no Body that is colourless, so there is no Colour that is bodiless.[9] Then the Empress desired to be informed, Whether all Souls were made at the first Creation of the World? We know no more, answered the Spirits, of the origin of humane Souls, then we know of our Selves. She asked further, Whether humane bodies were not burthensome to humane Souls? They answered, That Bodies made Souls active, as giving them motion; and if action was troublesome to Souls, then Bodies were so too. . . .

The Empress received the proffer which they made her, with all civility; and told them, that she desired a Spiritual Scribe. The Spirits answer'd, That they could dictate, but not write, except they put on a hand or arm, or else the whole body of Man. The Empress replied, How can Spirits arm themselves with gantlets of Flesh? As well, answered they, as Man can arm himself with a gantlet of steel. If it be so, said the Empress, then I will have a Scribe. Then the Spirits asked her, Whether she would have the Soul of a living or a dead Man? Why, said the Empress, can the Soul quit a living Body, and wander or travel abroad?

---

[9] See also *Observations Upon Experimental Philosophy*, section XXI, where Cavendish argues that "secondary qualities" like color are literally in objects.

Yes, answered they, for according to *Plato*'s Doctrine, there is a Conversation of Souls, and the Souls of Lovers live in the Bodies of their Beloved. Then I will have, answered she, the Soul of some ancient famous Writer, either of *Aristotle, Pythagoras, Plato, Epicurus,* or the like. The Spirits said, That those famous Men were very learned, subtile, and ingenious Writers; but they were so wedded to their own opinions, that they would never have the patience to be Scribes. Then, said she, I'le have the Soul of one of the most famous modern Writers, as either of *Galileo, Gassendus, DesCartes, Helmont, Hobbes, H. More, &c.* The Spirits answered, That they were fine ingenious Writers, but yet so self-conceited, that they would scorn to be Scribes to a Woman.[10] But, said they, there's a Lady, the *Duchess of Newcastle*; which although she is not one of the most learned, eloquent, witty and ingenious, yet she is a plain and rational Writer; for the principle of her Writings, is Sense and Reason, and she will without question, be ready to do you all the service she can. That Lady then, said the Empress, will I chuse for my Scribe, neither will the Emperor have reason to be jealous, she being one of my own sex. In truth, said the Spirit, Husbands have reason to be jealous of *Platonick* Lovers, for they are very dangerous, as being not onely very intimate and close, but subtil and insinuating. You say well, replied the Empress; wherefore I pray send me the *Duchess of Newcastle*'s Soul; which the Spirit did; and after she came to wait on the Empress, at her first arrival the Empress imbraced and saluted her with a Spiritual kiss; then she asked her whether she could write? Yes, answered the *Duchess*'s Soul, but not so intelligibly that any Reader whatsoever may understand it, unless he be taught to know my Characters; for my Letters are rather like Characters, then well formed Letters. Said the Empress, you were recommended to me by an honest and ingenious Spirit. Surely, answered the Duchess, the Spirit is ignorant of my hand-writing. The truth is, said the Empress, he did not mention your hand-writing; but he informed me, that you writ Sense and Reason, and if you can but write so, that any of my Secretaries may learn your hand, they shall write it out fair and intelligible. The Duchess answered, That she questioned not but it might easily be learned in a short time. But, said she to the Empress, What is it that your Majesty would have written? She answered, The *Jews* Cabbala. Then your onely way for that is, said the Duchess, to have the Soul of some famous *Jew*; nay, if your Majesty please, I scruple not, but you may as easily have the Soul of *Moses,* as of any other. That cannot be, replied the Empress, for no Mortal knows where *Moses* is. . . . If your Majesty were resolved to make a *Cabbala,* I would advise you, rather to make a

[10] Note that *Philosophical Letters* is a "correspondence" in which Cavendish engages the views of Hobbes, Descartes, More, and Van Helmont indirectly and through a third party, apparently on the assumption that men would not take her seriously enough to participate with her in a thorough exchange of ideas.

Poetical or Romancical *Cabbala*, wherein you may use Metaphors, Allegories, Similtudes, &c. and interpret them as you please.

With that the Empress thank'd the Duchess, and embracing her Soul, told her she would take her Counsel: she made her also her Favourite, and kept her sometime in that World, and by this means the Duchess came to know and give this Relation of all that passed in that rich, populous, and happy World; and after some time the Empress gave her leave to return to her Husband and Kindred into her Native World, but upon condition, that her Soul should visit her now and then; which she did: and truly their meeting did produce such an intimate friendship between them, that they became *Platonick* Lovers, although they were both Femals. One time, when the Duchess her Soul was with the Empress, she seem'd to be very sad and melancholy; at which the Empress was very much troubled, and asked her the reason of her Melancholick humour? Truly, said the Duchess to the Empress, (for between dear friends there's no concealment, they being like several parts of one united body)[11] my Melancholy proceeds from an extream Ambition. The Empress asked, What the height of her ambition was? The Duchess answered, That neither she her self, nor no Creature in the World was able to know either the height, depth, or breadth of her Ambition; but said she, my present desire is, that I would be a great Princess. The Empress replied, So you are; for you are a Princess of the fourth or fifth Degree; for a Duke or Duchess is the highest title or honour that a subject can arrive to, as being the next to a King's Title . . . Well, said the Duchess, setting aside this dispute, my Ambition is, That I would fain be as you are, that is, an Empress of a World, and I shall never be at quiet until I be one. I love you so well, replied the Empress, that I wish with all my soul, you had the fruition of your ambitious desire, and I shall not fail to give you my best advice how to accomplish it; the best informers are the Immaterial Spirits, and they'l soon tell you, Whether it be possible to obtain your wish. But, said the Duchess, I have little acquaintance with them, for I never knew any before the time you sent for me. They know you, replied the Empress; for they told me of you, and were the means and instrument of your coming hither: Wherefore I'le conferr with them, and enquire whether there be not another World, whereof you may be Empress as well as I am of this?

No sooner had the Empress said this, but some Immaterial Spirits came to visit her, of whom she inquired, Whether there were but three Worlds in all, to wit, the *Blazing World* where she was in, the World which she came from, and the

---

[11] This is an interesting aside from Cavendish, given that she holds that an individual is a cluster of smaller bodies that work in unison toward a common goal—to preserve the existence of the whole, and in some cases to support other bodies or alternately to dominate them. See for example *Philosophical Letters*, letter XVII of section two and letter II of section three; *Grounds of Natural Philosophy*, chapter XVII of the First Part; and *Philosophical and Physical Opinions*, chapter 22.

World where the Duchess lived? The Spirits answered, That there were more numerous Worlds then the Stars which appeared in these three mentioned Worlds. Then the Empress asked, Whether it was not possible, that her dearest friend the Duchess of *Newcastle*, might be Empress of one of them? Although there be numerous, nay, infinite Worlds, answered the Spirits, yet none is without Government. But is none of these Worlds so weak, said she, that it may be surprized or conquered? The Spirits answered, That *Lucian*'s World of Lights,[12] had been for some time in a snuff, but of late years one *Helmont* had got it, who since he was Emperour of it, had so strengthened the Immortal parts thereof with mortal out-works, as it was for the present impregnable. Said the Empress, If there be such an Infinite number of Worlds, I am sure, not onely my friend, the Duchess, but any other might obtain one. Yes, answered the Spirits, if those Worlds were uninhabited; but they are as populous as this your Majesty governs. Why, said the Empress, it is not possible to conquer a World. No, answered the Spirits, but, for the most part, Conquerers seldom enjoy their conquest, for they being more feared then loved, most commonly come to an untimely end. If you will but direct me, said the Duchess to the Spirits, which World is easiest to be conquered, her Majesty will assist me with Means, and I will trust to Fate and Fortune; for I had rather die in the adventure of noble achievements, then live in obscure and sluggish security; since the by one, I may live in a glorious Fame; and by the other I am buried in oblivion. The Spirits answered, That the lives of Fame were like other lives; for some lasted long, and some died soon. 'Tis true, said the Duchess; but yet the shortest-liv'd Fame lasts longer then the longest life of Man.[13] But, replied the Spirits, if occasion does not serve you, you must content your self to live without such achievements that may gain you a Fame: But we wonder, proceeded the Spirits, that you desire to be Empress of a Terrestrial World when as you can create your self a Celestial World if you please. What, said the Empress, can any Mortal be a Creator? Yes, answered the Spirits; for every human Creature can create an Immaterial World fully inhabited by Immaterial Creatures, and populous of Immaterial subjects, such as we are, and all this within the compass of the head or scull; nay, not onely so, but he may create a World of what fashion and Government he will, and give the Creatures thereof such motions, figures, forms, colours, perceptions, &c. as he pleases, and make Whirl-pools, Lights, Pressures and Reactions, &c. as he thinks best; nay, he may make a World full of Veins, Muscles, and Nerves, and all these to move by one jolt or stroke: also he may alter that World as often as he pleases, or change

[12] For the reference, see Lucian, *A True Story*, in *Lucian: Volume I*, ed. and trans. A. M. Harmon, Loeb Classical Library (Cambridge, MA: Harvard UP, 1915). Lucian crafted fictional worlds that were similar in their playfulness and eccentricity to the one we encounter in *Blazing World*.
[13] See also *Worlds Olio*, "Fame makes a difference between Man and Beast."

it from a Natural World, to an Artificial; he may make a World of Ideas, a World of Atoms, a World of Lights, or whatsoever his Fancy leads him to. And since it is in your power to create such a World, What need you to venture life, reputation and tranquility, to conquer a gross material World? For you can enjoy no more of a material world then a particular Creature is able to enjoy, which is but a small part, considering the compass of such a world; and you may plainly observe it by your friend the Empress here, which although she possesses a whole World, yet enjoys she but a part thereof; neither is she so much acquainted with it, that she knows all the places, Countries, and Dominions she Governs. The truth is, a Sovereign Monarch has the general trouble; but the Subjects enjoy all the delights and pleasures in parts; for it is impossible, that a Kingdom, nay, a Country, should be injoyed by one person at once, except he take the pains to travel into every part, and endure the inconveniencies of going from one place to another? Wherefore, since glory, delight and pleasure lives but in other mens opinions, and can neither add tranquility to your mind nor give ease to your body, Why should you desire to be Empress of a Material World, and be troubled with the cares that attend Government? When as by creating a World within your self, you may enjoy all both in whole and in parts, without controle or opposition; and may make what World you please, and alter it when you please, and enjoy as much pleasure and delight as a World can afford you? You have converted me, said the Duchess to the Spirits, from my ambitious desire; wherefore, I'le take your advice, reject and despise all the Worlds without me, and create a World of my own. The Empress said, If I do make such a world, then I shall be Mistress of two Worlds, one within, and the other without me. That your Majesty may, said the Spirits; and so left these two Ladies to create two Worlds within themselves: who did also part from each other, until such time as they had brought their Worlds to perfection.[14]

The *Duchess* of *Newcastle* was most earnest and industrious to make her World, because she had none at present; and first she resolved to frame it according to the opinion of *Thales*, but she found her self so much troubled with Daemons,

[14] See also "Epilogue to the Reader," and *Worlds Olio*, "Allegory 20." Here it is worth noting an important similarity (and also an important difference) between Cavendish and Mary Astell on the role of contemplation in human life, and on its relation to issues of social equality. Astell is a Platonist philosopher who holds that men and women are equal in terms of their intellectual capacities and in particular in terms of their capacity to introspect and reflect on abstract philosophical truth. She does not suppose that women (or men) should focus their time on improving their material earthly status, but instead that we should contemplate Platonic ideas to practice for the purely spiritual experience that we will enjoy in the afterlife. (See, for example, *A Serious Proposal to the Ladies*, 80–81.) Cavendish has a quite different view, of course, but both philosophers hold that one of the central ways that an individual can achieve fulfillment in the face of an unfulfilling external environment is by turning attention toward an introspective world that is more amenable to their interests.

that they would not suffer her to take her own will, but forced her to obey their orders and commands; which she being unwilling to do, left off from making a world that way, and began to frame one according to *Pythagoras*'s Doctrine; but in the Creation thereof, she was so puzled with numbers, how to order and compose the several parts, that she having no skill in Arithmetick, was forced also to desist from the making of that World. Then she intended to create a World according to the opinion of *Plato*; but she found more trouble and difficulty in that, then in the two former; for the numerous Ideas having no other motion but what was derived from her mind, whence they did flow and issue out, made it a far harder business to her, to impart motion to them, then Puppit-players have in giving motion to every several Puppit; in so much, that her patience was not able to endure the trouble which those Ideas caused her; wherefore she annihilated also that World, and was resolved to make one according to the Opinion of *Epicurus*; which she had no sooner begun, but the infinite Atoms made such a mist, that it quite blinded the perception of her mind; neither was she able to make a *Vacuum* as a receptacle for those Atoms, or a place which they might retire into;[15] so that partly for the want of it, and of a good order and method, the confusion of those Atoms produced such strange and monstrous figures, as did more affright then delight her, and caused such a Chaos in her mind, as had almost dissolved it.[16] At last, having with much ado cleansed and cleared her mind of these dusty and misty particles, she endeavoured to create a World according to *Aristotle*'s Opinion; but remembring that her mind, as most of the Learned hold it, was Immaterial, and that, according to *Aristotle*'s Principle, out of Nothing, Nothing could be made; she was forced also to desist from that work, and then she fully resolved, not to take any more patterns from the Ancient Philosophers, but to follow the Opinions of the Moderns; and to that end, she endeavoured to make a World according to *DesCartes* Opinion; but when she had made the Aethereal Globules, and set them a moving by a strong and lively imagination, her mind became so dizzie with their extraordinary swift turning round, that it almost put her into a swoon; for her thoughts, by their constant tottering, did so stagger, as if they had all been drunk: wherefore she dissolved that World, and began to make another, according to *Hobbs*'s Opinion; but when all the parts of this Imaginary World came to press and drive each other,[17] they seemed like a company of Wolves that worry Sheep, or like so many Dogs that hunt after

---

[15] Cavendish argues in her nonfictional writings that there is no such thing as empty space or vacuum and that a body is just identical with its place. See for example *Observations Upon Experimental Philosophy*, section XIX; *Observations Upon the Opinions of Some Ancient Philosophers*, section IV.1; and note 20 for *Worlds Olio*.

[16] See also *Observations Upon the Opinions of Some Ancient Philosophers*, section IV.2.

[17] See also *Philosophical Letters*, letter IV of section one.

Hares; and when she found a re-action equal to those pressures, her mind was so squeezed together, that her thoughts could neither move forward nor backward, which caused such an horrible pain in her head, that although she had dissolved that World, yet she could not, without much difficulty, settle her mind, and free it from that pain which those pressures and reactions had caused in it. At last, when the Duchess saw that no patterns would do her any good in the framing of her World; she was resolved to make a World of her own Invention,[18] and this World was composed of sensitive and rational self-moving Matter; indeed, it was composed onely of the Rational, which is the subtilest and purest degree of Matter;[19] for as the Sensitive did move and act both to the perceptions and consistency of the body, so this degree of Matter at the same point of time (for though the degrees are mixt, yet the several parts may move several ways at one time) did move to the Creation of the Imaginary World; which World after it was made, appear'd so curious and full of variety, so well order'd and wisely govern'd, that it cannot possibly be expressed by words, nor the delight and pleasure which the Duchess took in making this World-of-her-own.

In the mean time the Empress was also making and dissolving several Worlds in her own mind,[20] and was so puzled, that she could not settle in any of them; wherefore she sent for the Duchess, who being ready to wait on the Empress, carried her beloved World along with her, and invited the Empress's Soul to observe the Frame, Order and Government of it. Her Majesty was so ravished with the perception of it, that her Soul desired to live in the Duchess's World: But the Duchess advised her to make such another World in her own mind; for, said she, your Majesty's mind is full of rational corporeal motions; and the rational motions of my mind shall assist you by the help of sensitive expressions, with the best Instructions they are able to give you.

The Empress being thus perswaded by the Duchess to make an imaginary World of her own, followed her advice; and after she had quite finished it, and framed all kinds of Creatures proper and useful for it, strengthened it with good Laws, and beautified it with Arts and Sciences; having nothing else to do, unless she did dissolve her Imaginary World, or made some alterations in the *Blazing-World*, she lived in; which yet she could hardly do, by reason it was so well ordered that it could not be mended; for it was governed without secret and deceiving Policy; neither was there any ambitious, factions, malicious detractions, civil

---

[18] Cavendish speaks throughout her corpus to the benefits of crafting worlds of imagination that are less resistant and more accommodating than the environments that we actually inhabit. See *Worlds Olio*, "Allegory 35" and "Allegory 20," and *Grounds of Natural Philosophy*, chapter IV of the Sixth Part.

[19] See also *Grounds of Natural Philosophy*, chapter X of the First Part.

[20] See also note 23 for *Observations Upon Experimental Philosophy*.

dissentions, or home-bred quarrels, divisions in Religion, Foreign Wars, *&c.* but all the people lived in a peaceful Society, united Tranquillity, and Religious Conformity. She was desirous to see the World the Duchess came from, and observe therein the several Sovereign Governments, Laws and Customs of several Nations. The Duchess used all the means she could, to divert her from that Journey, telling her, that the World she came from, was very much disturbed with Factions, Divisions and Wars; but the Empress would not be perswaded from her design; and lest the Emperor, or any of his subjects should know of her travel, and obstruct her design, she sent for some of the Spirits she had formerly conversed withal, and inquired whether none of them could supply the place of her soul in her body at such a time, when she was gone to travel into another World? They answered, Yes, they could; for not onely one, said they, but many Spirits may enter into your body, if you please. The Empress replied, she desired but one Spirit to be Vice-Roy of her body in the absence of her Soul, but it must be an honest and ingenious Spirit; and if it was possible, a female Spirit. The Spirits told her, that there was no difference of Sexes amongst them; but, said they, we will chuse an honest and ingenious Spirit, and such a one as shall so resemble your soul, that neither the Emperor, nor any of his Subjects, although the most Divine, shall know whether it be your own soul, or not: which the Empress was very glad at; and after the Spirits were gone, asked the Duchess, how her body was supplied in the absence of her soul? Who answered Her Majesty, That her body, in the absence of her soul, was governed by her sensitive and rational corporeal motions.[21] Thus those two Female Souls travelled together as lightly as two thoughts into the Duchess her native World; and, which is remarkable, in a moment viewed all the parts of it, and all the actions of all the Creatures therein, especially did the Empress's Soul take much notice of the several actions of humane Creatures in all the several Nations and parts of that World, and wonder'd that for all there were so many several Nations, Governments, Laws, Religions, Opinions, *&c.* they should all yet so generally agree in being Ambitious, Proud, Self-conceited, Vain, Prodigal, Deceitful, Envious, Malicious, Unjust, Revengeful, Irreligious, Factious, *&c.* She did also admire, that not any particular State, Kingdom or Common-wealth, was contented with their own shares, but endeavoured to encroach upon their Neighbours, and that their greatest glory was in Plunder and Slaughter, and yet their victory's less then their expences, and their losses more than their gains; but their being overcome, in a manner their utter ruine: But that she wonder'd most at, was, that they should prize or value dirt more then mens lives, and vanity more then tranquility. . . .

---

[21] Cavendish holds that embodied intelligence is quite common in nature. See, for example, *Worlds Olio*, "Epistle"; *Further Observations Upon Experimental Philosophy*, section XIII; and *Philosophical Letters*, letter X of section one.

And now to return to my former Story; when the Empress's and Duchess's Soul were travelling into *Nottinghamshire*, (for that was the place where the Duke[22] did reside) passing through the Forrest of *Sherewood*, the Empress's Soul was very much delighted with it, as being a dry, plain and woody place, very pleasant to travel in, both in Winter and Summer; for it is neither much dirty nor dusty at no time: At last they arrived at *Welbeck*, a House where the Duke dwell'd, surrounded all with Wood, so close and full, that the Empress took great pleasure and delight therein, and told the Duchess she never had observed more Wood in so little compass in any part of the Kingdom she had passed through. The truth is, said she, there seems to be more Wood on the Seas (she meaning the Ships) than on the Land. The Duchess told her, The reason was, that there had been a long Civil Warr in that Kingdom, in which most of the best Timber-trees and Principal Palaces were ruined and destroyed; and my dear Lord and Husband, said she, has lost by it half his Woods, besides many Houses, Land, and movable Goods; so that all the loss out of his particular Estate, did amount to above Half a Million of Pounds. I wish, said the Empress, he had some of the Gold that is in the Blazing-world, to repair his losses. The Duchess most humbly thank'd her Imperial Majesty for her kind wishes; but, said she, Wishes will not repair his ruins: however, God has given my Noble Lord and Husband great Patience, by which he bears all his losses and misfortunes.

[The Duchess and the Empress soon return to the Blazing World, and shortly thereafter the Duchess departs to return home.] ...

But when she was just upon her departure, the *Empress* sent to Her, and desired that she might yet have some little conference with her before she went; which the *Duchess* most willingly granted her Majesty; and when she came to wait on her, the *Empress* told the *Duchess*, That she being her dear Platonick Friend, of whose just and Impartial Judgment, she had alwayes a very great esteem; could not for-bear, before she went from her, to ask her Advice concerning the Government of the *Blazing-world:* For, said she, although this World was very well and wisely or-dered and governed at first, when I came to be Empress thereof; yet the nature of Women being much delighted with Change and Variety,[23] after I had received an absolute Power from the Emperor, did somewhat alter the Form of Government from what I found it; but now perceiving that the World is not so quiet as it was at first, I am much troubled at it; especially there are such continual Contentions and Divisions between the *Worm-Bear*-and *Fly*-men, the *Ape*-men, the *Satyrs,*

---

[22] This is Cavendish's husband, William, the Duke of Newcastle.

[23] Cavendish argues in her nonfictional writing that nature appreciates variety and that the more variety and diversity that exist in nature, the more that different individuals and species will be striving to maintain themselves in existence, and the more conflict, struggle, and destruction there will be. See, for example, *Observations Upon Experimental Philosophy*, section XXVIII.

the *Spider*-men, and all others of such sorts, that I fear they'l break out into an open Rebellion, and cause a great disorder, and the ruin of the Government; and therefore I desire your advice and assistance, how I may order it to the best advantage, that this World may be rendred peaceable, quiet and happy, as it was before. Whereupon the Duchess answered, That since she heard by her Imperial Majesty, how well and happily the World had been governed when she first came to be Empress thereof, she would advise her Majesty to introduce the same form of Government again, which had been before; that is, to have but one Soveraign, one Religion, one Law, and one Language, so that all the World might be but as one united Family, without divisions; nay, like God, and his Blessed Saints and Angels: Otherwise, said she, it may in time prove as unhappy, nay, as miserable a World as that is from which I came, wherein are more Soveraigns then Worlds, and more pretended Governours then Government, more Religions then Gods, and more Opinions in those Religions then Truths; more Laws then Rights, and more Bribes then Justices; more Policies then Necessities, and more Fears then Dangers; more Covetousness then Riches, more Ambitions then Merits, more Services then Rewards, more Languages then Wit, more Controversie then Knowledg, more Reports then noble Actions, and more Gifts by partiality then according to Merit; all which, said she, is a great misery, nay, a curse, which your blessed *Blazing-World* never knew, nor 'tis probable, will never know of, unless your Imperial Majesty alter the Government thereof from what it was when you began to govern it: And since your Majesty complains much of the factions of the *Bear-* *Fish-* *Fly-* *Ape-* and *Worm*-men, the *Satyrs, Spider*-men, and the like, and of their perpetual disputes and quarrels, I would advise your Majesty to dissolve all their Societies; for 'tis better to be without their intelligences, then to have an unquiet and disorderly Government. The truth is, said she, wheresoever Learning is, there is most commonly also Controversie and quarelling; for there be always some that will know more, and be wiser then others: Some think their Arguments come nearer to Truth, and are more rational then others; some are so wedded to their own opinions, that they'l never yield to Reason; and others, though they find their Opinions not firmly grounded upon Reason, yet, for fear of receiving some disgrace by altering them, will nevertheless maintain them against all sense and reason, which must needs breed factions in their Schools, which at last break out into open Wars, and draw sometimes an utter ruin upon a State or Government.

PART II

The Empress having now ordered and setled her Government to the best advantage and quiet of her *Blazing-World*, lived and reigned most happily and blessedly, and received oftentimes Visits from the Immaterial Spirits, who gave her

Intelligence of all such things as she desired to know, and they were able to inform her of: One time they told her, how the World she came from, was imbroiled in a great War, and that most parts or Nations thereof made War against that Kingdom which was her Native Country, where all her Friends and Relations did live; at which the Empress was extreamly troubled; insomuch that the Emperor perceived her grief by her tears, and examining the cause thereof, she told him that she had received Intelligence from the Spirits, that that part of the World she came from, which was her native Country, was like to be destroyed by numerous Enemies that made War against it. The Emperor being very sensible of this ill news, especially of the Trouble it caused to the Empress, endeavoured to comfort her as much as possibly he could; and told her, that she might have all the assistance which the *Blazing-World* was able to afford. She answered, That if there were any possibility of transporting Forces out of the *Blazing-World*, into the World she came from, she would not fear so much the ruin thereof: but, said she, there being no probability of effecting any such thing, I know not how to shew my readiness to serve my Native Country. The Emperor asked, Whether those Spirits that gave her Intelligence of this War, could not with all their Power and Forces, assist her against those Enemies? She answered, That Spirits could not arm themselves, nor make any use of Artificial Arms or Weapons; for their Vehicles were Natural Bodies, not Artificial: Besides, said she, the violent and strong actions of war, will never agree with Immaterial Spirits; for Immaterial Spirits cannot fight, nor make Trenches, Fortifications, and the like. But, said the Emperor, their Vehicles can; especially if those Vehicles be mens Bodies, they may be serviceable in all the actions of War. Alas, replied the Empress, that will never do; for first, said she, it will be difficult to get so many dead Bodies for their Vehicles, as to make up a whole Army, much more to make many Armies to fight with so many several Nations; nay, if this could be, yet it is not possible to get so many dead and undissolved Bodies in one Nation; and for transporting them out of other Nations, it would be a thing of great difficulty and improbability: But put the case, said she, all these difficulties could be overcome; yet there is one obstruction or hindrance which can no ways be avoided: For although those dead and undissolved Bodies did all die in one minute of time; yet before they could Rendezvouze, and be put into a posture of War, to make a great and formidable Army, they would stink and dissolve; and when they came to a fight, they would moulder into dust and ashes, and so leave the purer Immaterial Spirits naked: nay, were it also possible, that those dead bodies could be preserved from stinking and dissolving, yet the Souls of such Bodies would not suffer Immaterial Spirits to rule and order them, but they would enter and govern them themselves, as being the right owners thereof, which would produce a War between those Immaterial Souls, and the Immaterial Spirits in Material Bodies; all which would hinder them from doing any service in the actions of War, against the

Enemies of my Native Countrey. You speak Reason, said the Emperor, and I wish with all my Soul I could advise any manner or way, that you might be able to assist it; but you having told me of your dear Platonick Friend the Duchess of *Newcastle,* and of her good and profitable Counsels, I would desire you to send for her Soul, and conferr with her about this business.

The Empress was very glad of this motion of the Emperor, and immediately sent for the Soul of the said Duchess, which in a minute waited on her Majesty. Then the Empress declared to her the grievance and sadness of her mind, and how much she was troubled and afflicted at the News brought her by the Immaterial Spirits, desiring the Duchess, if possible, to assist her with the best Counsels she could, that she might shew the greatness of her love and affection which she bore to her Native Countrey. Whereupon the Duchess promised her Majesty to do what lay in her power; and since it was a business of great Importance, she desired some time to consider of it; for, said she, Great Affairs require deep Considerations; which the Empress willingly allowed her. And after the Duchess had considered some little time, she desired the Empress to send some of her*Syrens* or *Mear*-men, to see what passages they could find out of the *Blazing-World,* into the World she came from; for, said she, if there be a passage for a Ship to come out of that World into this; then certainly there may also a Ship pass thorow the same passage out of this World into that. Hereupon the Mear-or Fish-men were sent out; who being many in number, employ'd all their industry, and did swim several ways; at last having found out the passage, they returned to the Empress, and told her, That as their *Blazing World* had but one Emperor, one Government, one Religion, and one Language, so there was but one Passage into that World, which was so little, that no Vessel bigger than a Packet-Boat could go thorow; neither was that Passage always open, but sometimes quite frozen up. At which Relation both the Empress and Duchess seemed somewhat troubled, fearing that this would perhaps be an hindrance or obstruction to their Design.

At last the Duchess desired the Empress to send for her Ship-wrights, and all her Architects, which were Giants; who being called, the Duchess told them how some in her own World had been so ingenious, as to contrive Ships that could swim under Water, and asked, Whether they could do the like? The Giants answered, They had never heard of that Invention; nevertheless, they would try what might be done by Art, and spare no labour or industry to find it out. In the mean time, while both the Empress and Duchess were in a serious Counsel, after many debates, the Duchess desired but a few Ships to transport some of the Bird- Worm-and Bear-men: Alas! said the Empress, What can such sorts of Men do in the other World? Especially so few? They will be soon destroyed, for a Musket will destroy numbers of Birds at one shot. The Duchess said, I desire your Majesty will have but a little patience, and relie upon my advice, and you shall not fail to save your own Native Country, and in a manner become Mistress of all that World you came from. The Empress, who loved the Duchess as her own Soul, did so; the Giants returned soon after, and told her Majesty, that they had found out the Art which the Duchess had mentioned, to make such Ships as could swim under water; which the Empress and Duchess were both very glad at, and when the Ships were made ready, the Duchess told the Empress, that it was requisite that her Majesty should go her self in body, as well as in Soul; but I, said she, can onely wait on your Majesty after a Spiritual manner, that is, with my Soul. Your Soul, said the Empress, shall live with my Soul, in my Body; for I shall onely desire your Counsel and Advice. . . .

Thus after all things were made fit and ready, the Empress began her Journey; I cannot properly say, she set Sail, by reason in some Part, as in the passage between the two Worlds (which yet was but short) the Ships were drawn under water by the Fish-men with Golden Chains, so that they had no need of Sails there, nor of any other Arts, but onely to keep out water from entering into the Ships, and to give or make so much Air as would serve, for breath or respiration, those Land-Animals that were in the Ships; which the Giants had so Artificially contrived, that they which were therein, found no inconveniency at all: And after they had passed the Icy Sea, the Golden Ships appeared above Water, and so went on until they came near the Kingdom that was the Empress's Native Countrey; where the Bear-men through their Telescopes discovered a great number of Ships which had beset all that Kingdom, well rigg'd and mann'd.[24]

The Empress before she came in sight of the Enemy, sent some of her Fish- and Bird-men to bring her intelligence of their Fleet; and hearing of their number, their station and posture, she gave order that when it was Night, her Bird-men should carry in their beeks some of the mentioned Fire-stones, with the tops thereof wetted; and the Fish-men should carry them likewise, and hold them out of the Water; for they were cut in the form of Torches or Candles, and being many thousands, made a terrible shew; for it appear'd as if all the Air and Sea had been of a Flaming-Fire; and all that were upon the Sea, or near it, did verily believe, the time of Judgment, or the Last Day was come, which made them all fall down, and Pray. . . .

In the mean while, the Empress knowing the Colours of her own Country, sent a Letter to their General, and the rest of the chief Commanders, to let them know, that she was a great and powerful Princess, and came to assist them against

---

[24] In her nonfictional work Cavendish expresses a general distrust of telescopes and other artefacts (note 19 for *Worlds Olio*), though does she suppose that these are reliable when used from distances that allow of confirmation with the naked eye (for example in *Observations Upon Experimental Philosophy*, section XXXIV).

their Enemies; wherefore she desired they should declare themselves, when they would have her help and assistance.

Hereupon a Councel was called, and the business debated; but there were so many cross and different Opinions, that they could not suddenly resolve what answer to send the Empress; at which she grew angry, insomuch that she resolved to return into her *Blazing-World*, without giving any assistance to her Countrymen: but the Duchess of *Newcastle* intreated her Majesty to abate her passion; for, said she, Great Councels are most commonly slow, because many men have many several Opinions: besides, every Councellor striving to be the wisest, makes long speeches, and raise many doubts, which cause retardments.[25] If I had long-speeched Councellors, replied the Empress, I would hang them, by reason they give more Words, then Advice. The Duchess answered, That her Majesty should not be angry, but consider the differences of that and her *Blazing-World*; for, said she, they are not both alike; but there are grosser and duller understandings in this, than in the *Blazing-World*.

At last a Messenger came out, who returned the Empress thanks for her kind proffer, but desired withal, to know from whence she came, and how, and in what manner her assistance could be serviceable to them? The Empress answered, That she was not bound to tell them whence she came; but as for the manner of her assistance, I will appear, said she, to your Navy in a splendorous Light, surrounded with Fire. The Messenger asked at what time they should expect her coming? I'le be with you, answered the Empress, about one of the Clock at night. With this report the Messenger returned; which made both the poor Councellors and Sea-men much afraid; but yet they longed for the time to behold this strange sight.

The appointed hour being come, the Empress appear'd with Garments made of the Star-stone, and was born or supported above the Water, upon the Fish-mens heads and backs, so that she seemed to walk upon the face of the Water, and the Bird- and Fish-men carried the Fire-stone, lighted both in the Air, and above the Waters.

Which sight, when her Country-men perceived at a distance, their hearts began to tremble; but coming something nearer, she left her Torches, and appeared onely in her Garments of Light, like an Angel, or some Deity, and all kneeled down before her, and worshipped her with all submission and reverence: But the Empress would not come nearer than at such a distance where her voice might be generally heard, by reason she would not have that any of her Accoutrements should be perceived, but the splendor thereof; and when she

---

[25] In other work Cavendish speaks against aristocracy and councils, and in favor of monarchy as the best form of government for securing unity, consistency, and stability. See, for example, *The She-anchoret*, in this chapter, the response to "The Eighth sort of Visiters."

was come so near that her voice could be heard and understood by all, she made this following Speech:

Dear Country-men, for so you are, although you know me not; I being a Native of this Kingdom, and hearing that most part of this World had resolved to make Warr against it, and sought to destroy it, at least to weaken its Naval Force and Power, have made a Voyage out of another World, to lend you my assistance against your Enemies. I come not to make bargains with you, or to regard my own Interest more than your Safety; but I intend to make you the most powerful Nation of this World, and therefore I have chosen rather to quit my own Tranquility, Riches and Pleasure, than suffer you to be ruined and destroyed. All the Return I desire, is but your grateful acknowledgment, and to declare my Power, Love and Loyalty to my Native Country: for, although I am now a Great and Absolute Princess, and Empress of a whole World, yet I acknowledg, that once I was a Subject of this Kingdom, which is but a small part of this World; and therefore I will have you undoubtedly believe, that I shall destroy all your Enemies before this following Night, I mean those which trouble you by Sea; and if you have any by Land, assure your self I shall also give you my assistance against them, and make you triumph over all that seek your Ruine and Destruction.

Upon this Declaration of the Empress, when both the General, and all the Commanders in their several Ships, had return'd their humble and hearty Thanks to Her Majesty for so great a favour to them, she took her leave, and departed to her own Ships. But, good Lord! What several Opinions and Judgments did this produce in the minds of her Country-men! Some said she was an Angel; others, she was a Sorceress; some believed her a Goddess;[26] others said the Devil deluded them in the shape of a fine Lady.

The morning after, when the Navies were to fight, the Empress appear'd upon the face of the Waters, dress'd in her Imperial Robes, which were all of Diamonds and Carbuncles; in one hand she held a Buckler, made of one intire Carbuncle; and in the other hand a Spear of one intire Diamond; on her head she had a Cap of Diamonds, and just upon the top of the Crown, was a Starr made of the Starr-stone, mentioned heretofore; and a Half-Moon made of the same Stone, was placed on her forehead; all her other Garments were of several sorts of precious Jewels; and having given her Fish-men directions how to destroy the Enemies of her Native Country, she proceeded to effect her design. The Fish-men were to carry the Fire-stones in cases of Diamonds (for the Diamonds in the *Blazing-World,* are in splendor so far beyond the Diamonds of this World, as Peble-stones are to the best sort of this Worlds Diamonds) and to uncase or

---

[26] In her nonfictional writing Cavendish speaks to the importance of ceremony and of the presentation of a monarch as supremely exalted. See, for example, *Worlds Olio,* "Of Ceremony."

uncover those Fire-stones no sooner but when they were just under the Enemies Ships, or close at their sides, and then to wet them, and set their Ships on fire; which was no sooner done, but all the Enemie's Fleet was of a Flaming fire; and coming to the place where the Powder was, it streight blew them up; so that all the several Navies of the Enemies, were destroyed in a short time: which when her Countrymen did see, they all cried out with one voice, That she was an Angel sent from God to deliver them out of the hands of their Enemies: Neither would she return into the *Blazing-World*, until she had forced all the rest of that World to submit to that same Nation.

In the mean time, the General of all their Naval Forces, sent to their Soveraign to acquaint him with their miraculous Delivery and Conquest, and with the Empress's design of making him the most powerful Monarch of all that World. After a short time, the Empress sent her self, to the Soveraign of that Nation to know in what she could be serviceable to him; who returning her many thanks, both for her assistance against his Enemies, and her kind proffer to do him further service for the good and benefit of his Nations (for he was King over several Kingdoms) sent her word, that although she did partly destroy his Enemies by Sea, yet, they were so powerful, that they did hinder the Trade and Traffick of his Dominions. To which the Empress returned this answer, That she would burn and sink all those Ships that would not pay him Tribute; and forthwith sent to all the Neighbouring Nations, who had any Traffick by Sea, desiring them to pay Tribute to the King and Soveraign of that Nation where she was born; But they denied it with great scorn. Whereupon, she immediately commanded her Fish-men, to destroy all strangers Ships that traffick'd on the Seas; which they did according to the Empress's Command; and when the Neighbouring Nations and Kingdoms perceived her power, they were so discomposed in their affairs and designs, that they knew not what to do: At last they sent to the Empress, and desired to treat with her, but could get no other conditions then to submit and pay Tribute to the said King and Soveraign of her Native Country, otherwise, she was resolved to ruin all their Trade and Traffick by burning their Ships. Long was this Treaty, but in fine, they could obtain nothing, so that at last they were inforced to submit; by which the King of the mentioned Nations became absolute Master of the Seas, and consequently of that World; by reason, as I mentioned heretofore, the several Nations of that World could not well live without Traffick and Commerce, by Sea, as well as by Land.

But after a short time, those Neighbouring Nations finding themselves so much inslaved, that they were hardly able to peep out of their own Dominions without a chargeable Tribute, they all agreed to join again their Forces against the King and Soveraign of the said Dominions; which when the Empress receiv'd notice of, she sent out her Fish-men to destroy, as they had done before, the remainder of all their Naval Power, by which they were soon forced again to submit, except some Nations which could live without Foreign Traffick, and some whose Trade and Traffick was meerly by Land; these would no ways be Tributary to the mentioned King. The Empress sent them word, That in case they did not submit to him, she intended to fire all their Towns and Cities, and reduce them by force, to what they would not yield with a good will. But they rejected and scorned her Majesties Message, which provoked her anger so much, that she resolved to send her Bird-and Worm men thither, with order to begin first with their smaller Towns, and set them on fire (for she was loath to make more spoil then she was forced to do) and if they remain'd still obstinate in their resolutions, to destroy also their greater Cities. The onely difficulty was, how to convey the Worm-men conveniently to those places; but they desired that her Majesty would but set them upon any part of the Earth of those Nations, and they could travel within the Earth as easily, and as nimbly as men upon the face of the Earth; which the Empress did according to their desire.

But before both the Bird-and Worm-men began their journey, the Empress commanded the Bear-men to view through their Telescopes what Towns and Cities those were that would not submit; and having a full information thereof, she instructed the Bird-and Bear-men what Towns they should begin withal; in the mean while she sent to all the Princes and Soveraigns of those Nations, to let them know that she would give them a proof of her Power, and check their Obstinacies by burning some of their smaller Towns; and if they continued still in their Obstinate Resolutions, that she would convert their smaller Loss into a Total Ruin. She also commanded her Bird-men to make their flight at night, lest they be perceived. At last when both the Bird-and Worm-men came to the designed places, the Worm-men laid some Fire-stones under the Foundation of every House, and the Bird-men placed some at the tops of them, so that both by rain, and by some other moisture within the Earth, the stones could not fail of burning. The Bird-men in the mean time having learned some few words of their Language, told them, That the next time it did rain, their Towns would be all on fire; at which they were amaz'd to hear Men speak in the air; but withall they laughed when they heard them say that rain should fire their Towns; knowing, that the effect of Water was to quench, not produce Fire.

At last a rain came, and upon a sudden all their Houses appeared of a flaming Fire; and the more Water there was poured on them, the more they did flame and burn; which struck such a Fright and Terror into all the Neighbouring Cities, Nations and Kingdoms, that for fear the like should happen to them, they and all the rest of the parts of that World, granted the Empress's desire, and submitted to the Monarch and Sovereign of her Native Countrey, the King of

ESFI;[27] save one, which having seldom or never any rain, but onely dews, which would soon be spent in a great fire, slighted her Power: The Empress being desirous to make it stoop as well as the rest, knew that every year it was watered by a flowing Tide, which lasted some Weeks; and although their Houses stood high from the ground, yet they were built upon Supporters which were fixt into the ground. Wherefore she commanded both her Bird-and Worm-men to lay some of the Fire-stones at the bottom of those Supporters, and when the Tide came in, all their Houses were of a Fire, which did so rarifie the Water, that the Tide was soon turn'd into Vapour, and this Vapour again into Air; which caused not onely a destruction of their Houses, but also a general barrenness over all their Countrey that year, and forced them to submit, as well as the rest of the World had done.

Thus the Empress did not onely save her Native Country, but made it the Absolute Monarchy of all that World; and both the effects of her Power and her Beauty, did kindle a great desire in all the greatest Princes to see her; who hearing that she was resolved to return into her own Blazing-World, they all entreated the favour, that they might wait on her Majesty before she went. The Empress sent word, That she should be glad to grant their Requests; but having no other place of Reception for them, she desired that they would be pleased to come into the open Seas with their Ships, and make a Circle of a pretty large compass, and then her own Ships should meet them, and close up the Circle, and she would present her self to the view of all those that came to see her: Which Answer was joyfully received by all the mentioned Princes, who came, some sooner, and some later, each according to the distance of his Countrey, and the length of the voyage. And being all met in the form and manner aforesaid, the Empress appeared upon the face of the Water in her Imperial Robes; in some part of her hair, near her face, she had placed some of the Starr-Stone, which added such a luster and glory to it, that it caused a great admiration in all that were present, who believed her to be some Celestial Creature, or rather an uncreated Goddess, and they all had a desire to worship her; for surely, said they, no mortal creature can have such a splendid and transcendent beauty, nor can any have so great a power as she has, to walk upon the Waters, and to destroy whatever she pleases, not onely whole Nations, but a whole World. . . .

But when it was upon break of day, the Empress ended her Entertainment, and at full day-light all the Princes perceived that she went into the Ship wherein the Prince and Monarch of her Native Country was, the King of ESFI, with whom

---

[27] ESFI is apparently England, Scotland, France, and Ireland. Note that Cavendish lived in exile from her native England for almost twenty years, to escape from the violent civil war that included the dethroning of Charles I. She returned to England upon the restoration of the monarchy and the ascension of Charles II.

she had several Conferences; and having assured Him of the readiness of her Assistance whensoever he required it, telling Him withal, That she wanted no Intelligence, she went forth again upon the Waters, and being in the midst of the Circle made by those Ships that were present, she desired them to draw somewhat nearer, that they might hear her speak; which being done, she declared her self in this following manner:

Great, Heroick, and Famous Monarchs, I come hither to assist the King of ESFI against his Enemies, He being unjustly assaulted by many several Nations, which would fain take away His Hereditary Rights and Prerogatives of the Narrow Seas; at which Unjustice, Heaven was much displeased, and for the Injuries He received from His Enemies, rewarded Him with an Absolute Power, so that now he is become the Head-Monarch of all this World; which Power, though you may envy, yet you can no wayes hinder Him; for all those that endeavour to resist His Power, shall onely get Loss for their Labour, and no Victory for their Profit. Wherefore my advice to you all is, To pay him Tribute justly and truly, that you may live Peaceably and Happily, and be rewarded with the Blessings of Heaven: which I wish you from my Soul.

THE EPILOGUE TO THE READER

By this Poetical Description, you may perceive, that my ambition is not onely to be Empress, but Authoress of a whole World; and that the Worlds I have made, both the *Blazing-* and the other *Philosophical* World, mentioned in the first Part of this *Description*, are framed and composed of the most pure, that is, the Rational parts of Matter, which are the parts of my Mind; which Creation was more easily and suddenly effected, than the Conquests of the two famous Monarchs of the World, *Alexander* and *Cesar.* Neither have I made such disturbances, and caused so many dissolutions of particulars, otherwise named deaths, as they did; for I have destroyed but some few men in a little Boat, which dyed through the extremity of cold, and that by the hand of Justice, which was necessitated to punish their crime of stealing away a young and beauteous Lady. And in the formation of those Worlds, I take more delight and glory, than ever *Alexander* or *Cesar* did in conquering this terrestrial world; and though I have made my *Blazing-world* a Peaceable World, allowing it but one Religion, one Language, and one Government; yet could I make another World, as full of Factions, Divisions and Warrs, as this is of Peace and Tranquility; and the Rational figures of my Mind might express as much courage to fight, as *Hector* and *Achilles* had; and be as wise as *Nestor*, as Eloquent as *Ulysses*, and as beautiful as *Hellen.* But I esteeming Peace before Warr, Wit before Policy, Honesty before Beauty; instead of the figures of *Alexander, Cesar, Hector, Achilles, Nestor, Ulysses, Hellen,* &c. chose rather the figure of Honest *Margaret Newcastle,* which now I would not change for all this Terrestrial World; and if any should like the World I have made, and be willing to be my Subjects, they may imagine themselves such, and they are such, I mean in their Minds, Fancies or Imaginations; but if they cannot endure to be Subjects, they may create Worlds of their own, and Govern themselves as they please. But yet let them have a care, not to prove unjust Usurpers, and to rob me of mine: for, concerning the *Philosophical-world,* I am Empress of it my self; and as for the *Blazing-world,* it having an Empress already, who rules it with great Wisdom and Conduct, which Empress is my dear Platonick Friend; I shall never prove so unjust, treacherous and unworthy to her, as to disturb her Government, much less to depose her from her Imperial Throne, for the sake of any other, but rather chuse to create another World for another Friend.

FINIS.

Playes—"The Dedication"

> To those that do delight in Scenes and wit,
> I dedicate my Book, for those I writ;
> Next to my own Delight, fir I did take
> Much pleasure and delight these Playes to make;
> For all the time my Playes a making were,
> My Brain the Stage, my thoughts were acting there.

Playes, "An Introduction"

Enter 3 Gentleman.

. . .

1. *Gentleman.*
Well, if I were to write a Play, I would write the length of a humour according to the strength of the humour and breadth of my wit. Let them judge me and condemn as they would; for though some of the past, and present ages be erroniously or malitiously foolish in such cases; yet the future Ages may be more wise, and better natur'd as to applaud what the others have condemned.

But prithy *Tom* let us goe.

2. Gentleman.

No, I will not goe for the reasons before mentioned, which is, they tire me with their empty words, dull speeches, long parts, tedious Acts, ill Actors; and the truth is, theres not enough variety in an old play to please me.

1. Gentleman.

There is variety of that which is bad, as you have divided it, but it seemes you love youth and variety in playes, as you doe in Mistresses.

3. Gentleman.

Playes delight Amorous men as much as a Mistris doth.

1. Gentleman.

Nay, saith more, for a man and his Mistris is soon out of breath in their discourse, and then they know not what to say, and when they are at a *Non-pluss*, they would be glad to be quit of each other, yet are ashamed to part so soon, and are weary to stay with each other long, when a Play entertaines them with Love, and requires not their answers, nor forceth their braines, nor pumps their wits; for a Play doth rather fill them than empty them.

2. Gentleman.

Faith most Playes doth rather fill the spectators with wind, than with substance, with noise, than with newes;

1. Gentleman.

This Play that I would have you go to, is a new Play.

2. Gentleman.

But is there newes in the Play, that is (is there new wit, fancyes, or new Scenes) and not taken out of old storyes, or old Playes newly translated?

1. Gentleman.

I know not that, but this Play was writ by a Lady, who on my Conscience hath neither Language, nor Learning, but what is native and naturall.

2. Gentleman.

A woman write a Play!

Out upon it; out upon it, for it cannot be good, besides you say she is a Lady, which is the likelyer to make the Play worse, a woman and a Lady to write a Play; sigh, sigh.

3. *Gentleman.*

Why may not a Lady write a good Play?

2. *Gentleman.*

No, for a womans wit is too weak and too conceived to write a Play.

1. *Gentleman.*

But if a woman hath wit, or can write a good Play, what will you
say then?

2. *Gentleman.*

Why, I will say no body will believe it, for if it be good, they will think she
did not write it, or at least say she did not, besides the very being a woman
condemnes it, were it never so excellent and care, for men will not allow
women to have wit, or we men to have reason, for if we allow them wit, we
shall lose our prehemency.

. . .

Bell in Campo

Part I. ACT I.

. . .

Scene 2.

Enter the Lord General, *and the Lady* Victoria *his Wife.*

General.

My dear heart, you know I am commanded to the Wars, and had I not such
Wife as you are, I should have thought Fortune had done me a favour to
imploy my life in Heroical Actions for the service of my Country, or to give
me a honourable Death, but to leave you is such a Cross as my Nature sinks
under; but wheresoever you are there will be my life, I shall only carry a
Body which may fight, but my Soul and all the powers thereof will remain
with thee.

Lady Victoria.

Husband, I shall take this expression of love but for feigning words, if you
leave me; for 'tis against Nature to part with that we love best, unless it be for
the beloveds preservation, which cannot be mine, for my life lives in yours,
and the comfort of that life in your Company.

Lord General.
I know you love me so well, as you had rather part with my life than I should part from my honour.

Lady Victoria.
'Tis true, my love perswades me so to do, knowing fame is a double life[28], as infamy is a double death; nay I should perswade you to those actions, were they never so dangerous, were you unwilling thereunto, or could they create a world of honour, fully inhabited with praises; but I would not willingly part with your life for an imaginary or supposed honour, which dyes in the womb before it is Born; thus I love you the best, preferring the best of what is yours; but I am but in the second place in your affections, for you prefer your honour before me; 'tis true, it is the better choice, but it shows I am not the best beloved, which makes you follow and glue to that and leave me.

Lord General.
Certainly Wife my honour is your honour, and your honour will be buried in my disgrace, which Heaven avert; for I prefer yours before my own, insomuch as I would have your honour to be the Crown of my glory.

Lady Victoria.
Then I must partake of your actions, and go along with you.

Lord General.
What to the Wars?

Lady Victoria.
To any place where you are.

Lord General.
But Wife you consider not, as that long marches, ill lodgings, much watching, cold nights, scorching dayes, hunger and danger are ill Companions for Ladyes, their acquaintance displeases; their conversation is rough and rude, being too boisterous for Ladyes; their tender and strengthless constitutions cannot encounter nor grapell therewith.

Lady Victoria.
'Tis said, that Love overcomes all things: in your Company long marches will be but as a breathing walk, the hard ground feel as a Feather-Bed, and

---

[28] See also *Worlds Olio*, "Fame makes a difference between Man and Beast."

the starry Sky a spangled Canopy, hot dayes a Stove to cure cold Agues, hunger as Fasting dayes or an eve to devotion, and danger is honours triumphant Chariot.

Lord General.
But Nature hath made women like China, or Pursleyn, they must be used gently, and kept warily, or they will break and fall on Deaths head: besides, the inconveniencies in an Army are so many, as put patience her self out of humour; besides, there is such inconveniences as modesty cannot allow of.

Lady Victoria.
[I]f you let me stay behind you, it will be a thousand to one but either you will lose me in Death, or your honour in Life, where if you let me go you will save both; for if you will consider and reckon all the married women you have heard or read of, that were absented from their Husbands, although upon just and necessary occasions, but had some Ink of aspersions flung upon them, although their wives were old, illfavoured, decrepid and diseased women, or were they as pure as light, or as innocent as Heaven; and wheresoever this Ink of aspersions is thrown, it sticks so fast, that the spots are never rubb'd out, should it fall on Saints, they must wear the marks as a Badge of misfortunes, and what man had not better be thought or called an uxorious Husband, than to be despised and laught at, as being but thought a Cuckhold? . . . [W]hat is more lawfull, fitting, and proper, than for a man and wife to be inseparable together?

Lord General.
Well, you have used so much Rhetorick to perswade, as you have left me none to deny you, wherefore I am resolved you shall try what your tender Sex can endure; but I believe when you hear the Bullets fly about you, you will wish your self at home, and repent your rash adventure.

Lady Victoria.
I must prove false first, for love doth give me courage.

Lord General.
Then come along, I shall your courage try.

Lady Victoria.
I'le follow you, though in Deaths Arms I ly.

. . .

Scene 4
Enter four or five other Gentlemen.

1 *Gent.*
The Lord *General* was accounted a discreet and wise man, but he shows
but little wisdome in this action of carrying his wife along with him to the
Wars, to be a Clog at his heels, a Chain to his hands, an Incumberance in his
march, obstruction in his way; for she will be always puling and sick, and
whining, and crying, and tir'd, and . . . , and if her Dog should be left in any
place, as being forgotten, all the whole Army must make a halt whilst the
Dog is fetcht, and Trooper after Trooper must be sent to bring intelligence
of the Dogs coming, but if there were such a misfortune that the Dog could
not be found, the whole Army must be dispersed for the search of it, and if
it should be lost, then there must seem to be more lamentation for it than if
the Enemy had given us an intire defeat, or else we shall have frowns instead
of preferments.

2 *Gent.*
The truth is, I wonder the General will trouble himself with his wife, when
it is the only time a married man hath to enjoy a Mistriss without jealousy, a
spritely sound wench, that may go along without trouble, with bag and baggage, to wash his linnen, and make his field Bed, and attend to his call, when
a wife requires more attendance than Centries to watch the Enemy.

3 *Gent.*
For my part I wonder as much that any man should be so fond of his wife as
to carry her with him; for I am only glad of the Wars, because I have a good
pretence to leave my wife behind me; besides an Army is a quiet, solitary
place, and yields a man a peaceable life compared to that at home: for what
with the faction and mutiny amongst his Servants, and the noise the women
make, for their tongues like as an Alarum beat up quaters in every Corner of
the House, that a man can take no rest; besides every day he hath a set Battel
with his wife, and from the Army of her angry thoughts, she sends forth
such vollies of words with her Gunpowder anger, and the fire of her fury,
as breaks all the ranks and files of content, and puts happiness to an utter
rout, so as for my part I am forced to run away in discontent, although some
Husbands will stay, and fight for the Victory.

4 *Gent.*
Gentlemen, Gentlemen, pray condemn not a man for taking his lawfull delight, or for ordering his private affairs to his own humour, every man is free

to himself, and to what is his, as long as he disturbs not his Neighbours, nor breaks the Peace of the Kingdome, nor disorders the Commonwealth, but submits to the Laws, and obeys the Magistrates without dispute; besides Gentlemen, 'tis no crime nor wonder, for a man to let his wife go along with him when he goeth to the Wars, for there hath been examples; for *Pompey* had a wife with him, and so had *Germanicus,* and so had many great and worthy Heroicks, and as for *Alexander* the great he had a wife or two with him; besides, in many Nations men are not only desired, but commanded by the Chiefs to let their wives go with them, and it hath been a practice by long Custome, for women to be spectators in their Battels, to encourage their fights, and so give fire to their Spirits; also to attend them in their Sicknesses, to clense their wounds, to dress their meat; and who is fitter than a wife? What other woman will be so lovingly carefull, and industriously helpfull as a wife? And if the *Greekes* had not left their wives behind them, but had carried them along to the *Trojan* Wars, they would not have found such disorders as they did at their return, nor had such bad welcome home, as witness *Agamemnons*; besides, there have been many women that have not only been Spectators, but Actors, leading Armies, and directing Battels with good success, and there have been so many of these Heroicks, as it would be tedious at this time to recount; besides the examples of womens courage in Death, as also their wise conduct, and valiant actions in Wars are many, and pray give me leave to speak without your being offended thereat, it is not Noble, nor the part of a Gentleman, to censure, condemn, or dispraise another mans private actions, which nothing concerns him, especially when there is so gallant a subject to discourse of as the discipline and actions of these Wars we are entring into.

1 *Gent.*
In truth Sir, you have instructed us so well, and have chid us so handsomely, as we are sorry for our errour, and ask pardon for our fault, and our repentance shall be known by that we will never censure so again.

Exeunt.

ACT II.
Scene 5.
Enter Captain Whiffell, *and Madam* Whiffell *his Wife.*

Captain Whiffell.
I have heard our Generals Lady goeth with the General her Husband to the Wars, wherefore I think it fit for the rest of the Commanders, if it were only

for policy, to let our General see that we approve of his actions so well, as to imitate him in ours, carrying our Wives along with us, besides the Generals Lady cannot chose but take it kindly to have our Wives wait upon her, wherefore Wife it is fit you should go.

Madam Whiffell.
Alas Husband I am so tender, that I am apt to catch cold if the least puff of wind do but blow upon me; wherefore to ly in the open Fields will kill me the first Night, if not, the very journey will shatter my small bones to peeces.

Captain Whiffell.
Why, our Generals Lady is a very fine young Lady, and she ventures to go.

Madam Whiffell.
There let her venture, for you must excuse me, for I will stay at home, go you where you please.

Captain Whiffell.
Well Wife consider it.

Exeunt.

Scene 6.
Enter Captain Ruffell, *and his Wife Madam* Ruffell.

Captain Ruffell.
Wife prepare your self to follow the Army, for 'tis now the fashion for Wives to march, wherefore pack up and away.

Madam Ruffell.
What with a Knapsack behind me as your Trull? Not I, for I will not disquiet my rest with inconveniences, nor divert my pleasures with troubles, nor be affrighted with the roring Cannons, nor indanger my life with every Potgun, nor be frozen up with Cold, nor stew'd to a gelly with heat, nor be powdered up with dust, untill I come to be as dry as a Neats-tongue; besides, I will not venture my Complexion to the wroth of the Sun, which will tan me like a Sheeps skin.

Captain Ruffell.
Faith Wife, if you will not go, I will have a Landery-Maid to ride in my Waggon, and ly in my Tent.

Madam Ruffell.
Prethee Husband take thy Kitchin Maid along too, for she may have as much Grease about her as will serve to make Sope to wash your Linnen with, and while you ride with your Landery-Maid in your Waggon, I will ride with my Gentleman-Usher in my Coach.

Captain Ruffell.
Why Wife, it is out of love that I would have thee go.

Madam Ruffell.
And 'tis out of love that I will stay at home; besides, do you think I mean to follow your Generals Lady as a common Trooper doth a Commander, to feed upon her reversions, to wait for her favour, to watch for a smile; no, no, I will be *Generalissimo* my self at home, and distribute my Colours to be carried in the Hats of those that will fight in my quarrel, to keep or gain the Victory of my favour and love.

. . .

Scene 9.
Enter the Lady Victoria *and a number of women of all sorts with her, she takes her stand upon a heap of green Turfs, as being in the Fields before the Garrison Town, and then speaks to those women.*

[The soldiers have commanded the women to remain at a distance from the battlefield.]

Lady Victoria.
Most Heroical Spirits of most chast and loving Wives, Mistrisses, Sisters, Children or Friends, I know you came not from your several Houses and homes into this Army meerly to enjoy your Husbands, Lovers, Parents and Friends in their safe and secure Garrisons, or only to share of their troublesome and tedious marches, but to venture also in their dangerous and cruell Battels, to run their Fortunes, and to force Destiny to joyn you to their Periods; but the Masculine Sex hath separated us, and cast us out of their Companyes, either out of their loving care and desire of preserving our lives and liberties, lest we might be distroyed in their confusions, or taken Prisoners in their loss, or else it must be out of jealousy we should Eclipse the fame of their valours with the splendor of our constancy; and if it be Love, let us never give the preheminence, for then we should lose that Prerogative that belongs to the Crown of our Sex; and if it be thorough Jealous mistrust of their Fame, it were poor for us to submit and quit that

unto men, that men will not unto us, for Fame makes us like the Gods, to live for ever; besides, those women that have staid at home will laugh at us in our return, and their effeminate Lovers and Carpet Knights, that Cowardly and Luxuriously Coin excuses to keep and stay them from the Wars, will make Lampons of us for them to sing of our disgrace, saying, our Husbands, Lovers, and Friends were so weary of us, as they were forced to take that pretence of affectionate love to be rid of our Companyes; wherefore if you will take my advise, let us return, and force those that sent us away to consent that we shall be partakers with them, and either win them by perswasions, or lose our selves by breaking their decrees; for it were better we should dy by their angry frowns, than by the Tongue of Infamy.

All the women call to her.

All the women.
Let us return, let us return.

Lady Victoria *waves her hand to them to keep silence.*

Lady Victoria.
Noble Heroickesses, I am glad to hear you speak all as with one voice and Tongue, which shows your minds are joyned together, as in one piece, without seam or rent; but let us not return unfit to do them service, so we may cause their ruin by obstruction, which will wound us more than can their anger; wherefore let us strive by our industry to render our selves usefull to their service.

All the women.
Propound the way, and set the Rules, and we will walk in the one, and keep strictly to the other.

Lady Victoria.
Then thus, we have a Body of about five or six thousand women, which came along with some thirty thousand men, but since we came, we are not only thought unusefull, but troublesome, which is the reason we were sent away, for the Masculine Sex is of an opinion we are only fit to breed and bring forth Children, but otherwise a trouble in a Common-wealth, for though we encrease the Common-wealth by our breed, we encomber it by our weakness, as they think, as by our incapacities, as having no ingenuity for Inventions, nor subtill wit for Politicians; nor prudence for direction, nor industry for execution; nor patience for opportunity, nor judgment for Counsellers, nor secrecy for trust; nor method to keep

peace, nor courage to make War, nor strength to defend our selves or Country, or to assault an Enemy; also that we have not the wisdome to govern a Common-wealth, and that we are too partial to sit in the Seat of Justice, and too pittifull to execute rigorous Authority when it is needfull, and the reason of these erronious opinions of the Masculine Sex to the Effeminate, is, that our Bodyes seem weak, being delicate and beautifull, and our minds seem fearfull, being compassionate and gentle natured, but if we were both weak and fearfull, as they imagine us to be, yet custome which is a second Nature will encourage the one and strengthen the other, and had our educations been answerable to theirs, we might have proved as good Souldiers and Privy Counsellers, Rulers and Commanders, Navigators and Architectors, and as learned Sholars both in Arts and Sciences, as men are;[29] for Time and Custome is the Father and Mother of Strength and Knowledge, they make all things easy and facil, clear and prospitious; they bring acquaintance, and make friendship of every thing; they make Courage and Fear, Strength and Weakness, Difficulty and Facility, Dangers and Securities, Labours and Recreations, Life and Death, all to take and shake as it were hands together; wherefore if we would but accustome our selves we may do such actions, as may gain us such a reputation, as men might change their opinions, insomuch as to be-lieve we are fit to be Copartners in their Governments, and to help to rule the World, where now we are kept as Slaves forced to obey; wherefore let us make our selves free, either by force, merit, or love, and in order, let us practise and endeavour, and take that which Fortune shall profer unto us, let us practise I say, and make these Fields as Schools of Martial Arts and Sciences, so shall we become learned in their disciplines of War, and if you please to make me your Tutoress, and so your Generalless, I shall take the power and command from your election and Authority, otherwise I shall most willingly, humbly, and obediently submit to those whom you shall choose.

All the women.
You shall be our Generalless, our Instructeress, Ruler and Commanderess, and we will every one in particular, swear to obey all your Commands, to submit and yield to your punishments, to strive and endeavour to merit your rewards.

. . .

[29] See also *Philosophical and Physical Opinions*, "To the Two Universities," and *Worlds Olio*, "The Preface," and the corresponding note 1.

Scene 13.
Enter the Lady Victoria and a number of other Women.

Lady Victoria.
Now we are resolved to put our selves into a Warlike body, our greatest difficulty will be to get Arms; but if you will take my advise we may be fur-
nished with those necessaries, as thus, the Garrison we are to enter is full of
Arms and Amunition, and few men to guard them, for not only most of the
Souldiers are drawn out to strengthen the Generals Army, and to fight in the
battel, but as many of the Townsmen as are fit to bear Arms; wherefore it
must of necessity be very slenderly guarded, and when we are in the Town,
we will all agree in one Night, when they shall think themselves most secure,
to rise and surprize those few men that are left, and not only disarm them
and possess our selves of the Town and all the Arms and Amunition, but we
will put those men out of the Town or in safe places, untill such time as we
can carry away whatsoever is usefull or needfull for us, and then to go forth
and intrench, untill such time as we have made our selves ready to march,
and being once Master or Mistriss of the Field we shall easily Master the
Pesants, who are for the most part naked and defenceless, having not Arms
to guard them, by which means we may plunder all their Horses, and victual
our selves out of their Granaries; besides, I make no question but our Army
will increase numerously by those women that will adhere to our party, either out of private and home discontents, or for honour and fame, or for the
love of change, and as it were a new course of life; wherefore let us march to
the Town and also to our design, but first I must have you all swear secrecy.

All the women.
We are all ready to swear to what you will have us.

Exeunt.
. . .

Scene 15.
Enter a Gentleman, and another meets him as in great haste.

1 Gent.
What news? What news?

2 Gent.
Sad news, for there hath been a Battel fought betwixt the two Armies, and
our Army is beaten, and many of our gallant men slain.

1 *Gent.*
I am sorry for that.

The second Gentleman goeth out.
Enter a third Gentleman.

1 *Gent.*
Sir I suppose you are come newly from the Army, pray report the Battel?

3 *Gent.*
Truly I came not now from the Army, but from the Town the Generals heroical Lady and the rest of the heroicks did surprize, seise and plunder.

1 *Gent.*
What the Garrison Town they were sent to for safety?

3 *Gent.*
Yes.

1 *Gent.*
And doth their number encrease?

3 *Gent.*
O very much, for after the suprisal of the Town the women in that Town did so approve of their gallant actions, as every one desired to be inlisted in . . . the *Amazonian* Army, but in the mean time of the forming of their Army, intelligence was brought of the Battel which was fought, and that there was such loss of both sides as each Army retir'd back, being both so weak as neither was able to keep the Field, but that the loss was greater on the reformed Army, by reason there was so many of their gallant men slain, but this news made many a sad heart and weeping eyes in the Female Army; for some have lost their Husbands, some their Fathers, others their Brothers, Lovers and Friends.

1 *Gent.*
Certainly this will fright them out of the Field of War, and cause them to lay by their Heroick designs.

3 *Gent.*
I know not what they will do, for they are very secret to their designs, which is strange, being all women.

ACT IV.
Scene 16.
Enter two women like Amazons.

1 *Woman.*
Our Generalless seems to be troubled, perceiving how heavily this Female Army takes their losses.

2 *Woman.*
She hath reason, for it may hinder or at least obstruct her high designs.

Exeunt.

Scene 17.
Enter the Lady Victoria and her Amazons, she takes her stand and speaks to them.

Lady Victoria.
Noble Heroicks, I perceive a mourning veil over the Face of this Female Army, and it becomes it well; for 'tis both natural and human to grieve for the Death of our friends; but consider constant Heroicks, tears nor lamentations cannot call them out of the grave, no petitions can perswade Death to restore them, nor threats to let them go, and since you cannot have them alive being Dead, study and be industrious to revenge their quarrels on their Enemies lives, let your justice give them Death for Death, offer upon the Tombs of your Friends the lives of their Foes, and instead of weeping Eyes, let us make them weep through their Veins; wherefore take courage, cast off your black Veil of Sorrow, and take up the Firematch of Rage, that you may shoot Revenge into the hearts of their Enemies, to which I hope Fortune will favour us; for I hear that as soon as the Masculine Army have recovered strength there will be another Battel fought, which may be a means to prove our love to our Friends, our hate to our Enemies, and an aspiring to our honour and renown; wherefore let us imploy our care to fit our selves for our march.

All the women.
We shall follow and obey you, where, and when, and how you please.
. . .

Scene 20.
Enter two Gentlemen.

1 *Gent.*

I wonder there is no news or Messenger come from the Army yet, when there usually comes one every day.

Enter a Messenger.

2 *Gent.*

O Sir, what news?

Messenger.

Faith there hath been nothing acted since the last Battel, but it is said there will be another Battel very suddenly, for the Enemy provokes our men to fight, by reason our Lord General lies sick of his wounds, having had a Feavour, caused by the anguish of his hurts, and by his Sickness the Enemies hope to gain an advantage of his absence, but he hath put a Deputy in his place to command in chief untill he recovers.

1 *Gent.*

What is become of the Female Army?

Messenger.

I hear they are marched towards the Masculine Army, but upon what design I cannot understand.

Part II. Act I.

. . .

Scene 2.

Enter two Gentlemen.

1 *Gent.*

Sir, you being newly come from the Army, pray what news?

2 *Gent.*

I suppose you have heard how our Army was forced to fight by the Enemies provocations, hearing the Lord General lay sick, whereupon the Generals Lady the Lady *Victoria*, caused her *Amazonians* to march towards the Masculine Army, and to entrench some half a mile distance therefrom, which when the Masculine Army heard thereof, they were very much troubled thereat, and sent a command for them to retreat back, fearing they might be a disturbance, so a destruction unto them by, doing some untimely or unnecessary action; but the Female Army returned the Masculine Army an Answer, that they would not retreat unless they were beaten back, which they did believe the Masculine Sex would not, having more honour than to fight with the Female Sex; but if the men were so base, they were resolved to stand upon their own defence; but if they would let them alone, they would promise them upon the honour of their words not to advance any nearer unto the Masculine Army, as long as the Masculine Army could assault their Enemies, or defend themselves, and in this posture I left them.

Exeunt.

Scene 3.
Enter the Lady Victoria, and her Heroickesses.

Lady Victoria.
Noble Heroickesses, I have intelligence that the Army of Reformations begins to flag, wherefore now or never is the time to prove the courage of our Sex, to get liberty and freedome from the Female Slavery, and to make our selves equal with men: for shall Men only sit in Honours chair, and Women stand as waiters by? Shall only Men in Triumphant Chariots ride, and Women run as Captives by? Shall only men be Conquerors, and women Slaves? Shall only men live by Fame, and women dy in Oblivion? No, no, gallant Heroicks raise your Spirits to a noble pitch, to a deaticall height, to get an everlasting Renown, and infinite praises, by honourable, but unusual actions: for honourable Fame is not got only by contemplating thoughts which lie lasily in the Womb of the Mind, and prove Abortive, if not brought forth in living deeds; but worthy Heroickesses, at this time Fortune desires to be the Midwife, and if the Gods and Goddesses did not intend to favour our proceedings with a safe deliverance, they would not have offered us so fair and fit an opportunity to be the Mothers of glorious Actions, and everlasting Fame, which if you be so unnatural to strangle in the Birth by fearfull Cowardize, may you be blasted with Infamy, which is worse than to dye and be forgotten; may you be whipt with the torturing tongues of our own Sex we left behind us, and may you be scorned and neglected by the Masculine Sex, whilst other women are preferrd and beloved, and may you walk unregarded untill you become a Plague to your selves; but if you Arm with Courage and fight valiantly, may men bow down and worship you, birds taught to sing your praises, Kings offer up their Crowns unto you, and honour inthrone you in a mighty power.

> *May time and destiny attend your will,*
> *Fame be your scribe to write your actions still;*
> *And may the Gods each act with praises fill.*

All the women.

Fear us not, fear us not, we dare and will follow you wheresoever and to what you dare or will lead us, be it through the jawes of Death.

THE PRAYER.

Lady Victoria.

Great Mars thou God of War, grant that our Squadrons may like unbroaken Clouds move with intire Bodyes, let Courage be the wind to drive us on, and let our thick swell'd Army darken their Sun of hope with black despair, let us powre down showers of their blood, to quench the firy flames of our revenge.

And where those showers fall, their Deaths as seeds
Sown in times memory sprout up our deeds;
And may our Acts Triumphant gat lands make,
Which Fame may wear for our Heroicks sake.

. . .

Act II.
Scene 5.
Enter two Gentlemen.

1 *Gent.*

Pray Sir what news from the Army? You are newly come from thence.

2 *Gent.*

I suppose you have heard how the Effeminate Army was some half a mile from the Masculine Armies; but the Masculine Army being very earnest to fight, not only to get Victory and power, but to revenge each others losses, as their Friends slain in the former Battel, which thoughts of revenge did so fire their minds and inflame their Spirits, that if their Eyes had been as much illuminated as their flaming Spirits were, there might have been seen two blazing Armies thus joining their Forces against each other; at last began a cruell fight, where both the Armies fought with such equal Courages and active Limbs, as for a long time neither side could get the better, but at the last the Army of Faction broak the Ranks and Files of the Army of Reformation, whereupon every Squadron began to fall into a Confusion, no order was kept, no charge was heard, no command obey'd, terror and fear ran maskerd about, which helpt to rout our Army, whereupon the Enemy kill'd many of our men, and wounded many more, and took numbers of Prisoners; but upon this defeat came in the Female Army, in the time that some of the Enemy was busy in gathering up the Conquered spoils, others in pursute

of the remainders of our men, others were binding up the Prisoners, others
driving them to their Quarters like a Company of Sheep to a Market there
to be sold; but when as some of the Commanders perceived a fresh Army
coming towards them, their General commanded the Trumpets to sound a
Retreat to gather them together, and also made haste to order and settle his
men in Battel Array, and desirous their General was to have all the Prisoners
slain; but the Female Army came up so fast and so close to prevent that
mischief, as they had not time to execute that design; but their General
encouraged his Souldiers, and bid them not to be disheartened, perswading
them not to lose what they had got from an Army of men to an Army of
boys, for said he they seem to be no other by the appearance of their shapes
and statures; but when the Female Army came to encounter them, they
found their charge so hot and furious as made them give place, which advantage they took with that prudence and dexterity, as they did not only
rout this Army of Faction, killing and wounding many, and set their own
Countrymen at liberty, and recovered their losses, and gained many spoils,
and took numbers of Prisoners of their Enemies with Bag and Baggage, but
they pursued those that fled into their Trenches, and beat them out of their
works, and took possession thereof, where they found much riches; these
Trenches being taken, the Lady *Victoria* took possession, and made them
her Quarters, calling all her Female Souldiers to enter therein by the sound
of Flutes, which they always used instead of Trumpets, and their Drums
were Kettel-Drums.

ACT III.
Scene 8.
Enter the Lady Victoria, *and many of her* Amazons, *then enters a Messenger
from the Masculine Army.*

Messenger.
May it please your Excellence, our Lord General and the rest of the
Commanders have sent you and your Heroicks a Letter, desiring it may be
read in a full Assembly.

Lady Victoria.
One of you take the Letter and read it.
One of the women takes the Letter and reads it to all the Company.

The Letter.
To the most Excellent of her Sex, and her most worthy Heroickesses,
You Goddesses on Earth, who have the power and dominion over men, 'tis
you we worship and adore, we pray and implore your better opinions of us,

than to believe we are so unjust as to take the Victory out of your fair hands, or so vain-glorious as to attribute it to our selves, or so ungratefull as not to acknowledg our lives and liberties from your valours, wisdoms, and good fortune, or so imprudent as to neglect your power, or so ill-bred as to pass by you without making our addresses, or so foolish as to go about any action without your knowledge, or so unmannerly as to do anything without your leave; wherefore we entreat you and pray you to believe that we have so much honour in us, as to admire your beauties, to be attentive to your discourses, to dote on your persons, to honour your virtues, to divulge your sweet graces, to praise your behaviours, to wait your commands, to obey your directions, to be proud of your favours, and we wear our lives only for your service, and believe we are not only taken Captives by your Beauties, but that we acknowledge we are bound as your Slaves by your valours: wherefore we all pray that you may not misinterpret our affections and care to your persons, in believing we sent you away because we were weary of you, which if so, it had been a sin unpardonable, but we sent you away for your safety, for Heaven knows your Departure was our Hell, and your Absence our Torments; but we confess our errours, and do humbly beg our pardons, for if you had accompanied us in our Battels, you had kept us safe, for had we fought in your presence, our Enemies had never overcome us, since we take courage from your Eyes, life from your smiles, and victory from your good wishes, and had become Conquerours by your incouragements, and so we might have triumpht in your favours, but hereafter your rules shall be our methods, by which we will govern all our actions, attending only wholy your directions, yet give us leave humbly to offer our advise as Subjects to their Princess . . . , we think it best to follow close the victory, lest that our Enemies recruit their forces, with a sufficient strength to beat us out of what we have gained, or at least to hinder and oppose our entrance, and hopes of Conquering them, where if you will give us leave we will besiege and enter their Towns, and rase their Walls down to the ground, which harbour their disorders, offending their Neighbours Kingdoms; yet we are not so ambitious as to desire to be Commanders, but to join our forces to yours, and to be your assistants, and as your Common Souldiers; but leaving all these affairs of War to your discretion, offering our selves to your service, We kiss your hands, and take our leaves for this time.

All the women fall into a great laughter, ha, ha, ha, ha.

Lady Victoria.
Noble Heroickesses, by your valours, and constant, and resolute proceedings, you have brought your Tyrants to be your Slaves; those that Commanded your absence, now humbly sue your presence, those that

thought you a hindrance have felt your assistance, the time is well altered since we were sent to retreat back from the Masculine Army; and now nothing to be done in that Army without our advise, with an humble desire they may join their forces with ours: but gallant Heroickesses, by this you may perceive we were as ignorant of our selves as men were of us, thinking our selves shiftless, weak, and unprofitable Creatures, but by our actions of War we have proved our selves to be every way equal with men; for what we want of strength, we have supplied by industry, and had we not done what we have done, we should have lived in ignorance and slavery.

All the Female Commanders.
All the knowledge of our selves, the honour of renown, the freedome from slavery, and the submission of men, we acknowledge from you; for you advised us, counselled us, instructed us, and encouraged us to those actions of War: wherefore to you we owe our thanks, and to you we give our thanks.

. . .

Scene 18.
Enter two Gentlemen.

1 *Gent.*
I hear the Army is returning home.

2 *Gent.*
Yes, for they are returned as far back as to the Effeminate Army, and all the Masculine Commanders have presented all the Female Commanders with their spoils got in the Kingdome of Faction, as a tribute to their heroical acts, and due for their assistance, and safety of their lives and Country.

1 *Gent.*
And do not you hear what privileges and honours the King and his Counsel hath resolved and agreed upon to be given to the Female Army, and the honours particularly to be given the Lady *Victoria*?

2 *Gent.*
No.

1 *Gent.*
Why then I will tell you some, the Lady *Victoria* shall be brought through the City in triumph, which is a great honour, for never any one makes triumphs

in a Monarchy but the King himself, then . . . there shall be a blank for the Female Army to write their desires and demands; also there is an Armour of gold and a Sword a making, the hilt being set with Diamonds, and a Chariot all gilt and imbrodered to be presented to the Lady *Victoria*, and the City is making great preparation against her arrival.

2 *Gent.*
Certainly she is a Lady that deserves as much as can be given either from Kings, States, or Poets.

ACT V
Scene 20

. . .

Enter many Prisoners which march by two and two, then enter many that carry the Conquered spoils, then enters the Lady Victoria *in a gilt Chariot drawn with eight white Horses, four on a breast, the Horses covered with Cloth of gold, and great plumes of feathers on their heads.*

The Lady Victoria *was adorned after this manner; she had a Coat on all imbrodered with silver and gold, which Coat reach'd no further than the Calfs of her leggs, and on her leggs and feet she had Buskins and Sandals imbroidered suitable to her Coat; on her head she had a Wreath or Garland of Lawrel, and her hair curl'd and loosely flowing; in her hand a Crystall Bolt headed with gold at each end, and after the Chariot marched all her Female Officers with Lawrel Branches in their hands, and after them the inferiour she Souldiers, then going through the Stage, as through the City, and so entring again, where on the midst of the Stage as if it were the midst of the City, the Magistrates meet her, so her Chariot makes a stand, and one as the Recorder speaks a Speech to her.*

Victorious Lady, you have brought Peace Safety and Conquest to this Kingdome by your prudent conduct and valiant actions, which never any of your Sex in this Kingdome did before you. Wherefore our Gracious King is pleased to give you that which was never granted nor given to any before, which is to make you Triumphant, for no triumph is ever made in Monarchies, but by the Kings thereof; besides our Gracious King hath caused an act to be made and granted to all your Sex, which Act I have order to declare, as

First, That all women shall hereafter in this Kingdome be Mistriss in their own Houses and Families.

Secondly, They shall sit at the upper end of the Table above their Husbands.

Thirdly, That they shall keep the purse.

Fourthly, They shall order their Servants, turning from, or taking into their service what number they will, placing them how they will, and ordering them how they will, and giving them what wages they will or think fit.

Fiftly, They shall buy in what Provisions they will.

Sixtly, All the Jewels, Plate, and Houshold Furniture they shall claim as their own, and order them as they think good.

Seventhly, They shall wear what fashioned Clothes they will.

Eightly, They shall go abroad when they will, without controul, or giving of any account thereof.

Ninthly, They shall eat when they will, and of what they will, and as much as they will, and as often as they will.

Tenthly, They shall go to Playes, Masks, Balls, Churchings, Christenings, Preachings, whensoever they will, and as fine and bravely attired as they will.

Lastly, That they shall be of their Husbands Counsel.

When those were read, all the women cryed out, God save the King, God save the King, and Heaven reward the Lady Victoria.

. . .

The She-Anchoret[30]

There was a Widower who had but one Child, and she a Daughter; which Daughter he bred with Pious Devotions, Moral Instructions, and Wise Advertisements; but he falling sick to death, called his Daughter unto him, and thus spake to her:

Farewell my dearest Child, for dye I must;
My Soul must flye, my Body turn to dust:
My only care is, that I leave thee young,
To wander in the World, Mankind among;
Few of them charitable are, or kind;
Nor bear they in their Breast a Noble Mind,
To help the Fatherless, or pity Youth,
Protect the Innocent, maintain the Truth:
But all their time's spent with laborious toil,
For to pervert, to ruin, and to spoil.
Flatter thy Beauty, and thy Youth betray,
To give thy Heart, and Virgin-flower away.
They will profess love, vow to be thy Friend,
Marriage will promise; yet they will pretend
Their Friends will angry be, or else they'l say,
Their Land's engag'd, they first their Debts must pay;
Or else that they during some time of life,
Have made a Vow, Not yet to take a Wife:
And twenty such Excuses they will find
For to deceive the simple Female-Kind.
And if you marry, Troubles you will find,
Pains, Griefs, and Cares, to vex a quiet Mind.
But here I charge you (lying in Death's Arms)
That you do stop your Ears against their Charms:
Live chast and holy, serve the Gods above,
They will protect thee for thy zealous Love.

[30] Note that there is a tremendous amount of overlap between the philosophical views that are advanced in *The She-Anchoret* and the views that Cavendish defends in her philosophical writings. Cavendish also remarks at the end of the prefatory remarks of *Natures Picture*, "If I cannot be so happy to deserve your Commendations, let me deserve your Censure, which cannot be (in relation to you) till you have read the whole Work; and chiefly, the Stories of the *Anchoret*, and of the *Experienced Traveller*; and then (I hope) that Prejudices you may have against an unlearned Woman, will be taken off."

Daughter.
I will obey whatever you command:
Although you dye, your will shall fixed stand.

Father.
Next, I do charge thee, Not to grieve nor mourn,
Since no redress will from the Grave return.

Daughter.
O do not so, said she;
But give Grief leave to flow out of my Eyes;
For if it be supprest, the Body dyes:
Whilst now you live, great wrong y'uld think you have,
If I should sit and laugh upon your Grave;
Or with neglect should I your Grave pass by,
And ne're take notice where your Ashes lye.

Father.
You cannot hinder Destiny's Decree.

Daughter.
O no! but Nature, Nature still will be:
Nature created Love within the Mind;
The Object dead, the Passion still is kind.
Had I as many Lives as Nature make,
I'de lay them on Death's Altar for your sake.
That single one I have, O Heavens me hear!
Exchange it for my Father's Life so dear.

But when her Father found that Death drew on,
He bid her lay her Hand his Eyes upon.

Father.
Close up my Eyes, *said he*, and then receive
Upon thy Lips my last Breath, let me breathe.

When he was dead, sh' amaz'd, long time sat still;
At last bethought her of her Father's Will:

After she had interred her Father's Corps, although she had rich, honourable, and importunate Suiters; yet she resolved to live like a kind of an Anchoret's Life, living encloistered by her self alone, vowing Chastity, and a Single-life; but gave leave for any to speak to her through a Grate. When she went first into her solitary Habitation, she thus spake:

Virtues are several Pathes which lead to Heaven;
And they which tread these Pathes, have Graces given:
Repentant tears allay the Dust of Pride;
And pious Sighs doth blow vain Thoughts aside:
Sorrow and Grief, which in the Heart doth lye,
Doth cloud the Mind, as Thunder doth the Skie:
But when in Thundring-groans it breaketh out,
The Mind grows clear, the Sun of Joy peeps out.
This pious Life I now resolve to lead,
Will in my Soul both Joy and Comfort breed.

She had not been long enclosed, but she grew as famous as *Diogenes* in his Tub; all sorts of people resorted to her, to hear her speak;[31] and not only to hear her speak, but to get knowledg, and to learn wisdom: for she argued rationally, instructed judiciously, admonished prudently, and perswaded piously; applying and directing her Discourse according to the several Studies, Professions, Grandeurs, Ages, and Humours of her Auditory.

The first that came to her, were *Natural Philosophers*; who asked her Opinion of Man's Soul: of which she discoursed in this manner:

She said, Man hath three different Natures or Faculties; A Sensitive Body, Animal Spirits, and a Soul: This Soul is a kind of Deity in it self, to direct and guide those things that are far above it, and to create by Invention; and though it hath not an absolute Power over it self, yet it is an harmonious and absolute thing in it self: and though the Sensitive Body hath a relation to it, yet no other ways than *Jove's* Mansion hath unto *Jove*; for the Body is only the residing-place, and the Animal Spirits are as the Angels of the Soul, which are Messengers and Intelligencers: All Animal Creatures have not this Soul, but only Man; for Beasts have none; nor every Man: for most Men are Beasts, and have only a Sensitive Body, and Animal Spirits, as Beasts have: but none know when this Soul is out or in the Body, but the Gods: and not only other Bodies and Spirits cannot know; but the Body where it resides, and the attending-spirits, are ignorant thereof: for this Soul is as invisible to the Body and the Animal Spirits, as the Gods to Men; for, though this kind of Soul knows, and hath intelligence by the Senses, and by the Animal Spirits; yet the Senses nor Animal Spirits have none from the Soul: for, as Gods know Men,

---

[31] Noteworthy is that although the She-Anchoret retreats to a "solitary Habitation," no fewer than nineteen audiences make the journey to visit her and hear her views on all manner of topics. She is in a world (crafted by Cavendish) in which she has a voice in the sense that others regard her as authoritative and as having something to say.

but Men know not Gods; so this Soul knows the Senses and Animal Spirits, but the Senses nor Animal Spirits know not this Soul.

Then they asked her, Whether Souls were Immortal?

She answered, That only the Life was Immortal, from whence all Souls are derived.

Then they asked her, What Deities she thought there were?

She answered, She thought but one, which was the Father of all Creatures, and Nature the Mother; he being the Life, and Nature the only Matter; which Life and Matter produceth Motion; and Figure, various Successions, Creations, and Dissolutions.

Then they asked her, What she thought *Time* was?

She said, *Time* was only the Variation and Alteration of Nature; for *Time* is only in respect to Creations, Alterations, and Dissolutions.

Then they asked her, What Eternal was?

She answered, An endless Succession.

Then they asked her, What Infinite was?

She said, A Numberless Succession: but, said she, Eternal is in respect to Infinite, as Infinite to Eternal.

Then they asked her, Whether she thought there were fixt Decrees, or all were governed by Chance?

She answered, That doubtless there were fixt Decrees, as Light, Darkness, Growth, Decay; as Youth, Age, Pain, Pleasure, Life, Death, and so in every thing else, for ought my Reason can perceive. For, said she, as Nature creates by Dissolution, and dissolves by Creation; so the Diattical Life (says she) decrees Rules, and ruleth by Decrees.

Then they asked her, What was Chance and Fortune?

Chances (said she) are visible Effects from hidden Causes; and Fortune, a conjunction of many sufficient Causes to produce such an Effect; since that Effect could not be produced, did there want any one of those Causes, by reason all of them together were but sufficient to produce;[32] but that one Effect, many times, produces many Effects upon several Subjects; and that

---

[32] See also *Grounds of Natural Philosophy*, chapter XVIII of the First Part.

one Effect, like the Sun, streams out into several rays, darting upon several Subjects: and again, as the Sun scorches and burns some things, and warms and comforts others; so this Effect advances some, and casts down others; cures some, and kills others; and when the Causes vary, and the Effects alter, it is called Change of Fortune.

Then they asked her, Whether she thought Faith could naturally produce any Effect?

She answered, That in her opinion it might: for, said she, why may not Faith, which is an undoubted Belief, joined to such a subject, produce or beget an Effect, as well as a Seed sown or set in the Earth, produceth a Flower, a Tree, or the like; or as one Creature begets another; especially if the Faith, and Subject whereon it is placed, have a sympathy; but by reason (said she) Faith is not so customary a way of producing, as other ways are, it causeth many Doubts, which Doubts are like cold Northern Winds, or sharp biting Frosts, which nip and kill the Buds of Faith, which seldom or never lets the Effects come to perfection.

. . .

The Third sort that visited her, were Moral Philosophers.
The Moral Philosophers asked her, If it were possible to alter or abate the Passions?

No, said she; you may pacifie or imprison them, and enforce them to conceal themselves in the heart, not only from outward appearance, but from the very understanding in the head; but never alter or change their natures, to weaken their natural strength, or abate their natural vigour: for Passions (said she) are like the Sun; they may be eclipsed, or clouded, but never can be alter'd: and as the Sun (saith she) draws forth Vapour from the Earth; so do the Imaginations draw forth Passions from the Heart; and as a Bucket draws up Water from the bottom of a Well, so do outward Objects draw up Passions from the Heart.

. . . Then they asked her, If she thought Beasts had a Rational Soul?

She answered, That if there could be no Sense without some Reason, nor Reason without the Sense, Beasts were as Rational as Men;[33] unless, said she, Reason be a particular Gift, either from Nature, or the God of Nature, to Man, and not to other Creatures: if so, said she, Nature, or the God of Nature, would prove partial or finite. As for Nature in her self, she seems

---

[33] See also *Philosophical Letters*, letter X of section one.

unconfined; and for the God of Nature, he can have no Biass, he ruling every thing by the straight Line of Justice; and what Justice, nay what Injustice would it not be, for Mankind to be supream over all other Animal-Kind; or some Animal-Kind over any other Kind?

Then they asked her, Why no Creature was so shiftless at his birth, as Man?

She answered, There were other Creatures as shiftless as Man; as for example, Birds are as shiftless before their Wings are fledged.

For, as Infants want strength in Arms to feed themselves, and Legs to go; so Birds want strength of Bills to feed themselves, and Feathers in Wings to flye.

Then they asked her, Whether she thought there were a Heaven and a Hell?

She answered, That in Nature there was a Hell and a Heaven, a God and a Devil, good Angels and bad, Salvation and Damnation; for, said she, Pain and Trouble is a Hell, the one to torment the Body, the other the Mind.[34]

Likewise, said she, Health and Pleasure is a Heaven, which gives the body rest, and the mind Tranquility; also, said she, the natural God is Truth; the natural Devil, Falshood; the one seeks to save, the other to deceive; the good Angels are Peace and Plenty; the evil are Warrs, and Famine; Light is the Beatifical Vision, Darkness the natural Dungeon, Death is the Damnation, Life the Salvation; and Moral Virtue is the natural Religion, and Moral Philosophers are Nature's Priests, which preach, and seem to practise a good life.

Then they asked, What Government for a Commonwealth was best?

She answered, Monarchical. For, as one Sun is sufficient to give Light and Heat to all the several Creatures in the World; so one Governour is sufficient to give Laws and Rules to the several Members of a Commonwealth. Besides, said she, no good Government can be without Union; and Union is in Singularity, not in Plurality; for Union is drawn to a Point, when Numbers make Division, Extraction, Subtraction; which often-times brings Distraction; and Distraction, Confusions.[35]

. . .

---

[34] See also *Appendix to Grounds of Natural Philosophy*, Chapter XI of the First Part.
[35] See also the response to "The Eighth Sort of Visiters."

The Fourth sort that visited her, were Scholars, that studied Theology; and they asked her, Whether she was of opinion that Man hath Free will?

She answered, That she was not so proud, nor so presumptuous, as to think that Man had Freewill: for, said she, if *Jove* had given Men Free-will, he had given the use of one of his Attributes to Man, as free Power; which, said she, *Jove* cannot do; for that were to lessen himself, To let any Creature have free power to do what he will: for, Free-will is an Absolute Power, although of the narrowest limits; and to have an Absolute Power, is to be a God; and to think Man had it only, and no other Creature, were to think *Jove* partial; but, said she, Man's Ambition hath bred this, and the like Opinions.

But, said they, *Jove* might permit Man, or suffer Man to do some things.

She said, That was as ill, or a worse Opinion: for, to think *Jove* permits Man to cross his will, and let him do that which he would not have him do, were to make *Jove* less than a God, as if his Decrees were to be alter'd by Man's Humour and Will; or, said she, to think that *Jove* requires of Man such things as his Nature suffers him not to do; and so, as it were, to force him to disobey him: or to think *Jove* suffers Man to do evil, when he could prevent it; or to think *Jove* permits Man to provoke his Justice, or to damn Man, when it is in *Jove's* power to save him, were to think *Jove* unjust and cruel; or to think *Jove* made Man, yet knew he would be damned; and might have saved him, in not making him; were make a malignity in the nature of *Jove*: for to make, and take delight to punish, is to be malicious; which cannot be, said she; for *Jove* is a God in Goodness, as well as a God in Power; and a God in Justice, as well as a God of Wisdom: for Justice and Knowledg is the Basis of Wisdom; but, said she, the Opinions Men have of *Jove,* are according to their own natures, and not according to the nature of *Jove,* which makes such various Religions, and such rigorous Judgment in every Religion, as to condemn all but their own Opinion; which Opinions are so many and different, as scarce any two agree; and every Opinion judges all damned but their own: and most Opinions are, That the smallest Fault is able to damn; but the most Vertuous Life, and innocent Thoughts, not sufficient to save them.[36]

Then they asked her, If she did believe Predestination?

She said, She believed that *Jove* did order all things by his Wisdom; and that his Wisdom knew how to dispose to the best; as also, that *Jove's* Will was the only fixt Decree; and that his Power establishes all that his Will decrees.

[36] See also *Appendix to Grounds of Natural Philosophy*, chapter VI of the First Part.

Then they asked her, What she thought *Jove* required from Man?

She answered, She thought *Jove* required nothing from man, but what he required from Nature; as Love, Praises, Admiration, Adoration, and Worship; to love his Goodness, praise his Justice, admire his Wisdom, adore his Power, and to worship all his Attributes; and *Jove* (said she) requires not only this in man, but of all the Creatures in Nature; for, said she, it were a sinful opinion to think none but man did love, praise, admire, adore, and worship *Jove*. . . .

The Fifth sort that visited her, were the Fathers of the Church; who desired her to speak: which she did as follows:

You Holy Fathers (said she), you will pardon me for what I shall speak, since it is your desire I should speak.

The Preachers for Heaven, said she, ought not to preach Factions, nor to shew their Learning, nor to express their Wit; but to teach their Flock to pray rightly: for hard it is to know, whether we pray, or prate; since none can tell the purity of their own heart, or number the Follies thereof, or cleanse out the muddy Passions that by Nature are bred therein, or root out the Vices the World has sown thereon: for, if we do not leave out the World, the Flesh, and the Devil, in our humble Petitions, and earnest Desires, we offer to Heaven, it may be said, we rather talk than pray: for, it is not bended knees, or a sad countenance, can make our Prayers authentical or effectual; nor words, nor groans, nor sighs, nor tears, that can pierce Heaven; but a zealous Flame, raised from a holy Fire, kindled by a spark of Grace in a devout heart, which fills the soul with admiration and astonishment at *Jove's* incomprehensible Deity:[37] for, nothing can enter Heaven, but Purity and Truth; all the gross and drossie parts fall back with greater force upon our Lives, and, instead of Blessings, prove Curses to us; and the Ignorant, not conceiving the difference, may be lost for want of instruction therein, being most commonly taught the varieties of Opinions, the Sayings and Sentences of the Fathers of the Church; or exclaimed against natural Imperfections, or threatned for slight Vanities; and many, by giving warning against Vices, raise those that have been dead and buried with former Ages, unaccustomed, and utterly unknown to the present Auditory. But one good Prayer that is directly sent to Heaven, buries a multitude of Errors and Imperfections, and blots out many a Sin. I speak not this to tax any one here; for I believe you are all Holy Men, and Reverend and Grave Fathers of the Church, who are blessed

[37] See also *Further Observations Upon Experimental Philosophy*, section XII.

Messengers and Eloquent Orators for Heaven, the true Guides to Souls, and the Example of a good Life.

Then they asked, How they ought to pray?

Whereupon, in a Zealous Passion, thus she said:

O Gods! O Gods! Mankind is much to blame;
He commits faults when he but names his Name:
This Name, saith she, that Deity hath none;
His Works sufficient are to make him known.
His wondrous Glory is so great, how dare
Man similize, but to himself compare?
Or, how durst Men their Tongues or Lips to move
In argument, his mighty Power to prove?
As if Men's Words his Power could circle in,
Or trace his ways, from whence he did begin
His mighty Works to make, or to what end;
As proudly placing Man to be his Friend:
Yet poor, proud, ign'rant Man, knows not the cause
Of any Creature made, much less his Laws:
Man's knowledg so obscure, not so much light
As to perceive the glimmering of his Might.
Strive not this Deity to comprehend;
He no beginning had, nor can have end:
Nor can Mankind his Will or Pleasure know,
It strives to draw Him to expression low.
Let Words desist, let's strive our Souls to raise:
Let our Astonishments be Glory's praise:
Let trembling thoughts of fear, as prayers, be sent;
And not leight words, which are by Men invent:
Let Tongues be silent, Adoration pray:
And Love and Justice lead us the right way.

The Eighth sort of Visiters were States-men, who ask'd her, What Government was best?

She answered, Monarchy: For (said she) a good King is the Center of a Commonwealth, as God is the Center of Nature, who orders and disposes all to the best, and unites and composes all differences, which otherwise would run into a confusion: and Unity, said she, is sooner found, and easier made by one, than by more, or many: Neither, said she, can one Man make so many Faults, as more or many may. Besides, said she, there is less Justice, and more Injustice in a Multitude, than in one.

Then they asked her, Whether it were lawful for a King to lay down his Scepter and Crown?

She answered, That Princes that voluntarily lay down their Royal Dignity, do either express some infirmity in Power, or weakness of Understanding, or imperfect Health of Body, or Effeminacy of Spirits, or doting Affection, or Vainglory: for Religion requires it not; nay, said she, it seems rather an Impiety for *Jove's* Annointed, being his chief Deputy on Earth, to leave, or be weary in governing the people, by which, and in which he serves *Jove*. And it was accounted (said she) a Blessing as well as an Honour, in the Ancient Writ, to go out and in before the People, most being inspired by *Jove* to that Dignity of Prophesying; and for the Great, Gallant, Heroick *Heroes*, as *Alexander* and *Caesar*, they left not their Crowns, nor parted with their Power, until Death uncrowned and divested them. Neither (said she) were there any that voluntarily laid down or yeelded up a Crown, but have had more Condemners and Dispraisers, than Commenders or Admirers. Thus, said she, neither the Laws of Honour or Religion allow it; nor can I perceive Morality approves it.

Then they asked her, If a foolish King might not bring a Commonwealth to ruin sooner, than a Council of Many?

She said, No: for, said she, the plurality breeds Faction; which Faction causeth more evil than one foolish Head can make or bring about.

Then they asked, If a Tyrant-King were not worse than a Factious Assembly?

She said, No: for, said she, a Tyrant-King may make good Laws, and keep Peace, and maintain Supreme Power and Authority; but a Factious Assembly (said she) will break all Laws, do no Justice, keep no Peace, obstruct Authority, and overthrow Supreme Power; and, said she, that Kingdom is happiest that lives under a Tyrant-Prince; for when the People are afraid of their Prince, there is Peace; but where the Prince is afraid of the People, there is Warr; and there is no Misery like a Civil-Warr: Nor is there a greater sign that a King is afraid of his People, than when he advances those that are, or seem to be his Enemies. Thus Subjects in general live happiest under a Tyrant, but not particular Courtiers, or busie prating Fools, or Factious Knaves: and a facil King causeth more Trouble, Distraction, and Ruin, by his soft easie nature, than a Cruel Tyrant with Executions, severe Laws, or heavy Taxes: for the greatest Tyrant that ever was, will not destroy all his Subjects, or take away all Substance, for his own sake; for if he did, he would destroy his Power, and ruin his Monarchy.

. . .

The sixteenth sort of Visiters, were Poets.

Who asked her, Why Poets were most commonly Poor?

She said, Poets are employed with Contemplations, that they have no time for Fruition; for Poets, said she, had rather have Fancies in their Heads, than Money in their Purse; and take more pleasure in expressing the one, than in spending the other; which makes their Imaginations their chiefest Possessions;[38] being careless of Fortune's Goods, despising her Service, regarding neither her Frowns nor her Favours; being entertained by Nature, whom they most industriously serve, and diligently attend.

Then they asked her, Who were most in Nature's favour, Poets or Philosophers?

She answered, There was no doubt to be made, but that she esteemed and loved Poets the best: for (said she) Natural Philosophers tire Nature with Enquiries, trouble her with searching and seeking about, anger her with their Erroneous Opinions, tedious Disputations, and sensless Arguments, and make her outragious with their cruel Extractions, Substractions, and Dissections.

As for Moral Philosophers, said she, they restrain, enclose, and tye Nature, as one that is mad, tormenting her beyond all reason: but sometimes, said she, with strugling and striving, she breaks out; but cannot get so far, but they straight get hold of her again; which makes them always at variance.

But Poets, saith she, never cross nor anger her, nor torment her; they please her all they can, and humour her every way; they sooth her Passions, feed her Appetites, delight her Senses, praise her Wit, admire her Beauty, adorn her Person, and advance her Fame.

Then they asked her, What the *Muses* were?

She said, That the *Muses* were Nature's Dressers, and Poet's Mistresses; to whom they made Love, and several Courtships.

Then they asked her, What Poets were?

She said, Poets were Nature's Painters, which drew her to the life; yet some do flatter her, said she, and some do her wrong; but those that flatter her, she favours most (as all great Ladies do).

---

[38] See also *Worlds Olio*, "Allegory 20," and *Blazing World*, "To all Noble and Worthy Ladies" and "The Epilogue to the Reader."

Then they asked her, What was the ground of Poetry?

She said, Distinguishing and Similizing, which is, said she, Judgment and Fancy: as for Numbers, Rhyme, and Rhetorick, they are but the several Accoutrements, but no part of the Body of Poetry.

Then they asked her, What was the Effect of Poetry?

She said, To move Passions, to describe Humours, to express Actions, to correct Errors, to condemn Follies, to persecute Vice, to crown Virtue, to adorn the Graces, to entertain Time, to animate Youth, to refresh Age, to encourage Noble Endeavours, to quicken the Spirits, to please the Senses, to delight the Mind, to recreate the Thoughts, to encrease Knowledg, to instruct the Understanding, to preserve the Memory, to refine Language, to praise Heaven, to enflame Zeal, to register Life, to in-urn Death, to pencil Nature, and raise Fame.

Then the Poets asked her, If Wit might not be gotten by Industry?

She said, Yes: for, though it is Nature's Work to make a Brain strong, and well-temper'd, or put it in tune; yet it is Learned Practice and Skill, that must play therewith; like a Lute, although it should be well strung, and justly tuned, yet if there were no hands, or other things, to set it in motion, it would become useless; and unless it were tried, it would not be known whether it could sound or no; and one that was not practised and learnt in the Art of that Instrument, might jangle, but hardly play a composed Tune, or make any Harmony therewith. So a Brain becomes dull for want of use, stupid for want of subject, and barren for want of learning; unless Nature doth play on the Instruments she makes, without the help of Art: which she can do, and doth sometimes; but so seldom, that it is a wonder.

But although she doth not always make use of Art, she never but doth make use of Time; for Time is her chief Instrument, with which she works, and produceth all things.

I perceive, said she, that few profit by reading over or repeating of their own Wit; for it is like the Breath of Water-Divers, who have two Bags, one filled with Air, the other to put in Breath that issues out; and that Breath that goes out, can never be drawn back for use; for the life of the Body must be fed with fresh Air, or else it is smuthered out: so the life of Wit must be fed with new Subjects; or else it becomes idle, or (panting) dyes.

LIST OF SUGGESTED SECONDARY READINGS

Neil Ankers, "Paradigms and Politics: Hobbes and Cavendish Constrasted," in Stephen Clucas (ed.), *A Princely Brave Woman: Essays on Margaret Cavendish, Duchess of Newcastle*, Hamsphire (England) and Burlington, VT: Ashgate Publishing (2003), 242–254.

Iva Apostalova, "Princess Elizabeth of Bohemia and Margaret Cavendish: The Feminine Touch in Seventeenth-Century Epistemology," *Maritain Studies/Etudes Maritainiennes* 26 (2010), 83–97.

Anna Battigelli, *Margaret Cavendish and the Exiles of the Mind*, Lexington: Kentucky UP (1998).

Sylvia Bowerbank, "The Spider's Delight: Margaret Cavendish and the 'Female' Imagination," *English Literary Renaissance* 14 (2004), 392–408.

Deborah Boyle, "Margaret Cavendish's Nonfeminist Natural Philosophy," *Configurations* 12 (2004), 195–227.

Deborah Boyle, "Fame, Virtue, and Government: Margaret Cavendish on Ethics and Politics," *Journal of the History of Ideas* 67 (2006), 251–289.

Deborah Boyle, "Margaret Cavendish on Gender, Nature, and Freedom," *Hypatia: A Journal of Feminist Philosophy* 28 (2013), 516–532.

Deborah Boyle, "Margaret Cavendish on Perception, Self-Knowledge, and Probable Opinion," *Philosophy Compass* 10 (2015), 438–450.

Deborah Boyle, *The Well-Ordered Universe: The Philosophy of Margaret Cavendish*, New York: Oxford University Press (2018).

Jacqueline Broad, "Margaret Cavendish and Joseph Glanvill: Science, Religion and Witchcraft," *Studies in the History and Philosophy of Science* 38 (2007), 493–505.

Jacqueline Broad, "Margaret Cavendish, Jan Baptista van Helmont, and the Madness of the Womb," in Judy A. Hayden (ed.), *The New Science and Women's Literary Discourse: Prefiguring Frankenstein*, New York: Palgrave Macmillan (2011).

Jacqueline Broad, "Is Margaret Cavendish Worthy of Study Today," *Studies in History and Philosophy of Science* 42 (2011), 457–461.

Jacqueline Broad, "Women on Liberty in Early Modern England," *Philosophy Compass* 9 (2014), 112–122.

Hero Chalmers, "'Flattering Division': Margaret Cavendish's Poetics of Variety," in Cottegnies and Weitz (2003), 123–144.

Colin Chamberlain, "Color in a Material World: Margaret Cavendish Against the Early Modern Mechanists," *The Philosophical Review* (forthcoming).

Stephen Clucas, "The Atomism of the Cavendish Circle: A Reappraisal," *The Seventeenth Century* 9 (1994), 247–273.

Stephen Clucas, "Variation, Irregularity and Probabilism: Margaret Cavendish and Natural Philosophy as Rhetoric," in Stephen Clucas (ed.), *A Princely Brave Woman: Essays on Margaret Cavendish, Duchess of Newcastle*, Hamsphire (England) and Burlington, VT: Ashgate Publishing (2003), 199–209.

Stephen Clucas, "'A Double Perception in All Creatures': Margaret Cavendish's Philosophical Letters and Seventeenth-Century Natural Philosophy," in Siegfried and Sarasohn (2014), 121–139.

Nicolas Correard, "Anti-Scientific Scepticism and Early Satires of the Royal Society: Exposing the Fictions of Experimental Science in Samuel Butler, Margaret Cavendish, and Jonathan Swift (1660–1730)," *Science et Espirit* 65 (2013), 325–342.

Line Cottegnies and Nancy Weitz (eds.), *Authorial Conquests: Essays on Genre in the Writings of Margaret Cavendish*, Madison: Fairleigh Dickinson UP (2003).

David Cunning, "Cavendish on the Intelligibility of the Prospect of Thinking Matter," History of Philosophy Quarterly 23 (2006), 117–136.

David Cunning, "Margaret Cavendish," *The Stanford Encyclopedia* (2012), ed. Edward Zalta, https://plato.stanford.edu/entries/margaret-cavendish/index.html.

David Cunning, *Cavendish*, in the series *The Arguments of the Philosophers*, London and New York: Routledge Publishing (2016).

David Cunning, "Cavendish on the Metaphysics of Imagination and the Dramatic Force of the Imaginary World," in Emily Thomas (ed.), *Early Modern Women on Metaphysics*, Cambridge UP (2018), 188–210.

David Cunning, "Cavendish on Material Causation and Cognition," in Dominik Perler and Sebastian Bender (ed.), *Causation and Cognition: Perspectives on Early Modern Philosophy*, Routledge (forthcoming).

David Cunning, "The Feminist Worlds of Margaret Cavendish," in Pamela Hammons and Brandie Siegfried (ed.), *World-making Women*, Cambridge UP (forthcoming).

David Cunning, "Cavendish, Philosophical Letters, and the Plenum," in Lisa Walters and Brandie Siegfried (ed.), *Margaret Cavendish: An Interdisciplinary Perspective*, Cambridge UP (forthcoming).

Karen Detlefsen, "Atomism, Monism, and Causation in the Natural Philosophy of Margaret Cavendish," *Oxford Studies in Early Modern Philosophy* 3 (2006), 199–240.

Karen Detlefsen, "Reason and Freedom: Margaret Cavendish on the Order and Disorder of Nature," *Archiv fur Geschichte der Philosophie* 89 (2007), 157–191.

Karen Detlefsen, "Margaret Cavendish on the Relation Between God and World," *Philosophy Compass* 4 (2009), 421–438.

Karen Detlefsen, "Margaret Cavendish and Thomas Hobbes on Reason, Freedom, and Women," in Nancy Hirschmann and Joanne Wright (eds.), *Feminist Interpretations of Hobbes*, University Park: Penn State UP (2012), 149–168.

Stewart Duncan, "Debating Materialism: Cavendish, Hobbes, and More," *History of Philosophy Quarterly* 29 (2012), 391–409.

James Fitzmaurice, "Fancy and the Family: Self-characterizations of Margaret Cavendish," *The Huntington Library Quarterly* 53 (1990), 199–209.

James Fitzmaurice, "Introduction," in James Fitzmaurice (ed.), *Sociable Letters*, New York and London: Garland Publishing (1997), xi–xxi.

James Fitzmaurice, "Paganism, Christianity, and the Faculty of Fancy in the Writings of Margaret Cavendish," in Siegfried and Sarasohn (2014), 77–92.

Jean Gagen, "Honor and Fame in the Works of the Duchess of Newcastle," *Studies in Philology* 56 (1959), 519–538.

Carrie Hintz, "'But One Opinion': Fear of Dissent in Cavendish's *New Blazing World*," *Utopian Studies* 7 (1996), 25–37.

Sarah Hutton, "In Dialogue with Thomas Hobbes: Margaret Cavendish's Natural Philosophy," *Women's Writing* 4 (1997), 421–432.

Sarah Hutton, "Cudworth, Boethius, and the Scale of Nature," in G.A.J. Rogers, J.M. Vienne, and Y.C. Zarka (eds.), *The Cambridge Platonists in Philosophical Context*, Boston: Kluwer Academic Publishers (1997), 93–100.

Sarah Hutton, "Science and Satire: The Lucianic Voice of Margaret Cavendish's *Description of a New World Called the Blazing World*," in Cottegnies and Weitz (2003), 161–178.

Susan James, "The Philosophical Innovations of Margaret Cavendish," *British Journal for the History of Philosophy* 7 (1999), 219–244.

Susan James, "Introduction," in Susan James (ed.), Margaret Cavendish: *Political Writings*, Cambridge and New York: Cambridge UP (2003), ix–xxix.

Kathleen Jones, *A Glorious Fame*, London: Bloomsbury Publishing (1988).

Claire Jowitt, "Imperial Dreams? Margaret Cavendish and the Cult of Elizabeth," *Women's Writing* 4 (1997), 383–399.

Ian Lawson, "Bears in Eden, or, This Is Not the Garden You're Looking For: Margaret Cavendish, Robert Hooke, and the Limits of Natural Philosophy," *British Journal for the History of Science* 48 (2015), 583–605.

Eric Lewis, "The Legacy of Margaret Cavendish," *Perspectives on Science* 9 (2001), 341–365.

Yaakov A. Mascetti, "A 'World of Nothing, but Pure Wit': Margaret Cavendish and the Gendering of the Imaginary," *Partial Answers: Journal of Literature and the History of Ideas* 6 (2008), 1–31.

Mary Ann McGuire, "Margaret Cavendish, Duchess of Newcastle, on the Nature and Status of Women," *International Journal of Women's Studies* 1 (1978), 193–206.

Kourken Michaelian, "Margaret Cavendish's Epistemology," *British Journal for the History of Philosophy* 17 (2009), 31–53.

Sarah E. Moreman, "Learning Their Language: Cavendish's Construction of an Empowering Vitalistic Atomism," *Explorations in Renaissance Culture* 23 (1997), 129–144.

Eileen O'Neill, "Introduction," in Eileen O'Neill (ed.), *Observations Upon Experimental Philosophy*, Cambridge: Cambridge UP (2001), x–xxxvi.

Eileen O'Neill, "Margaret Cavendish, Stoic Antecedent Causes, and Early Modern Occasional Causes," *Revue philosophique de la France et de l'étranger* 3 (2013), 311–326.

Dolores Paloma, "Margaret Cavendish: Defining the Female Self," *Women's Studies* 7 (1980), 55–66.

Alison Peterman, "Cavendish on Motion and Mereology." *Journal of the History of Philosophy* (forthcoming).

Alison Peterman, "Empress vs. Spiderman: Margaret Cavendish on pure and applied mathematics." *Synthese* (forthcoming).

Emma L. E. Rees, *Margaret Cavendish: Gender, Genre, Exile*, Manchester: Manchester UP (2003).

John Rogers, *The Matter of Revolution: Science, Poetry and Politics in the Age of Milton*, Ithaca: Cornell UP (1998).

Carlos Santana, "'Two Opposite Things Placed Near Each Other, Are the Better Discerned': Philosophical Readings of Cavendish's Literary Output," *British Journal for the History of Philosophy* 23 (2015), 297–317.

Lisa Sarasohn, "A Science Turned Upside Down: Feminism and the Natural Philosophy of Margaret Cavendish," *The Huntington Library Quarterly* 47 (1984), 289–307.

Lisa Sarasohn, "Leviathan and the Lady: Cavendish's Critique of Hobbes in the Philosophical Letters," in Cottegnies and Weitz (2003), 40–58.

Lisa Sarasohn, *The Natural Philosophy of Margaret Cavendish*, Baltimore: The Johns Hopkins UP (2010).

Lisa Sarasohn, "Fideism, Negative Theology, and Christianity in the Thought of Margaret Cavendish," in Siegfried and Sarasohn (2014), 93–106.

Londa Schiebinger, "Margaret Cavendish," in Mary Ellen Waithe (ed.), *A History of Women Philosophers*, Boston: Kluwer Academic Publishers (1991), 1–20.

Jonathan Shaheen, "Part of Nature and Division in Margaret Cavendish's Materialism," *Synthese* (forthcoming), doi:10.1007/s11229-017-1326-y.

John Shanahan, "From Drama to Science: Margaret Cavendish as Vanishing Meditator," *Literature Compass* 5 (2008), 362–375.

Sandra Sherman, "Trembling Texts: Margaret Cavendish and the Dialectic of Authorship," *English Literary Renaissance* 24 (1994), 184–210.

Brandy R. Siegfried, "The City of Chance, or, Margaret Cavendish's Theory of Radical Symmetry," *Early Modern Literary Studies*, Special Issue (2004).

Brandie Siegfried, "Conjuring Three Queens and an Empress: The Philosophy of Enchantment in Margaret Cavendish's *Blazing World*," in Anna Riehl Bertolet (ed.), *Queens Matter in Early Modern Philosophy*, London: Palgrave Macmillan (2018), 323–345.

Brandie Siegfried and Lisa Sarasohn (eds.), *God and Nature in the Thought of Margaret Cavendish*, London: Ashgate Publishing (2014).

Brandie R. Siegfried, "God and the Question of Sense Perception in the Works of Margaret Cavendish," in Siegfried and Sarasohn (2014), 59–76.

Tina Skouen, "Margaret Cavendish and the Stigma of Haste," *Studies in Philology* 111 (2014), 547–570.

Hilda L. Smith, "Claims to Orthodoxy: How Far Can We Trust Margaret Cavendish's Autobiography," in Siegfried and Sarasohn (2014), 15–26.

Ryan John Stark, "Margaret Cavendish and Composition Style," *Rhetoric Review* 17 (1999), 264–281.

G. Gabrielle Starr, "Cavendish, Aesthetics, and the Anti-Platonic Line," *Eighteenth-Century Studies* 39 (2006), 295–308.

Jay Stevenson, "The Mechanist-Vitalist Soul of Margaret Cavendish," *Studies in English Literature, 1500–1700* 36 (1996), 527–543.

Mihoko Suzuki, "Margaret Cavendish and the Female Satirist," *Studies in English Literature, 1500–1700* 37 (1997), 483–500.

Sophie Tomlinson, "'My Brian the Stage': Margaret Cavendish and the Fantasy of Female Performance," in Clare Brant and Diane Purkiss (eds.), *Women, Texts and Histories 1575–1760*, London: Routledge (1992), 134–163.

Elaine Walker, "Longing for Ambrosia: Margaret Cavendish and the Torment of a Restless Mind in Poems, and Fancies," *Women's Writing* 4 (1997), 341–351.

Elizabeth Walters, "Gender and Civil War Politics in Margaret Cavendish's 'Assaulted and Pursued Chastity'," *Early Modern Women: An Interdisciplinary Journal* 8 (2013), 207–240.

Lisa Walters, *Margaret Cavendish: Gender, Science, and Politics*, Cambridge: Cambridge UP (2014).

Erin Webster, "Margaret Cavendish's Socio-Political Interventions into Descartes' Philosophy," *English Studies* 92 (2011), 711–728.

Nancy Weitz, "Romantic Fiction, Moral Anxiety, and Social Capital in Cavendish's 'Assaulted and Pursued Chastity'," in Cottegnies and Weitz (2003), 145–160.

Katie Whitaker, *Mad Madge*, London: Chatto and Windus (2003).

Joanne H. Wright, "Darkness, Death, and Precarious Life in Cavendish's *Sociable Letters* and *Orations*," in Siegfried and Sarasohn (2014), 43–58.

INDEX

abstraction, 13–14, 71–72
action at a distance, 18–19, 62–63, 69–70, 82, 90, 118–19
action by contact, 69–70, 90
afterlife, 15, 25, 85–86, 141–42, 149–50
agency/authority, 13–14, 198–201, 216–17
air, 69–70, 73, 90
Alexander the Great, 171, 198–99
angels, 83–84
animals, 25, 33–34, 64–65, 74–75, 163, 225–26
animism. *See* vitalism
annihilation, 44–45, 48, 49–50, 77–78, 113, 145–46
antipathy, 44, 46
ants, 2, 165
archeus, 89
architects, 24, 208–9
aristocracy, 31, 230
Aristotle, 9–10, 48, 184–86
artefacts, 7–9, 52, 93, 97, 100–3, 107–9, 112–13, 120, 163–64, 232
Astell, Mary, 182–84
atheism, 28, 75
atomism, 11, 41–42, 110–11, 127–28, 151–53, 184–86

beauty, 30–31, 126, 142–43
bees, 64, 79
benefits of inquiry, 35–36, 46, 52, 97, 100–2, 108–9
birds, 34, 64
blas, 89

Cabbala, 180–82
canonicity, 3–4, 13–14, 18–19
castles in the air, 32, 53–54, 141
causation, 11–13, 17, 19–20, 51, 68–69, 134–35

Cavendish Circle, 6
Cavendish, William, 4–5, 6, 26–27, 188
ceremony, 29, 193–94, 197
chance, 134–35, 224–25
Charles I, 4
Charles II, 4, 171
Christ, 62, 76–77, 148–49
Church, 76–77, 86–87, 123–24
clemency, 28
cognition
    animal, 9–10, 34, 50, 64–65, 76, 124, 163, 166, 225–26
    insect, 2, 64, 78, 165
    mineral/vegetable, 45–46, 64–65, 78, 98
    unconscious, 9–10, 26–27, 116–17
color, 105–7, 114–15, 138–39, 179–80
communication, 9–10, 79, 81–82, 117, 134, 135–36, 137
Conway, Anne, 81–82
cooperation, 96, 110, 119–20, 135, 136, 141–42, 165
creation, 62, 138
    ex nihilo, 1–2, 113
crocodiles, 124
Cudworth, Ralph, 8–10, 26–27

De Beauvoir, Simone, 3–4
death, 44–45, 49–50, 78, 81, 85–86, 92, 109, 114, 141–42
democracy, 31
Descartes, René, 3–4, 6, 8–9, 10, 13–14, 41–42, 71–75, 114–15, 116–17, 180–82, 184–86
desire, 28, 30, 33–35, 154–55, 156, 159
devils, 83–84, 87–88
Digby, Kenelm, 6
disease, 38–39, 52, 56–57, 93–94
disorder. *See* irregularities

CPSIA information can be obtained
at www.ICGtesting.com
Printed in the USA
BVHW071454220821
614419BV00003B/18